Patisserie
Second Edition

L. J. Hanneman
FInstBB, FHCIMA, FCFA

*Formerly Head of Department of Service Industries
Lancaster and Morecambe College of Further Education*

BUTTERWORTH
HEINEMANN

Butterworth-Heinemann
Linacre House, Jordan Hill, Oxford OX2 8DP
225 Wildwood Avenue, Woburn, MA 01801-2041
A division of Reed Educational and Professional Publishing Ltd

 A member of the Reed Elsevier plc group

OXFORD   AUCKLAND   BOSTON
JOHANNESBURG   MELBOURNE   NEW DELHI

First Published 1971
Reprinted 1975, 1977, 1979, 1983, 1984, 1985, 1986, 1987, 1989, 199
Second edition 1993
Reprinted 1994, 1995, 1997, 1998, 1999, 2000, 2002

British Library Cataloguing in Publication Data
Hanneman, L. J
  Patisserie. - 2Rev.ed
  I. Title
  641.8

ISBN 0 7506 0430 1

For information on all Butterworth-Heinemann publications
visit our website at www.bh.com

Composition by Genesis Typesetting, Laser Quay, Rochester, Kent
Printed and bound in Great Britain by Scotprint

Contents

Preface to the Second Edition

In the twenty years since the first edition *Patisserie* was published, there have been great changes in almost every aspect of this art. Such changes are reflected in the book to bring it up to date without deviating too much from its original concept. The greatest change is the introduction of colour photography.

Comments received from many teachers overseas as well as in this country have influenced some of the changes made in this new edition. Thus some new ideas and recipes have been introduced while others have been either deleted or amended.

Although many changes have taken place in the education field this edition is still as valid as a textbook, giving as it does much of the underlying theory and fault-finding in recipes as well as sections on commodities, hygiene and equipment. The glossary has also been enlarged. Examinations now covered by this book include the following:

Union of Lancashire and Cheshire Institutes
  711 Basic patisserie
  711 Advanced patisserie
City and Guilds of London Institute
  706/1 Cookery for the catering industry
  706/2 Cookery for the catering industry
  706/3 Advanced cookery for the catering industry: pastry, parts 1 and 2
  332 Cooks professional, parts 1 and 2
  120/3 Bakery: cakes and pastry, part 3
National Vocational Qualifications
BTEC First and National Diplomas

Hopefully this new edition will be as popular in the next decade as in the last and will make a significant contribution to the catering industry.

L. J. Hanneman

Preface to the First Edition

This publication is designed to be used by all interested in patisserie. Designed especially for students who will need to learn patisserie as part of courses in catering, domestic science, and confectionery, it would also prove of great value to the practising chef and patissier, as well as the ambitious housewife.

The examination requirements of the following are also covered:

Union of Lancashire and Cheshire Institutes
    Basic patisserie
    Advanced patisserie
City and Guilds of London Institute (Patisserie section only)
    705 General catering
    706/1 Basic cookery for the catering industry
    706/2 Cookery for the catering industry
    706/5 Advanced cookery for the catering industry (pastry)

Precise instructions as to the method are given to help the student to use this book in preparation for the above examinations.

The quantities given in this book are fairly small, being mostly calculated for eight persons. However, for larger quantities it is an easy matter to divide the yield given into the required number and multiply the recipe by the factor which results.

Metric as well as imperial units have been given throughout. For simplicity, however, ounces have been calculated as being equivalent to 30 grammes instead of their value of 28.35 grammes. Since we are dealing in ratios in a recipe, this discrepancy does not alter the recipe and is small enough not to affect the yield appreciably.

Obviously no book can cover every aspect of patisserie the world over, but a serious attempt has been made to include most of the basic and a variety of the better known specialized, advanced dishes, many of which are continental in origin.

Illustrations have been included to show not only finished goods but also the techniques used.

This book is offered in the sincere hope that it will prove of great value to all those who enjoy good patisserie.

L. J. Hanneman

Acknowledgements

In producing this second edition, I was particularly fortunate in being allowed to use the facilities of the Department of Food, Tourism and Beauty at the Lancaster and Morecambe College and for this privilege my grateful thanks are due to its Principal and the Governors of the College.

My special thanks are given to the Director of this Department, Mr Graham Wilkinson and some of his staff of teachers and technicians who gave me considerable help in producing the examples of work which are photographed, namely, Mr Robert Glenn, Mr Anthony Blake and Miss Beverley Hemsill to whom I am especially indebted for her contributions in the chapter on sugar work.

My thanks are also due to the following:

Mr Steven F. Mann, BSc (Hons) MIEH, the Principal Environmental Health Officer of the Lancaster City Council who not only gave me valued advice but made a great contribution to the section on hygiene.
Mr William O'Brien for the contribution of moulded chocolate work.
Mr Tony Mercer for the excellence of the colour photography.
Mrs Marie Cooper for acting as my secretary and for proofreading.

Also to the many teachers both in this country and overseas who took the trouble to reply to a questionnaire sent by the publishers. Many suggestions for the improvement of this book have been adopted as a result.

L. J. H.

1 *Patisserie equipment, hygiene and ingredients*

Equipment (Figures 1, 2 and 3)

It is a legal requirement that equipment with which food comes into contact or is liable to come into contact is kept clean and kept in such good order, repair and condition to enable it to be effectively cleaned. Equipment must be non-absorbent. In the past, a lot of the equipment and utensils used by the patissier were constructed of wood. These should now be replaced with non-absorbent polypropylene or stainless steel alternatives.

A whole range of equipment is used by the patissier – from an oven to a patty pan – but some items merit special attention as follows.

Bain-marie

When in use, the main precaution is to see that the pan is never allowed to burn dry. When not in use, the bain-marie should be emptied, cleaned inside and out, washed in hot detergent water, then rinsed and dried.

Baking sheets

These are made of either aluminium or steel.

Aluminium

This has the advantage of being light in weight, rustless, and able to conduct heat more quickly. Its main disadvantage is that it is a softer metal and is, therefore, not so durable. It must, therefore, be treated with care. When scraping off food soils never use a steel scraper as this will scratch the surface and may remove some of the metal. The best method of cleaning is to use water with a mild disinfectant. If a scraper has to be employed, use either a celluloid or nylon one.

Steel

Although this will stand up to more harsh treatment, its obvious disadvantage is its liability to rust. If water is used to wash the tin, always thoroughly dry afterwards. Often the cause of rust can be traced back to buns being left on the tin to cool. When this happens, the steam trapped between the tin and the bun condenses to water and, if left, rusts away that part of the tin under the bun.

Of whatever metal the baking sheet is made, make sure that the corners are really well cleaned. It is here that the particles of food accumulate and if left will bake onto the surface of the tin to leave a soil which is difficult to remove. When cleaning baking tins, concentrate on the corners and the centre will clean itself!

Figure 1   *Equipment*

1 Rubber moulds for fondant centres
2 Marzipan and pastillage flower cutters
3 Copper boiling saucepan
4 Bomb mould
5 Pouding souffle moulds
6 Charlotte mould
7 Savarin mould
8 Danish mould
9 Ravioli roller
10 Petits florentine chocolate moulds
11 Croissant cutter
12 Seahorse fleuron cutter
13 Danish pastry cutter
14 Ribbed roller
15 Assorted cutters
16 Crimping tool
17 Petits torten moulds
18 Patterned roller
19 Petit torte mould
20 Basket roller
21 Tracy cutter
22 Roller docker
23 Small petits fours cutters
24 Aspic cutters
25 Sugar boiling thermometers
26 Dough thermometers
27 Saccharometers
28 Trellis cutter
29 Chocolate dipping forks

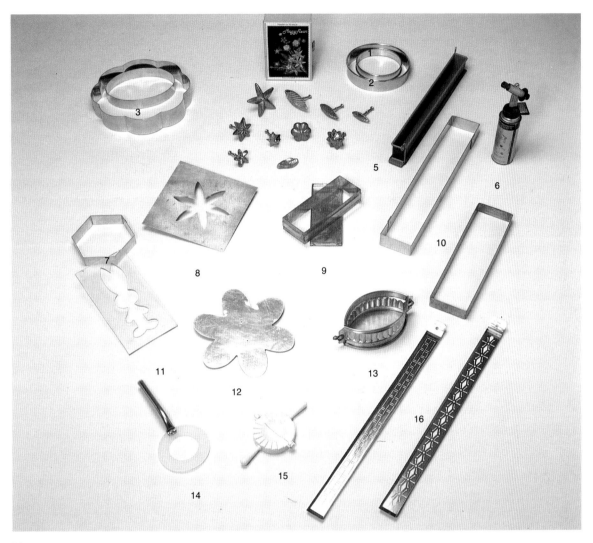

Figure 2 *Equipment*

1 Torten ring
2 Flan ring
3 Torten rings
4 Boiling sugar moulds
5 Pate croute mould
6 Blow torch
7 Torten ring
8 Tuille stencil

9 Glace bisquit mould
10 Torten mould for slices
11 Rabbit stencil
12 Metal template
13 Pie mould
14 Stencil for japs
15 Savoury pie crimper
16 French torten stencils

Brushes

These need washing and thoroughly drying at regular intervals. If left, there is a build up of food particles adhering to the bristles which quickly reduces the efficiency of the brushes. This is particularly prevalent with board brushes used for brushing such commodities as flour which, when wet, forms a tenacious paste which dries hard on the bristle.

Cake machines and attachments

These should be regularly serviced and lubricated to ensure freedom from breakdown. One of the most annoying faults with these machines is the leakage of oil which tends to drip into the mixing. If this happens when sponges or meringues are being made, they could be completely ruined. Cleaning of machines after each use is desirable but, if moving parts like the blade of a mincer are involved, thorough drying is essential to prevent rust formation. Traces of mixings left on the handles, etc. of the machine are not only unhygienic but can contaminate other mixings. It is important that these mixers should not be overloaded. This can easily happen by allowing them to mix stiff pastes and doughs. It is better to mix these by hand if in doubt.

Bowls, whisks, beaters, etc. should always be washed in very hot water to eliminate traces of grease which can have disastrous consequences to mixes such as meringues and sponges.

Cloths (muslin, jelly bags, and piping bags)

These should be regularly laundered and sterilized. Often pastry is left wrapped in a damp cloth. It should be remembered that such practice increases the risk of attack by mould and could infect the goods with this micro-organism and others.

Cutters

Pastry cutters are usually very poorly cared for. They are comparatively fragile utensils and, with misuse, quickly lose their shape. Always ensure that cutters are put away in their boxes clean and dry. If cutters are replaced in their boxes without proper cleaning, the food particles adhering can go bad without anyone noticing. When cleaning, special attention should be given to the rim where food particles can easily become lodged. If the cutters are washed, make sure that they are really well dried out before replacing in their boxes; otherwise rust will soon be apparent.

Cutting boards

A variety of non-absorbent hygienic cutting boards are now available, the majority of which can be obtained in different colours to minimize cross-contamination and the picking up of odours, for example fruit and chocolate will readily pick up the odour of onions.

Docker

This is a wooden disc with protruding points used to make a number of small holes in pastry. Roller dockers are now available which greatly speeds up this operation. When cleaning it, it is essential to remove any food soil from the points.

Dredgers

These are used for giving a light dusting of flour, icing sugar, etc. Since the same kind of dredger is used for these materials, it is important to have some means of identification; otherwise the flour could be mistaken for sugar and vice versa. Regular cleaning is again recommended with a regular change of contents.

Drying cabinet

This is a useful piece of equipment for keeping goods such as pulled and blown sugar pieces, nougat, etc., in perfect condition. It consists of an airtight, dust-proof cabinet on the base of which provision is made for a tray containing silica gel. This will absorb moisture in the cabinet, which if left would ruin such sugar goods by gradually reducing the sugar to syrup. The silica gel is removed and heated at regular intervals to evaporate the moisture collected and to revert the gel to its dry state before returning it to the cabinet. The silica gel is usually sold with a blue test paper which turns red when the gel needs reheating.

Showpieces made from boiled sugar will keep for a long period of time if kept under such conditions. The cabinet should be constructed of materials which can be easily dry cleaned and, if glass fronted, can be used as a showcase.

Fryers

Many goods are deep fried by the patissier. For the best results it is essential that frying oil should be as fresh as possible and screened free of foreign matter. The oil used by the patissier should never be used by the chef because of the risk of contamination from such commodities as fish and onions. The fryer should be cleaned out and restocked with fresh oil at regular intervals.

Knives

Besides ensuring that these are kept clean and free from rust, French knives, etc. need to be kept sharp for their efficient use. To achieve an edge, a stone should be used first, after which the knife edge should be kept keen by the use of a steel.

Measuring sticks

These are useful aids to achieve uniformity both in rolling pastry to a predetermined thickness and also for cutting goods to a uniform size. Pairs of sticks can be easily made out of wood of a rectangular cross-section so that two different thicknesses can be achieved using each strip. Moreover, the strips can be ruled off differently on each side according to the widths required. Thus two sticks can be used to produce two different thicknesses of pastry but four differently marked cutting widths. The use of such strips are shown in Figure 4.

Moulds

These should be kept in a clean condition both inside and outside, particularly if stacked. Never use a knife to scrape off adhering particles as this will damage the surface and could spoil the mould for future use – especially Easter egg moulds.

Patty pans

The cleaning of these is often neglected. Because they are stacked it is very easy to contaminate clean tins with dirty ones. If placed on a dirty tray, dirt becomes transferred to the underside of the tin which, if stacked in an unclean condition, makes the clean patty

Figure 3   *Equipment*

1 Fluted flan cases	20 Piping tubes
2 Chisel scraper	21 Pastry brush
3 Metal scrapers	22 Deep tart moulds
4 Plastic scrapers	23 Aerograph air brush
5 Plastic spoon	24 Plastic chocolate moulds
6 Plastic rolling pin	25 Barquette moulds
7 Japonaise rubber stencil	26 Petits fours tartlet tins
8 Pudding moulds	27 Steel
9 Wooden shortbread mould	28 Gateau knife
10 Individual quiche mould	29 French chef knives
11 Slice tray	30 Trowel palette knife
12 Patty tins	31 Palette knives
13 Brioche tins	32 Pastry wheel
14 Cream horn tin	33 Zester
15 Torten markers	34 Apple corer
16 Petit savarin moulds	35 Grapefruit knife
17 Savoy bag and tubes	36 Melon baller
18 Custard tins	37 Canella knife
19 Marzipan nippers	38 Jigger wheel

pan into which it nests also dirty. Always place these patty pans on a clean tray and ensure they are thoroughly cleaned before stacking.

Piping bags

Decoration executed in royal icing or buttercream is sometimes best done with a small tube placed into a bag which is made from either greaseproof or silicone paper as shown in Figure 5. This diagram is made simplistic to aid the novice and is suitable for most plastic tubes. However, small metal piping tubes have a better fit in

Figure 4   *Use of marking sticks to reduce pastry to a uniform thickness*

cones made more acute than the ones shown in Figure 5. This is done by wrapping the end *A* further round the cone and moving *C* further to the right to accommodate the extra layer so formed. *A* can still be folded over to secure the shape.

Obviously the size will be dictated by the type of tube chosen; large tubes require larger bags. If large areas have to be piped with a fairly large tube it is best to use a nylon bag. Special attachments are also available to enable savoy bags to accommodate small plastic tubes.

Never overfill the bag and sufficient space should be left at the top for it to be folded over and so seal in the icing or cream.

Stages in the making of a paper bag for icing

1 Cut a rectangle along the dotted line.
2 Lay out as shown.
3 Take *C* to approx a third down line *AB*.
4 Take *A* round *C* to *B*.
5 Fold *A* and *B* over.
6 Cut off the point of the bag and insert a piping tube.

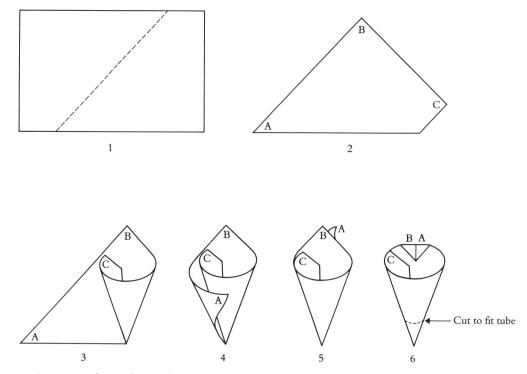

Figure 5   *Stages in the making of a paper piping bag*

Piping tubes

These should always be washed immediately after use. This is especially important if icing like royal icing is used, because of its rapid drying action. To remove hard sugar from piping tubes, they should be soaked in water, then either brushed out or a thin jet of water directed into the nozzles.

Preparation surfaces

Preparation surfaces should be jointless, durable, impervious and provide a firm base on which to work. If materials other than stainless steel are used, for example, plastic laminate, care should be taken to seal the edges and gaps which harbour food scraps. Flanged-lip designs which harbour food scraps and are difficult to clean, should be avoided.

Marble tops require special care to ensure they do not crack. Heavy concussion such as hitting with a rolling pin can cause this to happen.

Provers

These are cabinets in which steam can be generated and in which trays of fermented goods are left to prove. The steam can be made either by allowing a pan of water to boil (gas or electric ring) or injecting steam from a steam boiler. With the presence of so much water, deterioration by rust is a real problem in metal provers. Wiping out and drying after each use can greatly reduce this risk.

Refrigerators

Should be operating within the range 1–4°C. Separate refrigerators should be used for raw meats, fruit and vegetables and cooked foods. All refrigerators should be provided with indicating or, better still, recording thermometers. This should be supplemented by manual checks using a probe thermometer to take the temperature of the product itself.

For the rapid chilling of products the use of a blast chiller or liquid chiller is recommended. These allow foodstuffs to be chilled from around 70°C down to 3°C in 90 minutes if operated in accordance with the manufacturer's instructions.

Refrigerators should be readily accessible and should not be positioned near any heat source or in the direct rays of the sun. They should be constructed to facilitate easy cleaning. Large motors are best positioned outside as they generate heat and collect dust. Door seals should be checked regularly since they can become perished and difficult to clean.

Domestic refrigerators are generally not designed or suitable for use in commercial operations.

Refrigerators should be defrosted and cleaned frequently, for example once a week, using a suitable non-perfumed disinfectant. After cleaning the surfaces need to be completely dried.

Table-top refrigerated cream whippers require to be stripped down including all 'O'-rings and seals after each use and all parts washed and then disinfected in accordance with the manufacturer's instructions.

Deep freeze

These should operate at 0°F (−18°C) or below. Never overload and ensure all foodstuffs are wrapped to prevent dehydration of the product and subsequent freezer burn.

Siting should be the same as for refrigerators.

Salamanders

The bars and draining trays should be regularly cleaned with hot water containing a grease solvent. After rinsing, they should be replaced and the salamander turned on for a few minutes to dry out. Prevent waste of fuel by never having the salamander alight unnecessarily.

Saucepans

The type of pan used by the patissier is usually either copper or aluminium.

Copper pans are sometimes lined with tin. For these pans it is dangerous practice to leave them empty on too hot a stove since the tinning can melt. Copper has the advantage that food cooks more quickly and burns less easily because of its good heat conduction. Tarnishing is a problem which can only be eliminated by repeated use of a cleaning paste. Copper pans should be thoroughly washed in boiling soda water, scoured with a brush, wire wool, or powder, rinsed, and then placed upside down to dry.

Aluminium is suitable for most cooking purposes but there is a risk of discoloration of some foods when prepared in aluminium pans. The use of metal spoons and whisks should be avoided, a wooden or polypropylene spoon always being used to prevent risk of discoloration. This type of saucepan may be cleaned in the same way as copper except that a detergent should be used instead of soda.

Savoy bags and tubes

These are available in either nylon, plastic or cloth. Of these the plastic bags have a definite advantage in that they are not porous and, when used for creams, etc., no liquid can seep through. Whatever their composition savoy bags require to be sterilized before each use, especially when used for fresh cream and jelly concoctions (see food hygiene, page 11). After sterilizing in a suitable solution or by boiling, they should be thoroughly dried and stored in a very clean place. Tubes are made either of plastic or tinned metal; in the latter case rust must be guarded against.

Sieves

These may be very fine hair sieves, large meshes for sieving flour, or larger still for draining dried fruit after washing.

Sieves should be washed immediately after use. If this is not done, the food or liquid dries in the mesh, making it difficult to remove. To wash, the sieve should be placed upside down under running water, tapping vigorously with the bristles of a stiff brush. Always store sieves in a dry place to prevent risk of rusting the wire mesh.

Silicone paper

This is strongly recommended in place of greaseproof paper for lining baking tins and trays. Goods can be baked on silicone paper without the necessity for applying grease. Because of its non-sticking properties it is especially useful for good such as florentines and boiled sugar preparations.

Spatulas and spoons

Traditionally made from wood but should now be replaced with non-absorbent, hygienic types, for example stainless steel.

Steamers

For efficient working, this piece of equipment should be checked periodically by a qualified engineer to ensure that it is working correctly.

The trays, runners, and the inside of the steamer should be washed in hot detergent water and then rinsed. When not in use the steamer door should always be left open to allow free circulation of air.

To prevent scalding special care should be exercised when opening steamer doors and releasing their contents.

Stencils

These can be used for a number of purposes from stencilling japonaise bases to cast sugar work for which special rubber mats are available. They should be thoroughly cleaned after use and stored flat.

Storage bins

These may be made of metal or plastic; the latter is not as robust as metal but has the advantage of being more easily cleaned; they are often moulded with no corners in which food particles can be trapped. There should be a regular programme of cleaning. No storage bin should be refilled until it has been thoroughly washed in hot detergent water, rinsed, and dried. Storage of such goods as onions, spices, etc. should be confined to the same bin since washing is not always effective in removing the pungent aroma of such foods and this can easily be passed on to other commodities via the bin.

Hygiene (Figure 6)

Hygiene is playing an ever increasing part in our daily lives especially in so far as it affects our food. The patissier must be particularly conscious of the need for hygiene because many of his preparations have to be handled and passed on to the consumer without any further heat treatment, for example custards, cream filled confectionery, gâteaux, etc.

High standards of food hygiene are essential to prevent food poisoning, food spoilage, loss of productivity, pest infestation and prosecutions for contraventions of food legislation.

Food hygiene is much more than just cleanliness; it includes all practices, precautions and procedures involved in:

1 Protecting food from risk of contamination of any kind.
2 Preventing any organisms multiplying to an extent which would expose consumers to risk, or result in premature spoilage of food.
3 Destroying any harmful bacteria in the food by thorough cooking.

The above points may be considered in relation to three important areas:

1 Personnel
2 Premises and equipment
3 Handling and storage of food

Personal hygiene

Good personal hygiene stems from a healthy person with clean habits. The foundations of high standards of hygiene are built by the employment of the right calibre of staff and the provision of satisfactory training.

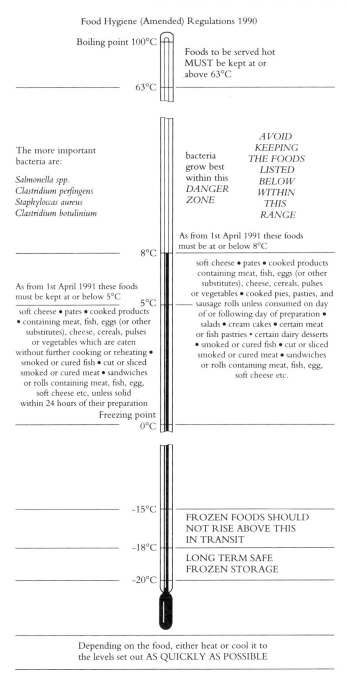

Food Hygiene (Amended) Regulations 1990

Boiling point 100°C

Foods to be served hot
MUST be kept at or
above 63°C

63°C

The more important
bacteria are:

Salmonella spp.
Clastridium perfingens
Staphyloccas aureus
Clastridium botulinium

bacteria
grow best
within this
DANGER
ZONE

AVOID
KEEPING
THE FOODS
LISTED
BELOW
WITHIN
THIS
RANGE

As from 1st April 1991 these foods
must be at or below 8°C

8°C

soft cheese • pates • cooked products
containing meat, fish, eggs (or other
substitutes), cheese, cereals, pulses
or vegetables • cooked pies, pasties, and
sausage rolls unless consumed on day
of or following day of preparation •
salads • cream cakes • certain meat
or fish pastries • certain dairy desserts
• smoked or cured fish • cut or sliced
smoked or cured meat • sandwiches
or rolls containing meat, fish, egg,
soft cheese etc.

As from 1st April 1991 these foods
must be kept at or below 5°C

5°C

soft cheese • pates • cooked products
• containing meat, fish, eggs (or other
substitutes), cheese, cereals, pulses
or vegetables which are eaten
without further cooking or reheating •
smoked or cured fish • cut or sliced
smoked or cured meat • sandwiches
or rolls containing meat, fish, egg,
soft cheese etc, unless solid
within 24 hours of their preparation

Freezing point

0°C

-15°C

FROZEN FOODS SHOULD
NOT RISE ABOVE THIS
IN TRANSIT

-18°C

LONG TERM SAFE
FROZEN STORAGE

-20°C

Depending on the food, either heat or cool it to
the levels set out AS QUICKLY AS POSSIBLE

Figure 6   *Food Hygiene (Amended) Regulations 1990*
(Reproduced by kind permission of HCIMA 1991)

Washing

Regular washing and bathing is necessary to prevent germs from being transferred from the body to clothes and thence food. Hands should be washed frequently and always after:

1 Using the toilet.
2 On entering the food room.
3 After handling raw foods and always before handling cooked foods.
4 After smoking, touching the hair and face, blowing the nose, etc.
5 Handling waste food, rubbish and dustbins.

Hand washing must always take place in a purpose-designed wash handbasin provided with bactericidal liquid soap, hot and cold water, disposable paper towels and a nailbrush. Finger nails should be kept short and clean. Nail varnish should not be used.

Hair

This should be washed regularly and kept covered. It should not be combed, scratched, or touched in the kitchen as bacteria, loose hair and dandruff could find their way into the food.

Nose, mouth and ears

Up to 40 per cent of adults carry *Staphylococcus Aureus* in the nose and 15 per cent on their hands. Coughs and sneezes can carry droplet infection for a considerable distance and people with bad colds should not handle open food. Soiled handkerchiefs should not be used, paper handkerchiefs being more hygienic, and hands should be washed after blowing the nose. The mouth is also likely to harbour *Staphylococci* and food handlers should not eat sweets while working, or spit. Tasting of food should be done with a separate spoon, and should be washed well after use.

Cuts, boils, whitlows and septic spots

Food handlers with boils and septic spots should be excluded from food handling areas as such lesions contain *Staphylococcus aureus*. Any wound must be covered with conspicuously *coloured* waterproof dressings. Cuts on hands may need the extra protection of waterproof fingerstalls.

Smoking

This is prohibited where food is being prepared because:

1 Of the danger of contaminating food by *Staphylococci* from fingers which touch the lips and from saliva from the cigarette end.
2 It encourages coughing.

3 Cigarette ends, contaminated with saliva, are placed on work benches.
4 Ash or cigarette ends may find their way into food.

Jewellery and perfume

Food handlers should not wear earrings, watches, rings or brooches which harbour dirt and bacteria. Only sleepers or plain bands are allowed. Strong smelling perfume which may cause taint problems should not be allowed.

Protective clothing

Every person handling food must wear clean protective clothing. It should be light weight, washable, strong, absorbent, and of a suitable colour. Most chefs' coats, overalls, aprons, hats, and trousers are made of white cotton because it has most of these qualities. White clothing has the advantage of showing the dirt more easily and keeping one's person cool.

Protective garments should be appropriate for the work being carried out and should completely cover ordinary clothing. Protective clothing is worn to protect the food from risk of contamination and not to keep the persons own clothes clean. Protective clothing must not be worn outside food premises and not for travelling to and from work.

Premises

The use of premises which are clean and can be kept clean is essential for the preparation of food. The layout should be designed to provide a continuous linear work flow, that is, from dirty processes through to clean operation. Cross-contamination should be minimized by providing separate preparation areas for the various raw and cooked foods. In bakeries and large catering operations a refrigerated cream room should be provided where all finishing work is carried out at an air temperature not exceeding 50°F (10°C).

Floors

These should be of some easily washed, durable and non-permeable material. Ideally they should be tiled, but terrazzo and granolithic surfaces are almost as good. They must be kept clean with repeated washes of hot detergent water.

Walls

The same requirements as with the floor, except that they should be light in colour. Tiles, special painted, or Melamine surfaces are best because they have an impervious smooth surface which can be washed easily. Corners should be rounded or coved for ease of cleaning.

Ceilings

These should be smooth without cracks or flaking.

Ventilation

Circulation of air is important for the well-being of the staff. Stale air and fumes must be taken away by extractor fans but these are a potential source of dirt and must be kept clean.

Lighting

Good lighting is essential to avoid eye strain and to detect dirt. Natural light is best but where artificial lighting is used some thought should be given to the type employed. Generally fluorescent lighting is best but this sometimes makes food colours look peculiar. If decorative patisserie is being carried out, this factor must be considered.

Windows

These should be cleaned inside and out to admit the maximum light. If opened for ventilation purposes, they have to be screened against entry of birds and insects.

Water and sanitation

A plentiful supply of hot and cold water should always be available. Separate toilets for men and women must be provided away from the rooms in which food is prepared. Facilities for washing hands must be furnished, separate from food preparation sinks.

Equipment

Equipment should be constructed from materials which are non-toxic, non-flaking, corrosion-resistant, smooth and free from breaks, open seams, cracks, chips, pits, and difficult to clean internal corners and crevices.

Food contact surfaces will need regular disinfection and care must be taken in selecting materials for these surfaces. The preferred material for most equipment is food-grade stainless steel 18/8 (18/8 contains 18 per cent chromium and 8 per cent nickel). Wood is absorbent and should not be used if suitable alternatives are available. Handles of knives, brushes and other equipment, rolling pins, spoons and paddles, and cutting boards can now be obtained from cleansable materials such as polypropylene and in different colours to assist in separation of activities and prevention of cross-contamination.

Food poisoning

Food poisoning may be defined as an illness which can cause stomach pains, acute diarrhoea, and vomiting within 1 to 36 hours after eating infected food. Such food might be infected by:

1 Chemicals which may have entered the food accidentally during its processing in cooking.
2 Bacteria which have contaminated food from animal, human, or other sources. Either the bacteria themselves or the toxins produced by them cause the food to be harmful.

Chemicals

Arsenic

Sometimes to be found in fruit after it is treated by special sprays during its growth.

Copper, antimony, or zinc

Acid foods can sometimes become contaminated if stored in poor quality enamelled galvanized containers or copper containers.

Lead

Water in contact with lead for long periods can become contaminated.

Poisonous plants

Certain fungi, rhubarb leaves.

Bacteria

Bacteriological contamination of food is by far the most common cause of food poisoning. Bacteria are microscopic single cell organisms which are present practically everywhere but can only be brought into contact with food by an outside agent, that is, human, air movement, insects, etc.

The toxins or poisons are produced by some bacteria outside their own bodies and thus the food itself is poisonous causing very rapid symptoms of food poisoning. Other bacteria produce the toxins in their own bodies and this is not released until the bacteria die. In these circumstances food poisoning is delayed until the bacteria die in sufficient numbers.

Some of these toxins are very resistant to heat; bringing food to boiling point may not be sufficient if the food has become heavily contaminated with this type of toxin.

Given the right conditions, bacteria will multiply at a fantastic rate, dividing into two every 10 to 20 minutes at room temperature so that, within 12 hours, one bacterium can multiply into several hundred million.

Some bacteria, like lactic, acetic, etc., are beneficial to humans and are utilized in the making of cheese and vinegar.

Diseases other than food poisoning are caused by certain types of bacteria, for example typhoid, paratyphoid, and dysentery. This type of bacteria does not multiply in the food like the food poisoning bacteria, but it can be carried by the food, thus causing the disease.

The symptoms of food poisoning are not always immediately apparent; the time between the consumption of the contaminated food and the onset of the illness depends upon the type of bacteria which has caused the illness.

Conditions for the multiplication of bacteria

1 The right type of food.
2 Suitable temperature.
3 Adequate moisture.
4 Sufficient time.

High risk foods

Are usually high in protein requiring refrigerated storage and intended to be eaten without further heat treatment. They include:

1 All cooked meat and poultry.
2 Cooked meat products, including gravy, stock and sauces.
3 Milk, cream, artificial cream, custards and dairy produce.
4 Cooked eggs and egg products, for example mayonnaise, but excluding pastry, bread and similar baked goods.
5 Shellfish and other seafoods.
6 Cooked rice.

Temperature

The ideal is body temperature at 98.6°F (37°C) but growth will take place within the temperature range of 50–145°F (10–63°C) commonly referred to as the 'danger zone'. Below 41°F (5°C) the bacteria lie dormant. Legislation introduced by the UK in April 1991 requires the above high risk foods to be kept at a maximum of 46°F (8°C) and from 1993 at a maximum of 41°F (5°C). See also Figure 6.

Temperatures in excess of 158°F (70°C) for 30 minutes will kill bacteria but some such as *Clostidium* and *Bacillus* species produce spores which can survive boiling for up to 2 hours. Some produce toxins, for example *Staphylococcus*, and the toxin will survive half hour boiling.

Moisture

Bacteria cannot grow on dry food but requires some moisture. Jellies, custards, creams, and sauces make ideal breeding grounds.

Time

Given ideal conditions bacteria, for example *Clostridium Perfringens*, will multiply by dividing into two every 10 minutes. This process is known as binary fission. If there is sufficient time, a few bacteria can multiply to such an extent that there are enough present to cause food poisoning. For example, in 1 hour 40 minutes 1000 bacteria can become in excess of 1,000,000. For this reason it is essential that high risk foods are not left in the *danger zone* for longer than is absolutely necessary.

Following cooking, high risk foods, if not intended to be eaten straight away, should be refrigerated within 1 hour 30 minutes.

Types of bacteria which cause food poisoning

The Salmonella group

There are approximately 2200 serotypes of salmonella, the commonest UK types being *Salmonella enteriditis* and *Salmonella typhimurium*. The organisms survive in the intestine and are presumed to cause food poisoning by the release of an endotoxin on the death of the cell. The primary source of salmonella is the intestinal tract of animals and birds and will therefore be found in:

1 Human and animal excreta.
2 Excreta from rats, mice, flies and cockroaches.
3 Raw meats and poultry.
4 Animal feeding stuffs.

The main source of salmonella is poultry. A recent survey revealed that 80 per cent of chicken may be contaminated. Of particular interest to the bakery trade is that desiccated coconut/creamed coconut has been found to be contaminated.

Use of fresh shell eggs

Since 1988 there has been a link between *Salmonella enteriditis* infection and the use of fresh shell eggs in their raw or undercooked state.

1 The UK's Department of Health issued advice on the safe use of eggs which will continue in force for the foreseeable future. The advice is not to eat raw eggs or food made with raw eggs, as there is a risk of salmonella food poisoning.
2 Caterers must use only pasteurized egg in any dishes requiring minimal or no cooking, for example mayonnaise, meringue, hollandaise sauce, mousse, light omelette, home-made ice cream etc. See note below. Unpasteurized eggs may only be used in dishes to be thoroughly cooked such that both the yolk and white are hard.
3 Shell eggs should be stored in a cool, dry place, preferably refrigerated and away from possible contamination, for example from raw meat. Rotate stock: first in, first out.
4 Cracked eggs must never be used, as they are more likely to be contaminated.
5 Wash hands before and after handling shell eggs.
6 Disinfect preparation surfaces, utensils and containers used for egg preparation.

Note The practice of splitting fresh eggs into yolks and whites to add separately to a recipe should now cease. These recipes have been modified in this book so that only pasteurized egg can be used. Whipped processed albumen may be added to such recipes to compensate for any loss of volume which may result.

Staphylococcus aureus

Approximately 40 to 50 per cent of adults carry the organism in their nose, throat, ears and hands. If present in food, *Staphylococcus aureus* under ideal conditions will produce an exotoxin which may survive boiling for 30 minutes or more.

The majority of outbreaks are caused by poor hygiene practices which result in direct contamination of the food by people from sneezing, uncovered septic cuts or boils etc.

Frequently the cooked food has been handled while warm and storage conditions have encouraged the organism to produce its toxin. Cream goods, custards, trifles, rum babas and sliced cooked meats, especially ham, have all been implicated in outbreaks.

Clostridium perfringens

Commonly found in human and animal faecal matter and is therefore present in raw meat and poultry. The organism forms spores which may survive boiling for several hours. Outbreaks usually involve stews, gravies and large joints of meat which have been allowed to cool slowly in a warm kitchen and either eaten cold or inadequately reheated the following day.

Bacillus cereus

This is another spore forming bacterium which is capable of causing two distinct forms of food poisoning. The commonest type in the UK is characterized by nausea and vomiting 1 to 5 hours after ingestion of contaminated food, usually rice dishes, although cornflour and vanilla slices (made from a hot mix) have been responsible. The spores survive normal cooking, and rapid growth and exotoxin production will occur if the food is not cooled quickly and refrigerated. The second type of *Bacillus cereus* food poisoning is rare in the UK and has an onset period of 8–16 hours. Toxins are produced in the intestine and symptoms are usually diarrhoea and abdominal pain.

Prevention of food poisoning

Upon investigation, all food poisoning outbreaks are usually due to ignorance and/or negligence of food handlers and failures with regard to time and temperature are always involved.

Prevent spread of contamination

1 Organization of processes and refrigeration to ensure separation of raw and cooked products to avoid cross-contamination.
2 Care on the part of the food handler – washing of hands between processes and especially after handling raw meat and poultry and manipulation of cooked food by utensils and not hands.
3 Efficient cleaning and disinfection of working surfaces and equipment.

Prevent bacteria already in food from multiplying

1 Efficient refrigeration of foods at below 41°F (5°C) before consumption.
2 Avoid long storage at warm temperatures – close time gaps between preparation and service.
3 Provide facilities for rapid cooling. Break down large bulks of food into smaller quantities.

Cook to destroy most bacteria

1 Careful preparation and adequate cooking. Ensure centre temperature of product reaches 158°F (70°C) for at least 30 minutes. If possible serve hot, if not:
2 Keep hot above 145°F (63°C) or cool rapidly and store below 41°F (5°C).
3 Reheating should be as thorough as the initial cooking, that is, 158°F (70°C) for 30 minutes.

Avoid re-contamination

1 Keep food covered wherever possible.
2 Prevent insects, animals and birds from entering food rooms.
3 Store food in rodent proof containers, ensuring that the lids are tightly replaced after use.
4 Do not use unsuitable, defective or dirty equipment.
5 Do not use dirty wiping cloths. Disposable colour coded cloths are preferable.
6 Keep food and equipment off the floor.

The dessert trolley*

A potential source of food poisoning can be found in the dessert trolley since it not only stands inevitably at room temperature but some of the food displayed such as trifles, gâteaux and desserts containing cream, eggs or custard are high risk foods. The Food Hygiene (Amendment) Regulations 1990 make these foods subject to temperature control which if strictly applied would prohibit the use of dessert trollies altogether. However codicils have been agreed that such food can be displayed at room temperature for up to 4 *hours* in total (not just at any one time) and it must be kept at the correct control temperature at all other times.

Restaurants should therefore:

1 Keep records for each dessert – when it was made and how long it has been displayed.
2 Invest in hand-held electric thermometers to obtain quick readings.
3 Make smaller desserts so that they can be consumed within a certain period. If necessary prepare more than one and keep the other cold until needed on the trolley.
4 Consider buying chilled display trolleys.

*Source: A–Z OF SAFE FOOD. Courtesy of Alfresco leisure publications plc, Taste Magazine, 35 Tadema Road, London SW10 0PZ.

Commodities used in patisserie

All commodities are perishable and have a certain shelf life depending upon the conditions under which they are stored. Therefore it is wise to keep an accurate stock keeping account, date stamping supplies to ensure that they are not used past their 'used by' date. Also it is recommended to keep stocks well rotated, buying in small amounts often rather than a large quantity infrequently.

Wheat flour and cereal products

Wheat flour

This may be obtained either white or brown as follows.

White flour

This flour is milled from the white floury *endosperm* of the wheat berry, the husk or *bran* and embryo *germ* being removed. According to the blend of wheats from which it is milled, this flour may be either: weak (soft); strong (hard); or medium.

Weak flour

Milled from predominantly English wheats, this flour is low in protein (gluten) content, that is, 8 per cent, and is ideally suited to rich cakes and sponges and especially short pastry. The flour may be labelled 'biscuit', 'cake', or merely 'English'. Some Australian flours are also soft and ideal for the making of cakes. Special cake flour is specially milled to a fine particle size to have great moisture adsorbing properties and is used for cakes having a high liquid/flour ratio.

Strong flour

Canadian and American wheats are usually used for the major part of the wheat blend from which this flour is milled. Their high protein (gluten) content enables a dough to be made which will hold its shape and become aerated with the gas of fermenting yeast, thus producing good bread and rolls. This flour is used for all fermented goods, and for puff pastry when a special puff pastry fat is used.

Medium flour

Between these two extremes we have a flour milled to provide medium strength. Such a flour is suitable for goods which have to be chemically aerated, that is, with baking powder. It is strong enough to withstand the pressures of gas which can cause aeration, yet weak enough to prevent undue toughening in the crumb of such goods.

Self-raising flour and scone flour

This is usually a medium strength flour in which has been blended a proportion of baking powder, at the rate of approximately ⅓ oz (10 g) to 1 lb (480 g) flour. Although this flour is handy for the novice to use to produce cakes, it is not recommended because:

1 The baking powder will react with dampness so that, if such a flour has been kept for a long time, its aerating properties will be seriously affected.
2 The proportion of baking powder required in mixings will vary to such an extent that this flour could not be used on its own anyway. The patissier would either have to add some plain flour or extra baking powder for certain goods.

It is best to use plain flour and baking powder. When the quantities of baking powder required are very small, a special blend may be used called scone flour made up as follows:

1 lb (480 g) medium flour   1 oz (30 g) baking powder

Sieve together at least 3 times.

Hand test for flour strength

Weak and strong flours may be identified by squeezing some in the hand. A weak flour will cling together after the hand is opened. A strong flour will crumble to flour again as soon as the hand is opened.
   If a strong flour has to be used for goods which are best made from a weak flour, some of the strong flour may be replaced with cornflour (up to 50 per cent).

Brown flour

This is made by blending a certain proportion of the brown skins of the wheat berry bran with the white flour.

Wholemeal

A true wholemeal is made from the whole of the wheat berry and contains the embryo germ in addition to the bran and white endosperm.

Special flours

There are many types of speciality flours on the market. Some are especially milled like cracked wheat. Others are either brown, malted white or brown, some of which could contain cereals other than wheat, for example rye, barley and oats.

Cornflour

This is a white powder milled from maize and consisting mainly of starch. It is the well-known thickening agent for all culinary purposes because in the presence of boiling water it forms a thick jelly. In patisserie it is used for thickening all types of sauces, glazes and custards and may also be an ingredient in some special cake mixes.

Arrowroot   This is mainly pure starch and therefore has the same properties of thickening as cornflour. However, because the jelly formed by boiling it in water is not as opaque as the cornflour gel, it is widely used for making glazes.

Rice   There are several types of rice but the type used for patisserie is the short grained soft Carolina. It should be perfectly white and free from any adhering husk and specks.

Riceflour   This is finely milled rice. It has several uses:

1 As an ingredient in various puddings and cakes. Its function in some cakes is to absorb moisture. In macaroons its use can reduce the cost of the mixture and at the same time help to produce a good looking macaroon biscuit with a crack on its surface.
2 In baking powder it is a useful additive to absorb any dampness and so keep the powder free flowing and inactive.

Rice-cones   These are rice granules, that is, not milled so finely as riceflour. Their use is confined to dusting purposes, for example marzipan and bread.

Semolina   Obtained from wheat, it is really the product from the first break mill of the flour mill and consists mainly of the starchy endosperm minus the bran and germ. Use mainly for puddings.

Tapioca   This is the hard white grains of the cassava plant. Its use is confined to puddings.

Oatmeal   This product from oats is obtained milled as coarse, medium, or fine (pinhead), and is used in goods such as parkins and scones. Rolled oats are the oats partially cooked and put through rollers and flattened. These are used for making flapjacks. Any of the varieties of oats may be made into porridge.

Sugar

Many different types of sugar are available to the patissier as follows.

Icing sugar   This is merely crystalline sugar crushed to a fine powder. There are usually several qualities, the best being of superfine texture and pure white in colour. Inferior brands are more gritty and grey in colour. For royal icing the superfine grade is recommended, while if an icing sugar is required in a cake mixing, the poorer and cheaper qualities can be used. Sometimes a small quantity of calcium chloride is added to absorb any moisture and improve its free flowing properties.

Pulverized sugar

This is really a poor quality icing sugar having a coarse, gritty texture and grey in colour. It is useful in goods like shortpastry where it can easily dissolve in the small amount of liquid available.

Castor sugar

Consists of small crystals of sugar evenly graded. It can be obtained either as fine, medium, or coarse grained according to the crystal size. For goods which are aerated by beating in air, for example sponges, the coarse (or hard) grained sugar is the best.

Granulated sugar

Here the crystals are larger. Such sugar may be used in any goods in which there is sufficient liquor for it to be dissolved, that is, syrups and general sweetening of sauces, etc.

Nib sugar

This is sugar crystals in clusters to form lumps about ⅛ in (3 mm) diameter. It is used for decoration mainly in such goods as bath buns.

Cube and preserving sugar

For sugar boiling, it is best to use a pure sugar not contaminated with dust in order to prevent the formation of scum. These types of sugar are best used for this purpose.

Demerara sugar

This is pale amber and really only suitable for decorative effect or for flavouring purposes. Because of its hard crystalline state it is not suitable for cake making unless it can be dissolved first.

Raw sugar

This can be obtained in a variety of shades of brown. It is of a fine crystal size and ideal for making cakes such as Dundee, Christmas, wedding, etc. The darker the sugar the more pronounced the flavour. Because of the syrup which adheres to the sugar crystals, this type of sugar will form into a hard solid lump if left in store for too long a period.

Confectioners' glucose

This is a thick viscous, clear, transparent syrup used by sugar confectioners in all types of boiling sugar preparations. It is a complicated mixture of various simple sugars and dextrin and must not be confused with the pure glucose available as an anhydrous powder at the chemist.

Golden syrup

This should not be kept too long in storage before it is used since crystallization can occur and the syrup may become discoloured. It should be perfectly clear and transparent and of a pale amber colour.

Fondant

Although this can be readily made by the patissier, fondant purchased from a manufacturer is usually of much superior quality. It should be pure white, plastic, and devoid of any hard crust if packed properly by the manufacturer. Fondant should be used as soon as possible and not left too long in store.

Dry fondant

Fondant may now be purchased as a powder like icing sugar, only requiring a certain quantity of water or fruit juice to reconstitute it. The use of fruit juice makes an icing of much superior flavour.

Honey

Obtained either as a clear, golden-coloured, thin syrup or as a thick opaque crystalline mass. For most patisserie uses, the clear thin syrup is best because it will blend more readily with other ingredients. There is no difference in flavour of either type.

Storage

All sugar products are hygroscopic, that is, they absorb moisture from the atmosphere. This is an advantage in the actual goods which contain sugar because it contributes to their keeping properties, but in storage dampness can cause considerable trouble. Dry storage is essential even if some form of heating has to be installed.

Milk and milk products

Milk

Most patissiers will use fresh milk whenever necessary, but there are other milk products on the market which may be used either when there are shortages or when special circumstances arise.

Sterilized and ultra heat treated (UHT) milk

This will lack the flavour of fresh milk but has a much longer storage life and is a useful standby in case of shortages.

Milk powders (spray dried and roller dried)

Available as full, half, or skimmed, this product is a very useful one and has a wide use in many recipes. It may be added in powder form or reconstituted as follows:

1 pint (6 decilitres) water to 2 oz (60 g) milk powder.

Whisk the milk powder into the water for a solution free from lumps.

The skimmed milk powder has the longest shelf life and its use is recommended in preference to the full and half cream variety which will soon deteriorate in storage. If skimmed milk powder is used, the patissier can easily replace the butter fat which is removed in its manufacture. The spray dried product is the best.

Evaporated milk

For many recipes such as creams and sauces, this product gives superior results because it is concentrated and smooth. To get the same degree of concentration, milk powder would have to be used and this would give a gritty result. Storage approximately 3 days once tin is opened.

Condensed milk

Similar to evaporated but has high concentration of sugar. If this sweetness is required, condensed milk may be used with advantage. Once the tin is opened it has a much longer storage life than evaporated milk.

Fresh cream

This is the butter fat separated from fresh milk. There are three types depending upon the percentage of butter fat present, that is:

Single cream   18% butter fat
Double cream   48–50% butter fat
Whipping cream 35–40% butter fat.

All three types of creams may be whisked to thicken them but the degree of thickening will depend upon the percentage of butter fat present. Although the double cream will give the thickest and most stable cream, it will not give an economic volume and so the whipping cream is recommended.

A suitable whipping can be made by whipping together 1 part of single cream and 2 parts of double cream.

If liqueurs or fruit juices are to be added to cream for flavouring purposes, double cream should be used on its own. The amount of liqueur used should not exceed one-quarter of the amount of cream.

Fresh cream should be stored at 40°F (4.5°C) and also whisked at this temperature for the best results.

Cream and milk must be handled in a hygienic way and refrigeration used to keep them cool. Given sufficient time in a warm temperature they are subjected to the action of *lactic acid bacteria* which will quickly turn them sour and unfit for use in most patisserie recipes. In extreme circumstances the milk will curdle as the protein becomes coagulated by the acid formed. Sometimes this can happen to stale milk when warmed in a pan or when it has acid added, for example lemon juice. It is essential to use fresh milk in all recipes in which milk needs to be heated.

Imitation cream

There are several products on the market which may be whipped to a stable thick cream resembling fresh whipped cream in texture and looks (though lacking in flavour). These creams contain milk solids but the butter fat is replaced with a vegetable fat which is finely dispersed by a homogenizer. To all intents and purposes such creams behave like fresh cream except that they will keep much longer, up to one month in a refrigerator, and the foam is more stable. However, they are subject to attack by lactic acid and other bacteria and, therefore, the same hygienic handling precautions should be taken (see page 17).

Eggs and egg products

Shell eggs

All varieties of birds' eggs may be used in cooking but the hen provides the bulk of our requirements. Fresh or pickled eggs in shell may be used but they must be sound, without any musty smell, and with a strong glutinous white.

Both egg whites and egg yolks form a skin and dry if exposed to the air for long. They should always be covered with a damp cloth and placed in a refrigerator until required to prevent this and also for hygienic reasons.

The weight of an egg varies considerably and since January 1978 the European Community has graded eggs as follows:

Grade	Weight in grams	Approximate weight in ozs	Termed as
1	70 or over	2½	Extra large
2	65–70	2	Standard
3	60–65	2	Standard
4	55–60	2	Medium
5	50–55	1¾	Small
6	45–50	1½	Extra small
7	Under 45	Under 1½	

The yolk of an egg constitutes about 30 per cent of the whole egg and the whites 58 per cent. All eggs used in patisserie should be fresh but if in doubt the following simple test can be given.

Place the cold whole egg in a solution of brine of approximately 4 oz salt in 2 pints water (100 g per litre). If the egg is fresh it will sink and stay at the bottom. If it is stale it becomes more buoyant and will tend to float.

Eggs are very prone to infection of the Salmonella food poisoning bacteria and should never be used in the raw state. Where the number of eggs in a recipe is stated, it is based upon the standard egg Grade 3 which is approximately 2 oz (60 g) in weight. Reference to the use of egg is to be found on page 18.

Pasteurized frozen egg

This is marketed in tins of approximately 14 lb (3.5 kg) and must be kept frozen at a temperature of approximately −5°F (−20°C) until required. When the egg is needed it must be slowly defrosted, preferably by leaving it overnight in the kitchen. Alternatively, it may be placed in the sink and *cold* water allowed to trickle over for several hours. Once defrosted, frozen egg should be used as soon as possible. It is dangerous practice to re-freeze any surplus egg.

Frozen whites and yolks

Both frozen whites and frozen yolks are obtainable and the same defrosting precautions apply.

Dried egg

Dried egg is reconstituted at the rate of 1 oz (30 g) to 3 oz (90 g) water when it makes a thick liquid, having nearly the same properties as fresh egg. Such egg lacks the whipping property of fresh egg and recipes in which this is required must be supplemented with baking powder. Once reconstituted, the egg must be used immediately and not left for any length of time before use. Such egg is a useful standby although it will not make such a good product as fresh egg. It also has the disadvantage of a limited shelf life.

Dried whites or albumen

This is obtainable in either powder or flake form, the former being preferred since it reconstitutes much more quickly. It is reconstituted at the rate of 3 oz (90 g) to 1 pint (600 g) water. The solution should stand for a few hours prior to use because it does not readily dissolve immediately.

Processed albumen

Several products are now on the market under various proprietary trade names. Used as directed, they may be reconstituted into albumen solutions from which meringues, royal icing, and other goods in which egg whites are used may be made. However, such albumen solution lacks the stability that fresh egg whites enjoy and therefore is not recommended for such goods as bavarois, japonaise, etc.

Fats and oils

Butter

Used for all high class patisserie. There are two types of butter available:

Sweet cream

This type has the longest storage life but is not so strongly flavoured as the other type. New Zealand, Australian, and English butters are usually in this group.

Soured

This has a limited storage life but is superior in flavour since it is made from soured cream. Danish is an example of this type of butter.

Salted and unsalted

Most butters contain some salt to enhance the flavour and also prolong their storage life. For certain goods, for example buttercream, the unsalted variety must be used.

Margarine

In many respects in cakemaking, margarine is superior to butter in every respect except flavour. It can be specially prepared for specific purposes:

Cake margarine   Suitable for all cakes.
Pastry margarine   Tougher than cake margarine and ideally suitable for manufacture of puff pastry.
Saltless margarine For use in creams.

Shortening (white or yellow)

This is ideal for most cooking purposes in which flavour is not of paramount importance. It may be used with advantage in all short pastry goods and small quantities may be incorporated with margarine or butter in cakes where it improves the shortness of the crumb.

Lard

Used for savoury pastry where the flavour is especially valued. It also imparts a shortness in pastry unequalled by other fats. It is unsuitable for use in cakes because it has poor creaming qualities.

Cooking oils

The use of oil is mostly confined to frying purposes where it can be heated to quite high temperatures without deterioration and the absorption rate of the goods being fried is kept to the minimum. Most of these oils are manufactured specifically for this purpose from blends of various nuts and vegetable oils. Some oils are sold under their own name, for example arachis or ground nut, cottonseed, palm nut, corn oil, etc.

Suet

Recommended for suet puddings, dumplings, Christmas puddings and mincemeat. It is available in a shredded form which makes it easily usable.

Dripping

Savoury pastry can be made with this commodity but it will not give such good pastry as the use of lard.

Dried fruit

Dried fruits not only refer to currants, sultanas, raisins, and peel, but also to figs, dates, apricots, peaches, apples, pears, and prunes. Sometimes glacé cherries and other glacé fruits are included in this general term.

Currants and sultanas

These should be of good size and colour and free from dirt, stones, and stalks. They may be obtained already washed and selected but another sorting and washing should always be given before use.

It is a good idea to wash this fruit in hot water and, if the fruit is very dry or hard, to actually soak it for 10 minutes to soften it. The fruit should then be well drained in a sieve, placed on a clean cloth, and left to dry for 12 hours or so before use. In this way a soft, juicy fruit will be obtained which will enhance the goods in which it is used.

Raisins

These are of two types, seedless and the larger ones with stones (Muscatel). For most goods, the seedless raisins are used, but in puddings the use of large stoned raisins will give a better flavour. This fruit will also benefit from the washing procedure previously described.

Dates

These are usually packed with the stones already removed and no further treatment is necessary before they are used.

Figs, apricots, peaches, apples, pears, prunes

Before these can be used they need a preliminary washing and then at least a 12-hour soaking in water. For compote, the fruit should be cooked in the liqueur in which it has been soaking.

Candied peel

Three types are available: Orange, Lemon and Citron.

A mixture of all three makes an interesting blend of colour. The peel should be cut finely into small cubes approximately ¼ in (0.5 cm) and mixed in with the other dried fruit used.

Glacé cherries and other glacé fruit

These are usually packed in thick syrup which must be washed off before their use in a mixing. The fruit may be used whole or chopped into pieces.

Ginger in syrup

In this product, the ginger rhizome is preserved in a heavy syrup. This preserved ginger may be used cut into pieces or crushed.

Nut products

Almonds

There are many types of almond products available to the patissier. The types prepared for decoration are as follows:

Unblanched whole almonds	May be roasted and salted.
Split almonds	May be roasted and salted.
Strip almonds	May be roasted.
Flaked almonds	May be roasted.
Nib almonds	May be roasted or coloured.

Ground almonds

When the true flavour of almonds is required, the use of a proportion of ground almonds is recommended in place of some of the flour used in the recipe. Ground almonds are also the main ingredient used for macaroons and almond paste.

Other nuts

The composition of most nuts is very similar and many products which are traditionally made with almonds can also be made with other types of nuts.

Walnuts

Available as broken or halves. May be used either as an ingredient in cakes or for decorative effect.

Brazil

Available as broken or whole.

Hazelnuts (Filberts and Barcelonas)

These may be used as decoration either blanched, unblanched, or roasted. Ground hazelnuts may be used in place of almonds in macaroon goods.

Pecan

Very useful as a decorative nut. Available as halves or broken.

Coconut

This is available as: strip (thread), desiccated, or flour. It can be used in place of ground almonds in many recipes. The desiccated coconut may be roasted to make an attractive decorative medium.

Chestnuts

These must first be cooked either by roasting or boiling. They can be made into a sweetmeat by preserving in sugar – marron glacé. This may be crushed or made into a purée and used to flavour many types of sweet dishes.

Peanuts

Ground peanuts may be used as a substitute for ground almonds but are not a very satisfactory alternative.

Pistachio

These are green coloured nuts similar to an almond in shape and size and used principally for decoration. After blanching to remove the skin they may be either used whole or nibbed to decorate high class products. Because of their high cost, green coloured almonds are often used as a substitute.

Macadamia

This dessert nut, grown principally in Queensland Australia and Hawaii, is similar in size to the hazel or Barcelona nut. It is usually available in the tinned form and as such is a useful decorative medium although expensive to use.

Raw marzipan

This product is made by mixing sugar and almonds in the proportion of one-third sugar and two-thirds almonds, cooking the mixture by steam heating, and milling it into a stiff paste, light grey in colour. It may be used for making modelling pastes and macaroons by the addition of sugar and may also be incorporated into a cake to achieve a flavour of almonds. This is a bakers' and confectioners' product and may not be readily known to many patissiers.

Praline

If croquant (nougat) is milled to a paste through granite or steel rollers, a product called praline paste is made. It can be made from any type of nut although usually almonds and hazelnuts are used. Praline is used for flavouring purposes.

Almond paste

Although this can easily be made (see page 241), many patissiers may wish to purchase this commodity already manufactured. The quality of the almond paste depends upon its almond content, the best being approximately 40 per cent. It is also available either neutral or in various colours.

Macaroon paste

This product is made from ground almonds, sugar, and egg whites. It may be made into a macaroon mixing by the addition of water, egg whites, or egg, in accordance with the instructions supplied by the manufacturer.

Storage of nut products

On prolonged storage, nuts are very prone to become rancid and become ravaged by weevils and moth. They are best stored in an airtight tin or jar in a cool, dry place.

Marzipan and almond paste readily forms a skin when exposed to air. To avoid this it should be wrapped in waxed paper or a plastic bag. However, raw marzipan will rapidly go mouldy if stored too long in a plastic bag. The real solution is not to keep marzipan for any longer than necessary but obtain fresh supplies from the manufacturer as and when required.

Flavouring materials

Besides the obvious natural flavours the patissier imparts to his goods by the use of butter, chocolate, fruit, etc., there are many materials which may be added, either to reinforce or modify the natural flavour. These materials may be classified into extracts, essential oils and essences.

Extracts

These are derived from the natural flavouring material. The flavour is extracted by macerating the natural source in ethyl alcohol and so such extractions contain its true bouquet. An example of such an extract is vanilla. These extracts are not only the best flavouring materials to use but, as one would expect, are also the most expensive.

Essential oils

All fruits, nuts, and flowers yield an oil which contains the principal flavour. However, only a few materials such as spices and citrus fruits can be used to yield this oil economically. The most useful of these are lemon and orange. Since these oils will withstand high temperatures without deterioration their use is favoured in biscuits which are baked at a high temperature.

Essences

Many flavours can now be made artificially from coal tar products; although the flavour does not have the true bouquet of the natural products, used with discretion, they are useful to reinforce natural flavours and are fairly inexpensive. They will not withstand high temperatures however, so their use should be confined to flavouring cream, jellies, icings, etc.

Blended flavours

Some of the most popular essences are compounded from both natural and artificial sources. Such essences have the true bouquet of the natural flavour, reinforced with the strength of the artificial essence.

In general the quality of essences may be indicated by the cost. The better essences will always be the most expensive.

Essences, extracts, or essential oils cannot always imitate the natural flavour on their own and may require certain additions. An example of this is in the use of lemon or similar fruit flavour which usually accompanies an acid taste. For the true flavour citric or tartaric acid should also be introduced.

Spices

These are available in three forms:

Spice oils   The essential oil of the spice.
Ground spice   Finely ground to a powder.
Preserved   Ginger.

Fruit pastes and concentrates

These are first class products which impart the true flavour of the fruit. As one would expect such products are expensive but their use to flavour creams, etc. cannot be excelled.

Spirits and liqueurs

These are used in high class patisserie to impart flavour. In Britain, because of the high excise duty, these special flavours are expensive and therefore should be used with discretion. Their use should be confined to creams, icings, etc., and they should rarely be used as ingredients in goods which are to be baked, since spirits and liqueurs are volatile substances which can vaporize when heated. If a spirit like rum is required to flavour cakes such as Christmas and wedding cakes, it is best added by pouring onto the cake after it is baked.

Highly concentrated spirits such as Kirsch and rum with a 60 per cent volume alcohol are now available for flavouring torten, filling creams, ice cream etc.

These products should always be stored in well-stoppered bottles.

Storage

All these flavouring materials (spirits excepted) have a limited storage life and should be used as soon as possible after purchase. If left in the presence of air for a period of time, they undergo a chemical change known as oxidation and objectionable off-flavours will develop. All flavours whether in liquid or powder form should be stored in airtight containers away from strong sunlight.

Chocolate and cocoa

Chocolate couverture

This is available either as milk, plain, or blended. Before it may be used satisfactorily, it must be tempered (see Chapter 18, page 234).

Block cocoa

This is chocolate devoid of sugar. Its use is confined to the flavouring of icings which are themselves very sweet.

Cooking chocolate

Available in either milk or plain, this chocolate does not need to be tempered before use but merely warmed (not above 110°F (43°C)).

White chocolate

This is really manufactured from cocoa butter, milk powder, and sugar, but must be treated in the same way as couverture.

Cocoa

There are two types available, ordinary and superfine, the latter being superior.

Cocoa butter

When the natural fat of chocolate is extracted the result is cocoa butter. It is used to thin couverture for use as a coating medium but can also be used to glaze marzipan fruits.

Coffee

Available as a flavouring agent in three forms:

1 Normal solution extracted from coffee beans in the normal way
2 Concentrated extract of coffee
3 Instant powdered coffee

Where flavour is required without dilution due to water only, products 2 and 3 can be used.
The product 2 may have chicory added.

Baking powder

Baking powder is made as follows:

2 parts cream of tartar or substitute (acid)
1 part bicarbonate of soda (alkali).

Sieve together about 6 times to ensure uniform dispersal. Store in an airtight tin in a dry atmosphere.

Cream of tartar baking powder

This type of baking powder is now practically unavailable to purchase and can only be made up by the patissier. Its great virtue is that it leaves no aftertaste in goods in which it is used and so these goods have a superior flavour. However, it reacts rather quickly once in contact with water, giving off its carbon dioxide gas. Therefore, goods containing cream of tartar baking powder need to be baked off fairly quickly.

Substitute 'cream' powders

Most of these are derivatives from phosphoric acid (phosphates) which, whilst harmless, imparts an aftertaste or 'bite' to goods in which this baking powder is used in large quantities, for example scones. Phosphates have the advantage that they do not react very quickly with water and so goods containing phosphate baking powder may be left standing prior to baking. The appearance of goods in which phosphate baking powders are used is usually superior.

Glucono delta lactone (GDL)

Another type of acid substitute for cream of tartar is GDL. This is superior both from the point of view of flavour and its slowness to react in the cold. Like phosphates, goods can be left standing prior to being baked.

VOL

This is ammonium bicarbonate. When heated this chemical produces carbon dioxide gas, ammonia gas, and water. Although it appears to be an ideal aerating agent, it can only be used in biscuits which have little moisture content and are thin and baked at a high temperature. In goods like cake, it is difficult to get rid of the ammonia gas which leaves an objectionable taint in the baked goods.

Jams and curds

Although these may be made by the patissier and there is a section dealing with this on page 274, probably most patissiers will use a product made by a reputable manufacturer. The price is a guide to quality but there are now regulations governing the minimum quality of jam. The use of a good full fruit jam will always pay dividend because of its flavour.

Storage

These products should not be stored for longer than absolutely necessary. They are prone to attack by moulds and yeasts.

If the product has not been packed hot in sterile containers or has been opened, mould or yeast spores can settle on its surface and bring about its deterioration. Mould will form a coloured growth (usually green) on the surface and can be removed, leaving the product perfectly usable afterwards. Yeast, on the other hand, will ferment the product and make it completely unsuitable for further use.

Jellies

Jellies may be divided into:

Concentrated gelatine or agar jellies

Available in various flavours and colours, these are used for making jellies by the addition of a quantity of boiling water. Provided they are stored in a dry place, they should not deteriorate.

Piping jelly

Ideal medium for decorative uses. Available in various flavours and colours.

Glazing jelly

This is similar to piping jelly but is neutral in colour and is used as a glaze for fruit flans, etc.

Quick set pectin jelly

This product is in the form of a syrup which will set to a jelly once a certain measured amount of citric acid is stirred in. It is an ideal jelly for the glazing of fruit flans.

Jellying agents

Gelatine

Available either as a coarse powder or in sheets. For the best results, the leaf gelatine should be used. A preliminary soaking in water is always recommended before the gelatine is used in various goods. Although heat is required to dissolve gelatine thoroughly in water it is a mistake to subject it to prolonged boiling as this will weaken it.

Agar

Available as a coarse powder or as strips. This is a difficult commodity to get into solution which can only be achieved by prolonged boiling. Its use is confined mainly to marshmallow.

Pectin

This is used to increase the setting properties of jellies and jams made from various fruits naturally deficient in pectin. Two types are available: either dry or liquid. The dry pectin powder is the most convenient to use and has the greater strength.

Gum tragacanth

This gum is available either as flakes or as a powder. With water it forms a mucilage which is used to stiffen various mixtures such as sugar and almond paste. The powder form is recommended for use in patisserie.

Gum arabic

This is also a gum which forms a solution only with difficulty. It is usually in powder form and has to be dissolved in hot water for use.

Decorating materials

Sugar-preserved fruits and flowers (and jellies)

Many decorating materials are fruits or flowers which are preserved in sugar or syrup. There are two groups:

Confiture fruits

In this category are glacé cherries, angelica, pineapple and ginger. These should be kept moist in store, preferably in a heavy syrup. Before use the syrup should be washed off and the fruit dried.

Crystallized fruits and flowers

Rose, lilac, violet petals, and mimosa are in this category. With crystallized fruits, the preserving sugar they contain has been allowed to crystallize. Keeping such goods in perfect condition requires a dry atmosphere. Dampness in store could cause the sugar crystals to soften and eventually dissolve away.

Jellies

Many decorations are made from pectin jelly shapes usually covered with sugar crystals. The most popular of these are orange and lemon slices which are available either natural size or smaller. Pineapple slices are also imitated in jelly.

Coralettes and vermicelli

These are very useful decorating mediums. They can be made from a variety of materials as follows:

Chocolate

Available as plain or milk.

Almonds

Nib almonds coloured in a variety of tints.

Sugar

Coloured icing dried in the form of short threads or very small grains.

Other materials which are used for decoration in a similar way to coralettes are flaked, nibbed, or strip almonds, and desiccated coconut. Both these may be roasted prior to their use.

Yeast

This is available as a grey plastic solid which can be easily broken into lumps. Its storage should not be prolonged more than absolutely necessary; it is always best used fresh. If it has to be stored, a cool moist place should be chosen, for example in a refrigerator at approximately 40°F (4.5°C). Yeast is also available in a dried granular form which requires to be reconstituted with water before use.

Bread

Many patisserie items contain bread and this commodity is usually purchased from the baker. It is essential that the bread chosen should have a stable and firm crumb to enable it to be cut (for example for charlottes). The best type to purchase is usually the sandwich loaf.

Storage

Bread is best kept stored at room temperature. As bread stales more rapidly at temperatures around the freezing point of water, it is a mistake to think that placing it in a normal refrigerator will delay its staling rate. Deep freeze, that is, −5°F (−20°C), will keep bread indefinitely.

Fruit

For high class patisserie, choice ripe fruit should always be used. Choosing the best fruit for the purpose required is not always an easy task, especially if it is outside the fruit's normal season.

Apples

These are of two types: dessert and cooking.

Dessert apples

These should be sweet and juicy and of good flavour. The most well known are: Cox's Orange Pippin, Laxton's Superb, James Grieve, Golden Delicious, Epicure and Jonathon.

Cooking apples

These are sour and more suitable for cooking purposes. The best known and most reliable is Bramley's Seedling which has a season from October to March.

The number of different varieties of apples is considerable and even a normal English catalogue would list about fifty. Many of the apples sold on the market are imported from France, Italy, South Africa, Canada, USA, Australia, and New Zealand; therefore, with our own season, apples are available all the year round.

Selection and storage

Apples easily bruise when handled roughly or knocked against something hard, and this is enough to start the deterioration of the apple to the state when it is rotten. If apples have to be stored for any length of time, they should be individually wrapped in oiled tissue so that if decomposition sets in it will be confined to that particular apple only. One rotten apple will easily cause adjacent sound apples to turn rotten also. Always store in a dry place.

Use

Once the apple has been cut open and exposed to the air, oxidation occurs which causes the surface to brown. The use of lemon juice, salt, or ascorbic acid prevents or retards this action but sliced apples should not be exposed to the atmosphere for too long a period before use.

Pears

Most of what has been written about apples can also refer to pears.

The most well known are Conference, Doyenné du Comice, William Bon Chretien and Buerre Hardy.

Selection and storage

To be in the correct condition for eating, a ripe pear should be soft but with the flesh still firm, sweet, and juicy. Pears readily become over-ripe with a soft sleepy interior sometimes starting at the centre. For this reason, it is unwise to store pears for too long. Storage in a refrigerator slows down the ripening of pears but with some varieties, for example William Bon Chretien, they can become overripe with a sleepy interior in spite of the outside being firm.

Usually pears are purchased slightly underripe and allowed to ripen by the patissier. If a dessert pear yields to slight pressure at the stalk end, it is ready for eating.

Apricots, peaches, and nectarines

Most of these are imported, Italy being one of the main exporting countries. These fruits readily bruise and are usually carefully packed wrapped in tissue paper in moulded trays. If possible they are best purchased in this way to eliminate handling by a third person. Choice ripe fruits should be semi-firm but juicy.

Storage

In a refrigerator or cold store.

Cherries

These are mostly home-grown. There are many different varieties with colours ranging from yellow to very dark crimson, almost black. Most cherries are dessert but the one exception is Morello, which is sour but in great demand for making jam, tart fillings, etc.

Unless preserved in some way the cherry season is a short one, the dessert varieties being available in June and July and the Morello in August and September.

Storage

In a dry cool place and remove any blemished cherries as soon as they appear.

Plums, greengages, mirabelle and damsons

These are also mainly a home crop although a few large dessert plums are imported from abroad, mainly Italy. Like the cherries, there are many varieties of varying sizes and with colours ranging from green, yellow, blue, purple, and almost black. Most of the plums are suitable for either dessert or cooking purposes and a few, such as damsons, for cooking only.

The season for plums is fairly short, from July to September depending upon variety. When ripe, the flesh should be very juicy and fall away from the stone.

Storage

This fruit does not keep for long in store without becoming rotten. A cool, dry store is required and any plums showing signs of decay should be removed at once to prevent contamination of the rest.

Gooseberry

This is another home-grown fruit. The unripe green gooseberry is available from the end of April and is used extensively for cooking purposes. As the gooseberry ripens it also becomes sweeter and it may then be used for dessert purposes. Some varieties of ripe fruit are milky white in colour, others are yellow-green or deep red.

Storage

The unripe gooseberries will have a fairly good storage life provided they are kept dry and cool. The ripe fruit will rapidly deteriorate and should not be kept too long in store. Any blemished fruit should be removed at once as soon as it becomes apparent.

Use

Before use, gooseberries need to be washed and 'topped' and 'tailed'.

Soft fruits (raspberries, loganberries, strawberries, blackberries, blackcurrants, red currants and white currants)

All these soft fruits are very perishable and great care should be exercised in their selection. Mould will rapidly manifest itself especially if picked in wet weather. When buying, examine the underneath of the container. The presence of fruit stains is a sure indication that the fruit at the base is wet or damaged.

Storage

Soft fruits should be stored in shallow trays in a cool dark place or a refrigerator. Even with every precaution, deterioration will set in within three days from the time of packing.

Selection

Raspberries and loganberries   When purchasing make sure the fruit looks really fresh and clean and of good colour. The fruit should be firm but juicy without blemishes.

Strawberries   The same considerations as for raspberries. If the strawberries are to be used as a dessert fruit, the calyx and leaves should still be attached.

Blackberries   This fruit is liable to go bad very quickly so if possible it should be eaten or cooked on the day of purchase.

Black currants, red currants and white currants   When these are purchased, check that they are firm, clean, and glossy, not withered or dusty looking. Ensure that there are not very many leaves or strings without berries on them. Black currants should not be bought which have more than 15 per cent of dark berries or 5 per cent green berries turning red.

Citrus fruits (oranges, lemons, limes, grapefruit and kumquat)

These have to be imported, the main exporting countries being Spain, South Africa, and Israel.

Oranges

These may be sweet or bitter. Among the different sweet types available are mandarins, tangerines, and clementines which are small, Navels which are seedless, and the large thick skinned and very juicy Jaffas. Seville is the most widely known bitter orange which is used extensively in preserves.

Lemons

These should be full of juice with a fresh clear skin. Since the zest is often used for flavouring patisserie, this latter point is important.

Limes

These are like small green lemons widely used for flavouring purposes and for preserves.

Grapefruit

This fruit should be large and firm and full of juice. Brown marks which appear on the skin indicate that the grapefruit is perfectly ripe for eating.

Pink Grapefruit

This is slightly sweeter than the usual variety and the flesh is pale pink.

Kumquat

These are dwarf lemons and oranges and are a native of China and Japan. Being small they are useful in the decoration of tarts, etc.

Melons

There are several types, the following being the most widely known and used:

Cantaloup

These are large round melons with a rough skin mottled orange and yellow. The flesh is light orange in colour. These melons are imported mainly from France and Holland in the late summer.

Honeydew

Imported from North Africa and Spain in the late summer, autumn and winter. These melons are oval-shaped with dark green or yellow skins. The flesh is white with a greenish tinge.

Charentais

This melon, which is imported from France in the late summer, is small and round with a mottled green and yellow skin. The flesh is orange coloured.

Water melon

These are not often to be found in this country because they rapidly deteriorate. They are grown in the warm Mediterranean regions where there is an abundance of water. They are rather large, about the size of a football and green in colour. The flesh is very sweet, red, and juicy with a certain crispness. When chilled or refrigerated, a slice of this melon makes a very refreshing 'drink'.

Galia

These have a greenish skin covered with a rough yellow net pattern. The flesh is a pale green.

Ogen

Originating in Israel, these have a green-coloured skin streaked with a paler green. The flesh is pale orange.

Selection and storage

Care must be exercised in buying melons. They should not be either too under- or overripe. The ripeness can be detected by gently pressing the top when it should be soft. If the melon is underripe, it should be stored until the top softens.

Quince

This is not unlike an apple in appearance. It has a golden-yellow skin and a tough yellow flesh which turns pink on cooking. Because of its high pectin and acid content, quince is used extensively in making preserves.

Prunes

Prunes are dried plums and require first soaking and then cooking to make them suitable for eating. They may be obtained graded in different sizes. The large Californian prune is one of the best but also the most expensive.

Banana

Most of our bananas are imported from the Windward Islands. Here they are cut down in an unripe green condition and, with carefully controlled temperature conditions, are allowed to ripen to a golden yellow (tinged with green at the ends), before being placed in the shops for sale.

Selection

If bananas are required to be cooked, they should be as just described. For eating, however, it is best to wait until the skin has begun to show freckles of brown. This is the stage at which the banana is fully ripe and at its best.

Use

Once exposed to the air, banana slices will quickly brown and become unsightly. To prevent this they may be dipped in lemon juice or the slicing may be left to the last possible moment. Besides slicing bananas in various ways, they may also be pulped and incorporated into such dishes as ice-cream.

Grape

Although grapes may be grown in a hothouse in this country, the bulk of our requirements are imported from the Mediterranean countries, particularly North Africa. Supplies also reach us from South Africa and America. Four types are usually to be found on the market: large blue-black, large green, medium-sized red, and small sultana. The last variety is the least expensive and is ideally suitable for macédoine of fruits. The first variety above is usually the most expensive.

Selection

Make sure the grapes are sound, the bunch not containing any bruised or mouldy ones. Before use, the grapes should be washed and allowed to drain thoroughly and dry. Large grapes included in a fruit salad may have their skins and pips removed.

Storage

In a refrigerator or a cold dry store.

Rhubarb

Although not strictly a fruit, this is treated as such. Forced rhubarb is usually available in January. It has slender, light pink stems. The garden grown variety is much darker in colour and has thicker stems. After washing, the rhubarb stems should be cut into suitable sized lengths, after removing any unwanted fibre or skin. It requires a considerable amount of sweetening to overcome the acid taste and to make it palatable.

Pineapples

These have to be imported into this country. The largest and best are obtained from Hawaii but the fresh variety is very expensive.

Selection

The flesh should be of a deep yellow colour with a noticeable fragrance. When ripe the leaves or spikes at the top should loosen easily when pulled.

Except for special sweets in which the outside case of a fresh pineapple is required (for example Ninon), the tinned variety fulfils the needs of most patissiers. Tinned pineapple may be obtained in the following cuts: small slices or rings, large slices, cubes, titbits, and crushed. The first two types may also have a fancy cut at the edges of the ring.

Fig

Although figs are grown in this country, they seldom ripen sufficiently to become the delicious dessert fruit that they undoubtedly are. Fresh figs may be cooked in the same way as plums.

Selection

Most of the figs used by the patissier will be the dried imported variety. These should not be too dried and should be fairly clean.

Uses

Dried figs may be used in three ways:

1 Soaked in water and then stewed until soft (same as for other dried fruit).
2 Chopped into pieces and incorporated into puddings, etc.
3 Chopped or minced and cooked with a little water to make a paste to use as a filling.

Date

This is the fruit of a certain species of palm which grows in hot climes, that is, North Africa, Western Asia, etc.

Fresh dates are seldom available in this country but the dessert dates loosely packed in small boxes, unstoned, are a very acceptable substitute.

Selection

Apart from the dessert type which are used for petits fours, etc., dates may be obtained stoned and packed in bulk in a solid pack. Once washed, they are quite acceptable for cooking purposes.

Dessert dates should be very moist and purchased in as fresh a condition as possible. If kept too long in storage these dates will dry out and lose their palatability.

Kiwi

This very popular fruit is also known as the Chinese gooseberry. It is about the size of a large plum with a thin but tough brown skin with a rough surface. The skin is removed with a knife to reveal the flesh which is bright green with a centre of small seeds arranged in a decorative manner. This is cut into thin slices for use as decoration of many patisserie items.

Lychee

This Chinese fruit resembles a small nut about the size of a Mirabelle plum. The brown skin is removed to expose a pearly white aril which surrounds an inedible black stone. The aril which is the fruit has a delicate sweet fragrance not unlike nutmeg. This fruit is available in a canned form.

Mango

In shape this looks like a gigantic plum, the skin of which can be of various colours from yellow to green and brown. The golden flesh is firmly attached to a large flat stone which has to be removed before the fruit can be served. It can be used in fruit salads and ice cream dishes.

Paw paw	These are pear-shaped fruits about the size of a melon and are grown on trees in the tropics. When cut open they resemble a melon with seeds in the centre which have to be removed before the fleshy sweet surrounding fruit is used. It is excellent in fruit salads, creams and ice cream dishes.
Pomegranates	These are about the size of a large apple with a tough skin. Cut open it reveals a lot of small red and pink seeds which can be eaten with a spoon or used in fruit salads, purées, conserves, compotes or juices.
Persimmons	These resemble a tomato in shape and size. When ripe the skin looks glassy and the fruit soft. It can be made into a compote, purée, juice or a conserve. The flavour resembles apricot.
Guavas	These fruits can be round, egg or pear shaped with a yellowish waxy skin which encloses a delicate flesh being white, yellow, pink or red. For use it must first be peeled and the seeds removed. It can be used for fruit salads, jams and jellies, juices, compotes and purées.

Tinned fruits

Size of tins	*Approximate net weight*	
Picnic	8 oz	227 g
A 1	10 oz	284 g
E 1	14 oz	397 g
No. 1 tall	1 lb	454 g
1 lb flat	1 lb	454 g
A 2	1¼ lb	567 g
A2½	1¾ lb	794 g
A 10	6¾ lb	3006 g

Note: These may be canned in either their own juice or with added syrup. The weights given here are approximate only, since the canning industry have not standardized on tins.

Selection

When selecting tins of fruit, make sure that they are not dented, punctured, or 'blown'. Rust indicates that the tin has either been in store for a long time or has been stored in a damp place; all such tins should be discarded.

Uses

Once opened, the fruit should never be left in the tin. It should be transferred to a clean basin, preferably china or earthenware, and used as soon as possible. Fruit in syrup may be safely left up to 3 days provided it is placed in a refrigerator. Prolonged storage will encourage fermentation and spoil the product. Unsweetened tinned fruit will deteriorate more rapidly.

Measurements of small quantities in this book

Recipes in this book are given in the imperial as well as the metric scale and since direct equivalents are impractical the ounce is taken as the equivalent to 30 g (its true value being 28.35 g).

Because these recipes are very small scale, problems arise when measuring very small quantities of materials such as the gram equivalent of ¼ oz. Most metric scales are calibrated in 5 g divisions and the temptation therefore is to either round up to 10 g or round down to 5 g instead of measuring 7.5 g which is the true equivalent. For some commodities the slight imbalance which results from such practice does not drastically affect the result, but with others such as baking powder, gum tragacanth, etc., it can have a disastrous effect and utterly spoil the product. Rounding up from ¼ oz to 10 g, for example, is an increase of 50 per cent. An increase of this magnitude of baking powder in a cake would completely ruin it!

Fortunately we have an easy solution to weighing small quantities of baking powder by first blending a fixed proportion, that is, 1 to 16 into flour and then using the appropriate amount of this flour in the recipe. We call this special blend of baking powder and flour scone flour, the recipe appearing on page 52.

Where the amounts are not critical, gram equivalents have been rounded up but for others the following is recommended:

1 *Equivalent of ¼ oz*
   Weigh 15 g of the material and only use *half*. If the material is a dry powder, deposit on to smooth paper and, with the aid of a knife or scraper, physically divide the amount into two and only use one part.
2 *Equivalent of ¾ oz*
   Weigh 45 g and repeat the above procedure using only one *half*.
3 *Equivalent of ⅛ oz*
   Use 2 level teaspoonsful (1 level teaspoonful is approximately 2 g)

Weights

Grammes to ounces

28.35 g	1 oz		50 g	1 ¾ oz
10 g	0.353 oz		100 g	3½ oz
25 g	0.882 oz		150 g	5¼ oz
50 g	1.764 oz		200 g	7 oz
75 g	2.645 oz		250 g	8¾ oz
100 g	3.523 oz		500 g	17⅔ oz
250 g	8.818 oz		1 kg	2 lb 3 oz
500 g	1 lb 1.637 oz		1.5 kg	3 lb 5 oz
			2 kg	4 lb 6 oz
			2.5 kg	5 lb 8 oz
			3 kg	6 lb 10 oz

Ounces to grammes

---

1 oz	28.35 g		12 oz	340.20 g
2 oz	56.70 g		13 oz	368.55 g
3 oz	85.05 g		14 oz	396.90 g
4 oz	113.40 g		15 oz	425.25 g
5 oz	141.75 g		16 oz	453.60 g
6 oz	170.10 g		17 oz	481.95 g
7 oz	198.45 g		18 oz	510.30 g
8 oz	226.80 g		19 oz	538.65 g
9 oz	255.15 g		20 oz	567.00 g
10 oz	283.50 g		21 oz	595.35 g
11 oz	311.85 g		22 oz	623.70 g

---

1 cubic centimetre (cc) of water weighs 1 g, which can then be
converted as above

Capacity

0.5	decilitre		= ⅓ gill	= ¹⁄₁₂ pt	=	1¾ oz (approx.)
1	decilitre		= ⅔ gill	= ⅙ pt	=	3⅓ oz (approx.)
1.5	decilitres		= 1 gill	= ¼ pt	=	5 oz (approx.)
3	decilitres		= 2 gill	= ½ pt	=	10 oz (approx.)
5.75	decilitres		= 4 gill	= 1 pt	=	20 oz (approx.)
7	decilitres		= 5 gill	= 1¼ pt	=	25 oz (approx.)
9	decilitres		= 6 gill	= 1½ pt	=	30 oz (approx.)
10	decilitres = 1	litre	= 7 gill	= 1¾ pt	=	35 oz (approx.)

11.5 decilitres = 1.14 litre	= 8 gill	= 2 pt	= 40 oz (approx.)
2 litres		= 3½ pt	= 70 oz (approx.)
3.785 litres	= 1 American gallon		
4.546 litres	= 10 lb distilled water = 1 Imperial gallon		

Linear measure

1 millimetre	= 0.001 metre	= 0.0394 in	= 1/20 in
10 millimetres	= 1 centimetre	= 0.3937 in	= 3/8 in
10 centimetres	= 1 decimetre	= 3.937 in	= 4 in
10 decimetres	= 1 metre	= 39.37 in	= 39¼ in

Temperature

To change Celsius (Centigrade) into Fahrenheit:

Method 1 multiply by 9/5 and add 32.
Method 2 add 40, multiply by 9/5 and subtract 40.

To change Fahrenheit into Celsius:

Method 1 subtract 32 and multiply by 5/9.
Method 2 add 40, multiply by 5/9 and subtract 40.

Examples

1 Change 5°C into Fahrenheit.

Method 1 $\not{5} \times \frac{9}{\not{5}} = 9$

$9 + 32 = \underline{41°F \text{ Answer}}$

Method 2 $5 + 40 = 45$

$^{9}\not{45} \times \frac{9}{\not{5}} = 81$

$81 - 40 = \underline{41°F \text{ Answer}}$

2 Change 41°F into Celsius.

Method 1 $41 - 32 = 9$

$\not{9} \times \frac{5}{\not{9}} = \underline{5°C \text{ Answer}}$

Method 2　41 + 40 = 81

$$^9\cancel{81} \times \frac{5}{\cancel{9}} = 45$$

45 − 40 = 5°C Answer

Note: Celsius and Centigrade degrees are exactly the same thing, but Celsius is the preferred designation. A temperature conversion table appears on page 324.

Equivalents for oven temperatures

Gas mark	Approximate temperature at centre of oven		Heat of oven
	°F	°C	
¼	240	115 ⎫	
½	265	129 ⎬	Very slow or very cool
1	290	143 ⎭	
2	310	154	Slow or cool
3	335	168	Very moderate or warm
4	355	180	Moderate
5	380	193 ⎫	
6	400	204 ⎬	Moderately hot or fairly hot
7	425	218	Hot
8	445	230 ⎫	
9	470	243 ⎬	Very hot
10	500	260	

2 *Short pastries, flans and tarts*

General points

Service of flans and tarts

These look attractive when displayed on a doily on a round silver dish. When served, however, it is advisable not to use a doily as it becomes soiled and is likely to stick to the flan.

If the flan or tart is to be served hot, it is advisable to place it on the dish when cold and warm the dish and tart just prior to service. Transferring a hot flan from the oven to the dish very often results in damage.

Scone flour

For short, flan, or pie pastry, a flour containing a little baking powder is recommended. Because of the difficulty of accurately weighing and distributing small amounts of baking powder, a special scone flour is used. This is made up as follows:

1 lb (480 g) flour   1 oz (30 g) baking powder

Sieve together at least 3 times.

Soft flour

For a short eating pastry, a flour weak in protein content is recommended, such as English or biscuit or a proprietary cake flour.

Short pastry

There are three methods of making pastry as follows:

Method 1
1 Rub the fat, margarine, or butter, into the flour until no lumps are left.
2 Make a bay and in this place the liquid (egg, milk, or water) and the sugar or salt. These may be previously dissolved in the liquid.
3 Mix ingredients to a smooth paste.

Method 2
1 Cream the sugar and fat together until light.

2 Add the egg or liquid and beat in.
3 Stir in the flour and mix ingredients to a smooth paste.

Method 3
1 Cream the fat with an equal quantity of flour.
2 Add the liquid in which has been dissolved the sugar or salt.
3 Stir in the flour and mix ingredients to a smooth paste.

Note: Method 3 is the only one which guarantees that there is no undissolved sugar and will give the shortest eating paste.

Flans

The amount of pastry used per person for flans is largely a matter of taste. In some books 1 oz (30 g) flour per person is recommended, whilst in the recipes which follow the minimum of ½ oz (15 g) per person is given. Much depends upon the attitude of the patissier and the preference of his customer. The author believes that the main use of the pastry is to hold the filling and it is in the latter that the customer is really interested. If, however, it is felt that the pastry ranks equal in importance to the filling, or the edge is raised for applied decoration, the larger quantity of flour will be required and the quantity of pastry per person given would need to be increased.

Flan pastry – Sweet pastry – Pâte sucrée

1 oz (30 g) scone flour (page 52)
3 oz (90 g) soft flour
2½ oz (75 g) butter
1 oz (30 g) sugar
1 teaspoonful lemon juice
¾ oz (22.5 g) eggs (see page 48)

Short pastry (for fruit pies and tarts) – pâte à foncer

1 oz (30 g) scone flour (page 52)
3 oz (90 g) soft flour
1 oz (30 g) lard or cooking fat
1 oz (30 g) butter or margarine
½ oz (15 g) sugar
½ oz (15 g) water

Method 1 or 3   Mix ingredients to a light short dough.

Short pastries, flans, and tarts

In the above recipe the sugar can be omitted. However, its use will impart a sheen and bloom to pastry which will improve its appearance. For savoury pastry omit sugar and add salt.

Suet pastry (for baked and steamed rolls, dumplings, etc.)

2 oz (60 g) scone flour (page 52)
2 oz (60 g) soft flour
2 oz (60 g) finely chopped suet
2 oz (60 g) water
A pinch of salt

Method 1   Mix lightly to a stiff paste.

Chopping suet

1 Break into pieces removing all sinew.
2 Place on a chopping board with some flour.
3 Chop finely with a large knife.

Baked flan cases

(Yield 8 covers using 8 in (20 cm) flan ring)

1 Make flan paste using 4 oz (120 g) flour (scone and soft flour).
2 Place an 8-in (20-cm) flan ring on a disc or square of clean silicone paper on a thin card or strawboard (no flour or grease is required).
3 Make a ball of the paste and then roll out with the rolling pin to approximately 10 in (25 cm) diameter.
4 Carefully pick up the pastry by wrapping it around the rolling pin and lay it over the flan ring.
5 Remove rolling pin and with the fingers gently ease the pastry so that it fills the ring and extends up the sides.
6 Press pastry firmly against the sides and then trim off surplus by running a knife against the edge of the ring. If done properly there should not be very much pastry to trim off.
7 The walls or top edge of the flan ring may be crimped either with a pair of metal nippers or with the fingers to give a decorative effect but, if this treatment is contemplated, 6 oz (180 g) flour into paste must be allowed so that the walls are thicker and higher.
8 Prick the pastry in the base of the flan ring with a knife or docker.
9 Transfer the prepared flan ring to a clean baking tray. The use of the silicone paper greatly helps speed production and allows the flan to be easily moved back in its uncooked and cooked state.
10 Bake in an oven at 420°F (215°C) until light golden brown in colour.

Notes:

1 In many books it is recommended that before baking the flan should be covered with a disc of greaseproof paper and filled with dried peas, beans or ceramic balls. If the flan has been made as described, this is unnecessary; but if either more paste is used or the walls are made higher than the ring, then such a precaution is wise, to eliminate risk of the walls of pastry collapsing. If beans, peas or ceramic balls have been used, they should be removed before the flan is cooked through and the

flan returned to the oven for completion of baking. The flan ring should in any case be removed prior to the finish of the baking, so that the walls of pastry are nicely coloured. These may be egg washed if desired.

2 The use of ceramic balls is strongly recommended and is shown in Figure 11.

Figure 7   *Flans*

1 Fruit using mandarin oranges, peach and pears
2 Apple
3 Fruit using cherries and pears
4 Banana
5 Bakewell
6 Strawberry
7 Apple meringue
8 Centrepiece of puff pastry with black grapes, mandarin oranges, nectarines, pineapple, kiwi and strawberry with a star fruit and kumquat placed in the centre

Soft and tinned fruit

The base of the flan may be first covered with either pastry cream or custard. Drain the fruit well and then arrange it as a pattern on the pastry cream. The quantity of fruit will vary according to type but should never exceed 2 oz (60 g) per head. The following shows how much tinned fruit is approximately equal to 2 oz (60 g):

1 pineapple ring	4 apricots
16 mandarin oranges	20 cherries
1 peach	1 pear

Finish off by masking with a glaze (see pages 289–90).

Banana flan – flan aux bananes
(Figure 7(4))

Yield 8 covers

4 oz (120 g) flour into flan pastry
½ pint (3 dl) pastry cream or thick custard
3 bananas
1 oz (30 g) apricot jam (for glaze)

1 Cook flan unfilled and allow to cool.
2 Make custard or pastry cream and, while still hot, pour into flan case. Allow to set.
3 Peel and slice the banana evenly and neatly dipping each slice as it is cut into pure lemon juice before arranging them on top so they overlap each other. Start at the edge first.
4 Coat with the apricot glaze.

Note: The apricot glaze is made by boiling apricot jam with a little water and passing it through a sieve (see page 289).

Fresh cherry flan – Flan aux cerises

Yield 8 covers

4 oz (120 g) flour into flan pastry
1 lb (480 g) cherries
4 oz (120 g) sugar
1 oz (30 g) red glaze (see page 290)

1 Line an 8-in (20-cm) flan ring with flan paste and prick the bottom.
2 Remove the stones from the fresh cherries.
3 Carefully arrange the cherries in the flan case.
4 Sprinkle on the sugar.
5 Bake in the oven at 420°F (215°C).
6 Remove flan ring after 15 minutes baking and return flan to oven for a further 10 minutes (approximately) or until flan is coloured and cooked.
7 Cover top with the hot red glaze.

Fresh strawberry flan – Flan aux fraises
(Figure 7(6))
Fresh raspberry flan – Flan aux framboises

Proceed as for Fresh cherry flan

Gooseberry flan – Flan aux groseilles

Yield 8 covers

4 oz (120 g) flour into flan pastry
1 lb (480 g) gooseberries (washed, topped, and tailed)
8 oz (240 g) sugar
1 oz (30 g) apricot glaze

Same method as for Fresh cherry flan.

Plum, apricot and rhubarb flans

Same method and quantities as for Gooseberry flan. The fruit is first cut into suitable sized pieces. For red plum and rhubarb use the red glaze, and for apricot and yellow plum, the apricot.

Note: The amount of sugar mentioned in the recipes above must be regarded as the maximum and is governed by the type of fruit used, for example Morello cherries would require considerably more sugar than eating cherries. Red gooseberry require less than the traditional green gooseberry. Ripe fruit will not require as much sugar as unripe fruit.

High sugar quantities might also cause the pastry at the base of the flan to become soggy and difficult to bake out. Adjustment to the sugar content might have to be made for this reason or alternatively cake crumbs inserted at the base of the flan to absorb the excess juice.

Apple flan – Flan aux pommes
(Figure 7(2))

Yield 8 covers

4 oz (120 g) flour into flan pastry
6 oz (180 g) sugar
2 lb (960 g) cooking apples, fresh
1 oz (30 g) apricot jam (for glaze)

For tinned apple allow only 1½ lb (720 g) (25% waste in peel and core of fresh apples).

1 Make the flan pastry and line an 8-in (20-cm) flan ring. Trim edge and prick base with fork.
2 Half cook the flan in an oven approximately 400°F (204°C) and allow to cool.
3 Select two of the best apples and make apple purée with the remainder (see next recipe).
4 Place the cooled apple purée in the flan and spread level.
5 Peel, core, and then thinly slice the apples selected. Place slices in cold, salt water as they are cut (to prevent discoloration).
6 Wash slices with fresh water and remove one by one, placing each slice on top of the purée so that they overlap. Start at the edge of the flan and make each slice point to the centre. When a complete circle has been made, it will be necessary to lift up the first slice laid and tuck the last slice under it.
7 Sugar may be sprinkled on top and the flan baked in an oven approximately 400°F (204°C). Since the flan case has already been half baked, it is only necessary to complete the baking and soften the apple slices. If these are thin enough this should be completed in 10 to 15 minutes. Further, because the pastry has been half baked, it is possible to complete the baking without the ring which is removed at the first stage. This allows the flan casing to be baked to a nice golden brown which can be improved by previous egg-washing.
8 Finally mask the top with the apricot glaze.

Apple purée – Marmelade de pommes

Suitable for the flans for 8 covers

1 lb (480 g) cooking apples
4 oz (120 g) sugar
½ oz (15 g) butter

Wash, peel, core, and slice the apples. Melt the butter in the saucepan over heat and add the apples and sugar. Cover with a lid and gently cook until apples are soft. Remove and pass through a sieve.

Notes:
1 Take care to see that neither the chopping board, saucepan, knives, or sieve have been contaminated with strong flavoured substances like onions as this will be transferred to the apple and spoil its flavour.
2 The apples should not be cooked for longer than is necessary for them to soften. The action of passing through the sieve will reduce them to a purée even if the slices are still whole.
3 The quantity of sugar can be adjusted to suit the individual taste and also the type of apple used. Some apples require more sweetening than others.
4 If tinned apples are used reduce to ¾ lb (360 g). (There is a 25% waste in the peel and core of fresh apples.)

Apple meringue pie – Flan aux pommes meringuées

Yield 8 covers

4 oz (120 g) flour into flan pastry
1½ lb (720 g) apples into purée
2 egg whites
4 oz (120 g) sugar

1 Using an 8-in (20-cm) flan ring, prepare and cook an apple flan but without the slices. For this purpose the flan case can be completely cooked prior to the purée being added: it need not be replaced in the oven until the meringue has been piped on top.
2 Using 2 egg whites and 4 oz (120 g) sugar, make an Italian meringue (page 92) and pipe this in a decorative pattern on top.
3 Place into an oven approximately 450°F (232°C) for a few minutes until meringue is coloured.

Note: The meringue could be in two colours for a more decorative effect. In some books this is referred to as *Apple amber*.

Lemon meringue pie – Flan aux citrons meringués

Yield 8 covers

1 Using an 8-in (20-cm) flan ring and 4 oz (120 g) flour, make and bake an unfilled flan case.
2 Make the filling (see opposite) and pour into the baked flan case.
3 When this has set, make an Italian meringue (page 92) with 2 egg whites and 4 oz (120 g) sugar and pipe it on top in a decorative fashion.
4 Place into a hot oven at 450°F (232°C) for a few minutes to colour.

Filling for lemon meringue pie

4 oz (120 g) sugar
5 oz (150 g) water
¾ oz (22.5 g) cornflour (see page 48)
1 oz (30 g) butter
2 egg yolks
1 large or 2 small lemons or 2 oz (60 g) lemon juice

1 Dissolve sugar in half of the water and bring to the boil.
2 Add the cornflour mixed with the remaining half of the water and cook mixture until it thickens: stir well.
3 Whisk in the two yolks.
4 Lastly add the zest and juice of the lemon and the melted butter.

Figure 8　*Fruit tarts*

Decription from left to right:
Row 1　Top: Pineapple
Row 2　Top: black grapes
Row 3　Top: kiwi
Row 4　Top: Strawberries

Bottom: Peaches
Bottom: Nectarines
Bottom: Mandarin oranges
Bottom: Green grapes

 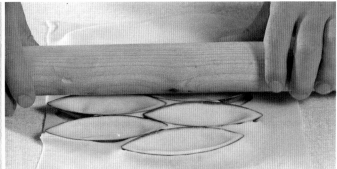

Figure 9　*Lining tins for tarts. Left: After covering with pastry press into the tins with a piece of scrap pastry. Right: Use of rolling pin to remove unwanted pastry*

Tarts

Individual fruit tarts
(Figure 8)

Yield 12 tarts

1 Use 4 oz (120 g) flour and make into flan pastry.
2 Roll out pastry ¹⁄₁₀ in (2.5 mm) thick.
3 Cut out with a round cutter and line small patty tins.
4 Press pastry firmly into the tin and trim off edge.

} For alternative method see Figure 9

5 Prick base with a fork and bake in an oven approximately 400°F (204°C) until golden brown.
6 When cold remove from patty tins and add a suitable piece or pieces of fruit, preferably forming a pattern.
7 Glaze with either a pectin quick-set jelly or the fruit juice gelled with arrowroot.

Large fruit tarts

Yield 8 covers, using an 8-in (20-cm) pie plate

1 Make shortpastry using 6 oz (180 g) flour.
2 Using just over half, make a round ball and pin out sufficient to just cover the plate.
3 Put in the fruit filling (see below).
4 Pin out remainder of paste to cover the plate.
5 Brush edges of bottom paste with egg or water and cover the plate with the paste.
6 Press paste firmly around the edge and trim off with a knife.
7 Using the thumb and a knife, notch the edge as illustrated in Figure 10.
8 Make two or three cuts in the top, wash with egg or water, and sprinkle with castor sugar.
9 Bake in oven at approximately 420°F (215°C).

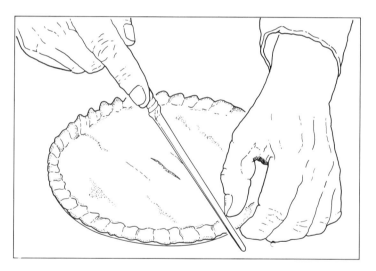

Figure 10   *Method of knotching the edge of a fruit tart, using a pie plate*

Fruit filling for tarts

Apple, plum, blackberry, bilberry, gooseberry, damson, cherry, red currant, black currant, rhubarb, dates, etc.
    The fruit filling should be ¾ to 1 lb (480 g) of which not more than 2 oz (60 g) is juice. Alternatively 8 oz (240 g) of solid fruit and 4 oz (120 g) juice thickened with cornflour could be used.

Dutch apple tart

Yield 8 covers

6 oz (180 g) flour into shortpastry
1 lb (480 g) cooking apples
2 oz (60 g) sultanas
8 oz (240 g) sugar

Same method as for Fruit tarts except for the filling which should be prepared as follows:

1 Peel, core, and wash the apples.
2 Partly cook in a saucepan with a little water and the sugar.
3 Add the cleaned sultanas and allow to cool.

Mincemeat tart

Yield 8 covers

6 oz (180 g) flour into shortpastry
12 oz (360 g) mincemeat (see page 225)

Same method as for Fruit tarts, using mincemeat as the filling.

Jam or curd tarts

Yield 8 covers

6 oz (180 g) flour into shortpastry
8 oz (240 g) jam or curd (for example lemon, orange, pineapple, etc.)

1 Make shortpastry and line an 8-in (20-cm) tart plate or flan ring.
2 Trim and notch the edge and prick the base.
3 Spread the jam evenly in the tart.
4 Using the trimmings of pastry, pin out and cut thin strips, either plain or fluted using a jigger wheel.
5 Lay these over the jam in a criss-cross fashion.
6 Bake in an oven at 420°F (215°C) until golden brown in colour.

Note: Make sure that the jam is free of lumps. If too stiff it should be reduced slightly with water.
   When cold this tart could be decorated or served with fresh whipped cream.

Individual jam tarts

Yield 12 tarts

4 oz (120 g) flour into shortpastry
6 oz (180 g) jam or curd

1 Make shortpastry using 4 oz (120 g) flour.
2 Roll out pastry to ¹⁄₁₀ in (2½ mm) in thickness.
3 Cut out with round cutter and line patty pans. (A fluted cutter may be used or the tart may be hand notched with the use of a plain cutter.)
4 Reduce the jam or curd to the correct consistency with water and pipe it into each tart through either a savoy bag with ⅛ in (3 mm) tube or a greaseproof or silicone paper bag.
5 Bake in oven at 420°F (215°C) until pastry is golden brown in colour.

Note: These also may be decorated or served with fresh whipped cream.

Syrup or treacle tart

Yield 8 covers

8 oz (240 g) syrup or treacle
1½ oz (45 g) white bread-crumbs
1 teaspoonful lemon juice

Individual mince or fruit pies
(Figure 60, page 224)

Yield 8 tarts

4 oz (120 g) flour into shortpastry
6 oz (180 g) mincemeat (see page 225) *or 8 oz (240 g) fruit*

1 Make shortpastry using 4 oz (120 g) flour.
2 Roll out shortpastry ⅒ in (2.5 mm) in thickness.
3 Cut out with round plain cutter and line patty pans.
4 Place a teaspoonful of mincemeat or fruit filling in the centre of each tart.
5 Roll out remaining paste very thinly ¹⁄₁₆ in (1½ mm) and cut out with a smaller cutter.
6 Damp the edges of the tarts with water. (Water may be sprinkled on.)
7 Lay on the smaller disc of pastry.
8 Press down with the rolled edge of a smaller cutter so that the top is secured to the bottom.
9 Prick with a fork or spear with a knife.
10 Bake in an oven at 420°F (215°C) until a golden colour.
11 Dredge liberally with icing sugar.
12 Place on a doily on a silver dish and serve warm with an appropriate sauce, for example custard, brandy, etc.

Figure 11   *The upper part of the figure shows a filled and unfilled individual quiche tin. The unbaked tart tins are filled with ceramic balls preparatory to baking 'blind'*

Bakewell tarts
(Figure 7(5))

Yield 8 covers in 8-in (20-cm) ring

4 oz (120 g) flour into flan pastry
2 oz (60 g) icing sugar
2 oz (60 g) raspberry jam

Frangipane filling

Recipe 1 (best quality)

4 oz (120 g) castor sugar
4 oz (120 g) butter or margarine
4 oz (120 g) eggs
4 oz (120 g) ground almonds
¼ oz (7.5 g) flour (see page 48)

Recipe 2 (medium quality)

4 oz (120 g) castor sugar
4 oz (120 g) butter or margarine
4 oz (120 g) eggs
2 oz (60 g) ground almonds
4 oz (120 g) sponge crumbs
¼ oz (7.5 g) flour (see page 48)

Method for filling

Cream and butter and sugar, beat in the egg, and lastly stir in the dry material.

Method for tart

1 Line flan ring with ¾ of the pastry.
2 Prick the base well with a fork.
3 Spread on the jam.
4 Place on the frangipane filling and spread evenly.
5 Pin out the remaining pastry, cut into strips approximately ¼ (6 mm) wide and place on top to form a lattice pattern (as for large jam tarts). Alternatively, use the trellis cutter (Figure 12).
6 Bake in an oven at 360°F (180°C) for approximately 30 minutes until cooked and golden in colour.
7 When baked, brush over thin water icing.

Date and apple filling

Yield 8 covers

4 oz (120 g) chopped dates
1 lb (480 g) cooking apples
4 oz (120 g) castor sugar

1 Make a purée with the apples and sugar.
2 When cold mix in the chopped dates.

Note: The covered fruit slices are suitable for such fruits as fresh gooseberries, cherries, plums, etc., which may be baked into the slice. The tops could be made of puff pastry if desired.

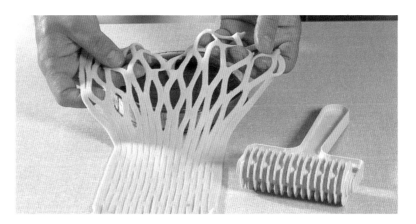

Figure 12   *Use of trellis cutter to cover the bakewell flan in Figure 7(5)*

Baked jam roll

Yield 8 covers

Use 3 times the shortpastry recipe, replacing the flours with:
6 oz (180 g) flour
6 oz (180 g) scone flour (see page 52)
5 oz (150 g) jam

1 Roll out the pastry to approximately 18 in × 12 in (45 cm × 30 cm).
2 Spread with jam to within ½ in (1.25 cm) of edge.
3 Roll up Swiss roll fashion starting at the short edge.
4 Moisten the edge to seal the roll.
5 Place on a clean baking sheet and bake in an oven at 400°F (204°C) for approximately 30 minutes.
6 Serve on an oval flat silver dish with jam sauce or custard served separately in a sauce-boat. Cut the slices on the slant.

Fruit slices

Yield 8 covers

4 oz (120 g) flour into shortpastry
6 to 8 oz (180 to 240 g) fruit, that is date and apple (tinned, fresh, or cooked)
2 oz (60 g) apricot jam

Method for open slice

1 Pin out the pastry to approximately ¹⁄₁₀ in (2.5 mm) thick.
2 Lift up with the rolling pin and lay the sheet on a baking tray.
3 Prick well with a fork or docker.
4 Cut into strips 4 in (10 cm) wide and bake in oven at 420°F (215°C).
5 Place on the pieces of fruit.
6 Cover with apricot glaze.
7 Cut into slices approximately 2 in (5 cm) wide.
   Note: This is only suitable for fruits which can be cut, for example peaches, or whole fruits, for example cherries, gooseberries, etc.

Method for covered slices

6 oz (180 g) flour into shortpastry
   Other ingredients same as for Fruit slices.

1 Repeat (1) to (3).
2 Cut into strips 4 in (10 cm) wide.
3 Place the fruit in the centre leaving about ½ in (12 mm) along each edge which should be dampened.
4 Pin out another piece of pastry and cut into strips slightly wider, that is 4½ in (11.5 cm).
5 Carefully lay this strip over the fruit and seal each edge by pressing down with the fingers. The edge can be notched if required.

6 Wash top with milk or water, sprinkle on castor sugar, and make cuts with a knife.
7 Mark into slices approximately 2 in (5 cm) wide and bake at 420°F (215°C).

Other baked rolls

1 Mincemeat.
2 Date and apple – *3 oz (90 g) diced apple; 3 oz (90 g) chopped dates.*
3 Syrup – *4½ oz (135 g) syrup, 1½ oz (45 g) breadcrumbs.*

Baked apple dumpling

Yield 8 covers

8 small cooking apples (approximately 4 oz (120 g) each)
8 cloves
4 oz (120 g) sugar
8 oz (240 g) flour into shortpastry

1 Roll out the pastry approximately ⅛ in (3 mm) thick.
2 Cut into 8 squares, each sufficient to completely cover the apple.
3 Damp the edges of the squares.
4 Peel and core the apples and place one in the centre of each square.
5 Place a clove in each apple.
6 Fill the centre of the apple with sugar.
7 Cover the apple with the pastry, making sure that it is completely sealed without the pastry breaking.
8 From the trimmings, cut out a round using a fancy cutter and place one on each apple.
9 Egg wash the pastry and place each on a clean baking tray.
10 Bake in an oven at 380°F (193°C) for approximately 30 minutes.
11 Serve on a silver dish with a sauce-boat of custard.

Shortbread

4 oz (120 g) butter
2¼ oz (70 g) castor sugar
5½ (165 g) soft flour
½ oz (15 g) ground rice

1 Cream the butter and sugar together until light.
2 Sieve the ground rice and flour together and blend into the butter/sugar cream.
3 Mix lightly into a smooth paste.

This mixing may now be made into individual biscuits, a large shortbread, or fancy biscuits by means of a wooden block (mould). All three are now described.

Finger biscuits
(Figure 60, page 224)

Yield 12

1 Roll out the paste to ½ in (1.25 cm) in thickness.
2 Transfer to a clean baking tray.
3 Prick all over with a fork or docker.

4 Trim and cut or mark into slices approximately 1 in × 2½ in (2.5 cm × 6.5 cm).
5 These slices can be individually baked or the whole piece may be just deeply marked so that it will break into fingers after it is baked.
6 Bake at 400°F (204°C) until golden brown in colour.
7 As soon as they are baked and whilst still hot, dredge with fine castor sugar.

Note: These slices may be individually crimped with the fingers or marzipan nippers for decoration.

Large shortbread

Yield on 9-in (23-cm) or two 6-in (15-cm)

1 Mould into a ball and roll this out to the sizes recommended above.
2 Prick all over with a fork or docker.
3 Crimp the edge using either the fingers or a marzipan nipper.
4 Bake at 380°F (193°C) until golden brown in colour.
5 When baked and whilst still hot, dredge with fine castor sugar.

Small moulded shortbreads

Yield 12

1 Divide the paste into approximately 1-oz (30-g) pieces.
2 Mould round and flatten to approximate size of the impression of the wooden block.
3 Dust the moulded pieces lightly with rice flour and press this surface into the mould, levelling the base.
4 Reverse and allow the moulded shortbread to drop onto a papered baking sheet.
5 Proceed as for fingers.

Petticoat tails
(Figure 60, page 224)

1 Divide mixture into 4.
2 Mould into round balls and roll out to approximately 5 in (130 cm) in diameter on a disc or square of silicone paper on a card or strawboard.
3 Crimp the edges with either the hands or a crimper.
4 Transfer to a clean baking tray and prick over with a fork or docker.
5 Mark into 6 divisions using a knife and only cutting through halfway.
6 Bake at 420°F (215°C) until golden brown.

Notes:
1 As the name suggests, these goods should be very short eating and crisp. To preserve their crispness they should be stored in an airtight tin in a dry atmosphere.
2 Shortbreads, particularly the large ones, may be decorated either with glacé fruits or royal icing. Traditional Scottish messages like 'For Auld Lang Syne' may be piped on in sugar for festive occasions.

3 Puff pastries

Notes on puff pastry manufacture

Puff pastry fat or margarine

This is a product made specially for puff pastry from oils and fats having a high melting point. It enables puff pastry to be made under warm conditions, that is, in summer, and will enable the pastry to withstand rough handling. Puff pastry fat does not usually contain moisture, although there are puff pastry emulsions which can be used which contain up to 20% moisture. If this type of margarine is used more must be used in the recipe, for example 14 oz (420 g) of margarine equates to 12 oz (360 g) of a 100% fat.

Use of butter

Undoubtedly butter produces the most deliciously flavoured puff pastry and is recommended where first quality goods are demanded. Care must be taken in its handling, however. The paste must be gently rolled and preferably refrigerated between turns. Plenty of rest must also be given and a softer dough made. The type of butter should be tough and waxy, Dutch being well recommended.

Consistency

The consistency of the dough should equal that of the fat. For a tough puff pastry, fat or margarine, a strong flour made into a tight dough is recommended. Butter or margarine demand a softer dough, preferably one made from a softer flour.

Turns

The number of turns normally given is such that about 700 to 1500 layers of fat in the dough should be built up. This may be done in two ways: by rolling out and folding into three, or by folding the ends in first and then folding together like a book (*book turn*). A combination of both methods may also be used. What seems to matter is that the layers should be even and properly insulated. Too many layers (over-rolling) will break down this insulation to render a product more like shortpaste. Too few layers (under-rolling) will result in coarse layers with perhaps uneven lift and the fat running out during baking. Each method has its advocates. The one favoured by the author is the French method in which six half turns are given.

Quantity of fat

Provided there is sufficient fat available to provide the insulation between the dough layers, the quantity of fat is not critical. It can vary between 8 oz (240 g) and 1 lb (½ kilo) of flour. For the lower quantities, however, less rolling must be given and this will mean slightly less and irregular lift. The lower quantity of fat will also give a harsher tasting pastry. Usually a small quantity of fat is rubbed in to bring about a shortening effect. Three-quarter paste is made with 12 oz (360 g) of fat to the pound (approximately ½ kilo) of flour and this makes an ideal good quality puff pastry.

Thickness of paste

Provided the paste is rolled out sufficiently to enable the operative to fold it and give it the required number of turns, there is no virtue in pinning out the pastry very thinly. Indeed this might damage the structure by breaking the layers. The smaller the quantity of paste the less it needs to be rolled out.

Oven temperature

Puff pastry requires a hot oven. Egg washed varieties, for example sausage rolls, should be baked at about 400° to 450°F (232°C), while the sugared varieties, because of the nature of the sugar, require a slightly lower temperature, that is, 420°F (215°C). A low baking temperature will prevent the pastry lifting.

Resting

The resting periods between the turns and on the tray prior to baking are essential to ensure even rolling without the risk of the layers breaking down. However, too long a rest just prior to baking will result in a loss of lift even though it aids the perfection of shape.

Use of scrap

Some pastries, for example vol-au-vent, require a virgin pastry, whilst others like palmiers require to be made from the pastry scraps. Most items can be made from pastry to which a proportion of scrap is added. The usual method is to turn back the top fold, cover with the scrap, and fold back, so that the cuttings are rolled into the virgin paste. For lift it is essential to use virgin pastry, but where only flakiness is required the use of cuttings is perfectly satisfactory.

Yields for items made from virgin pastry can only be calculated by taking into account the amount of scrap pastry which remains after these items have been cut out.

Whenever puff pastries are being made, the range of items should always include some in which the scrap pastry can be utilized.

Storage of puff pastry

Puff pastry can be stored indefinitely in the deep freeze. Since it is a time-consuming process to make puff pastry, it is always wise to have some in stock. To de-frost, it should be left in the kitchen for at least 2 hours or removed to the normal refrigerator where it can be left overnight or up to two days.

Faults in puff pastry

Uneven lift

(a) Incorrect rolling technique, for example uneven.
(b) Fat not evenly distributed prior to rolling.
(c) Insufficient resting for pastry to recover prior to baking.
(d) Uneven distribution of heat in the oven.

Poor lift

(a) Too much rolling, either by giving too many turns or pinning out too thinly.
(b) Either insufficient or too much fat employed.

Excessive shrinkage

This results in distorting the shape and is the result of insufficient rest prior to baking.

Fat running out during baking

It is inevitable that some fat will run out but this will be excessive if: too cold an oven temperature is used, paste is under-rolled giving too thick fat layers, or too much fat has been used.

Basic full paste (English and French methods)

8 oz (240 g) flour
4–4½ oz (120–135 g) cold water
1 oz (30 g) lard, butter, or margarine
5–7 oz (150–210 g) butter or margarine (or special fats)
2 teaspoonsful lemon juice (optional)

Dough making

1 Rub the 1 oz (30 g) lard into the flour.
2 Add the water and make into a well mixed dough.

English method

1 Roll out the dough to a rectangle approximately 8 in × 12 in (20 cm × 30 cm).
2 Plasticize the butter or margarine and spread it over ⅔ of the dough. To facilitate this it is recommended that the fat is first rolled between two sheets of silicone paper to the appropriate size.
3 Fold the remaining ⅓ of dough over the portion spread with the butter or margarine and fold over again so that there are two layers of fat and three layers of dough (Figure 13).
4 Roll out this piece to about the same size as previously and fold

into three. This constitutes a normal *turn*, sometimes referred to as a *half-turn* (Figure 13).

5 Repeat (4) another five times so that six turns have been given with resting periods between. If two turns are given in succession, it is advisable then to leave the dough to rest for at least 30 minutes.

Alternatively, four book turns may be given.

French method

1 Mould the dough into a ball, make a knife cut at right angles, and with the rolling pin form a square with the corners rolled extra thinly.
2 Plasticize the butter or margarine and form it into a square.
3 Place this diagonally in the centre of the dough and fold over each corner of the dough to meet in the centre, so completely enveloping the fat (Figure 13).
4 Proceed to give the required turns as in (4) and (5) above. (See Figure 13.)

Scotch or rough puff

In this method, the butter, margarine, or fat is chopped into cubes about 1 in (2.5 cm) and mixed into the dry flour. To this the water is added and a dough made, keeping the cubes of fat intact. Proceed to give turns in any of the conventional ways.

This pastry is suitable only for varieties in which scrap would normally be used, especially for pies.

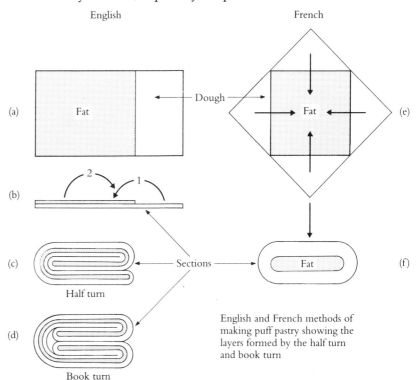

English   French

(a)   Fat   Dough   Fat   (e)

(b)

(c)   Half turn   Sections   Fat   (f)

(d)   Book turn

English and French methods of making puff pastry showing the layers formed by the half turn and book turn

Figure 13   *Methods of making puff pastry*

Varieties using virgin pastry

Vol-au-vent
(Figure 14)

This is an open baked puff pastry case which is usually filled with a savoury filling. They can be made either large, approximately 6 in (16 cm), or individual, 2½ in (6 cm).

1 Pin out the paste to ⅛ in (3 mm) in thickness and cut out discs, using a 2½–3-in (6–8 cm) round cutter.
2 Using a 1½-in (4-cm) cutter, cut out the centre from half of the discs.
3 Lay the remaining discs on a clean baking tray and damp tops with water.
4 Place on the discs cut out in (2).
5 Egg wash the top outside edge.
6 Let pieces rest for 30 minutes to one hour and egg wash a second time if desired.
7 Bake in a hot oven at 440°F (226°C) until crisp and light brown in colour.
8 If lids are required, the pieces cut out with the 1½-in (4-cm) cutter must also be egg washed and baked off separately. (Not on same tray, as these will take less time to bake.)

Figure 14 *Puff pastry varieties*

Description from left to right:
Top row: Coventry; Banbury; cream puff; cream horn
Middle row: turnover; Eccle; cream puff; cream slice
Bottom row: sausage roll; vol-au-vent; palmier; fleurons

Bouchées

Same method as for vol-au-vent but using smaller cutters, that is 1¾ and 1 in (4.5 and 2.5 cm).

Large vol-au-vent

Suitable for 4 covers For this the paste needs to be slightly thicker, about ³⁄₁₆ in (0.5 cm) and cut out with a 6–8-in (15–20-cm) cutter. Use a cutter about 1½ in (4 cm) smaller for the hole. Bake in a cooler oven at approximately 420°F (215°C).

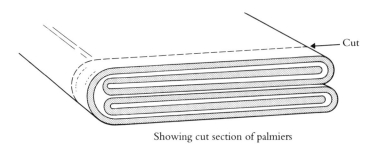

Figure 15   *Palmiers.*
Showing how the pastry is
folded and cut

Showing cut section of palmiers

Yields from 1 lb virgin pastry

		Scrap over
Large vol-au-vent 1 @ 7 in (18 cm)		6 oz (180 g)
Individual vol-au-vent 6 @ 3 in (7.5 cm)		7 oz (210 g)
Bouchées 16 @ 1¾ in (4.5 cm)		6 oz (180 g)

Cream puffs
(Figure 14)

Yield 12

10 oz (300 g) puff pastry, leaving 5 oz (150 g) scrap
⅓ pint (2 dl) fresh cream
2 oz (60 g) jam

1 Roll out the puff pastry to ⅛ in (3 mm) in thickness and approximately 12 in × 9 in (30 cm × 24 cm).
2 Prick the surface with a docker or fork and cut into twelve squares or circles approximately 3 in (8 cm).
3 Before they are baked, dress the surface in one of the following ways:
   (a) *Puff royal.* Spread over with royal icing. Pipe a thin line of jam from corner to corner in the form of a cross for additional effect.
   (b) *Sugar dressed.* Wash with either water or egg whites and dip into castor sugar.
   (c) *Egg washed.* If the top is egg washed the finished piece is left plain.
   (d) *Dusted.* If the puff is to be dusted with icing sugar after baking, it should be left plain.
4 Let the pieces rest for at least 30 minutes.
5 Bake in an oven at 420°F (215°C) for varieties (a) and (b) and 440°F (226°C) for varieties (c) and (d).
6 When baked and cold, split into two and remove the top piece.
7 Pipe a small bulb of jam onto the bottom piece and then pipe on a bulb of sweetened, whipped fresh cream.
8 Replace top.
9 With the (d) variety, dust top with icing sugar.

Slices
(Figure 14)

Yield 8

8 oz (240 g) puff pastry, leaving 2 oz (60 g) scrap
(This will make one strip, 4 in × 12 in (10 cm × 30 cm) = 8 slices)
¼ pint (1.5 dl) fresh cream
1½ oz (45 g) jam

1 Roll out a piece of well rested virgin puff pastry to ⅛ in (3 mm) in thickness and approximately 4 in × 12 in (10 cm × 30 cm).
2 Lay this piece of pastry on a clean baking tray.
3 Prick well with a fork or docker.
4 Allow to rest for at least 30 minutes and bake in an oven at 440°F (226°C) until crisp and light golden brown in colour.
5 When baked turn over and split the pieces in two lengthwise.
6 Remove the top piece (which was the base) and on the remaining piece spread on a layer of jam followed by a layer of either whipped fresh cream or custard.
7 Spread the top piece first with boiling apricot purée and then suitably flavoured and coloured warm fondant.
8 Allow the fondant to set and then cut the piece into slices approximately 1½ in (4 cm) wide.
9 Replace the cut slice on top of the creamed base and finish by cutting through.

Notes:
1 The top or edge could be suitably decorated with coralettes, browned desiccated coconut, etc.
2 The cream sides could also be spread evenly and masked with a suitable dressing, for example browned nibbed almonds, etc.
3 Instead of one piece of virgin pastry, the slice could be made from two strips of thinly rolled pastry ¹⁄₁₆ in (1.5 mm) in thickness. In this event some scrap pastry could be worked in.

Varieties using proportion of scrap pastry

Sausage rolls
(Figure 14)

Yield 8

6 oz (180 g) puff pastry, leaving 1 oz (30 g) scrap
4 oz (120 g) sausage meat

1 Roll out the pastry to about ¹⁄₁₀ in (2.5 cm) in thickness and into a rectangle approximately 10 in × 6 in (25 cm × 15 cm).
2 Cut pastry into two strips 3 in (8 cm) wide.
3 Mould the sausage meat into 2 long ropes approximately ¾ in (2 cm) in diameter and lay these in the centre of each strip.
4 Wash with egg or water between each roll of sausage meat so that the edge of each strip is dampened.
5 Fold over and press edges together firmly.
6 Cut lengths of roll into suitable length of approximately 2½ in (6 cm).
7 Mark surface with back of a knife.

8 Wash over with a mixture of egg and water.
9 Place the individual rolls on a clean baking sheet.
10 Allow a resting period of at least 30 minutes.
11 Bake in an oven at approximately 450°F (232°C) until crisp and light golden brown in colour.

Note: The sausage rolls described are dainty enough for a cocktail buffet. If larger rolls are required, the quantities of pastry and sausage meat would have to be increased proportionally.

Apple or jam turnovers – Chaussons
(Figure 14)

Yield 8

12 oz (360 g) pastry, leaving 5 oz (150 g) scrap
4 oz (120 g) jam
or
6 oz (180 g) apple
1 oz (30 g) sugar

1 Roll out pastry to ¹⁄₁₀ in (2.5 mm) thick.
2 Cut out with a 4-in (10-cm) fluted cutter.
3 With a rolling pin, elongate these discs, keeping the centre thin and the edges thick.
4 Place in a quantity of jam or sweetened apple.
5 Damp the edges with edge or water and fold over so that the two meet.
6 Wash with egg whites or water and dip into castor sugar.
7 Place on a clean baking tray and leave to rest for at least 30 minutes.
8 Bake in an oven at 420°F (215°C) until crisp and golden brown in colour.

Eccles
(Figure 14)

Yield 8

12 oz (360 g) pastry, leaving 5 oz (150 g) scrap
6 oz (180 g) Eccles or Banbury filling

Filling A
3 oz (90 g) currants
1 oz (30 g) brown sugar
½ oz (15 g) golden syrup
1½ oz (45 g) cake crumbs
Pinch mixed spice

Filling B
4 oz (120 g) mincemeat
2 oz (60 g) cake crumbs

Filling C
1 oz (30 g) butter
1 oz (30 g) brown sugar
4 oz (120 g) currants
Pinch mixed spice

Mix all ingredients together thoroughly.

1 Roll out the pastry to ¹⁄₁₆ in (1.5 mm) in thickness.
2 Cut out discs using a 4-in (10-cm) cutter.
3 Place a tablespoonful of the filling A, B or C in the centre of each piece.
4 Fold the edges into the centre, sealing in the filling and then turn over.
5 Either flatten with the palm of the hand or roll out with a rolling pin to approximately 3 in (7.5 cm) diameter.
6 Wash the tops with egg white or water and dip into castor sugar.
7 Place the pieces on a clean baking sheet.
8 Make two or three slits in the top with a knife so that the filling shows through.
9 Allow a 30-minute resting period.
10 Bake at 420°F (215°C) until crisp and golden brown in colour.

Figure 16 *Pithiviers. Showing the cutting of the top and the baked gateau*

Banburys
(Figure 14)

Yield 8

Ingredients same as for Eccles.

1 Repeat (1), (2), and (3) as for Eccles.
4 Fold over the top and bottom edges to meet in the centre but mould it into a boat shape, keeping the filling sealed in.
5 Flatten with the palm of the hand or rolling pin to approximately 2 in × 4 in (5 cm × 10 cm).
6 Finish off as for Eccles.

Mince pies
(Figure 60)

Yield 8

1 lb (480 g) puff pastry, leaving 6 oz (180 g) scrap
6 oz (180 g) mincemeat
½ oz (15 g) icing sugar

1 Roll out the paste to ¹⁄₁₀ in (2.5 mm) thick.

2 Cut out half the paste with a 2¾-in (7-cm) cutter, either fluted or plain.
3 Place the pieces on a clean baking sheet.
4 Damp the edges with water or alternatively splash the whole tray with water.
5 Place about a teaspoonful of mincemeat in the centre of each cut out piece.
6 Cover the pieces with discs cut from the remaining half of the paste with a 3-in (8-cm) cutter, rolling the paste slightly thinner to enable the same number of tops to be cut out.
7 Using the back rolled rim of a 2-in (5-cm) cutter, press down the edges to seal in the mincemeat.
8 Brush over with egg wash and pierce the top with a fork or knife.
9 Allow to rest for half an hour.
10 Bake in an oven at 450°F (232°C) until golden brown in colour.
11 Sprinkle with icing sugar when baked.
12 Place on a doily on a silver dish and serve warm with an appropriate sauce, for example custard or brandy (see page 185).

Pithivier
(Figures 16 and 19)

Yield 1 (suitable for 8 covers)

8 oz (240 g) puff pastry, leaving 1½–2 oz (45–60 g) scrap
1 oz (30 g) apricot jam
6 oz (180 g) frangipane filling (1½ oz (45 g) butter, etc.) (see page 62)
½ oz (15 g) icing sugar

1 Roll out a little less than half of the pastry to a thickness of 1¹⁄₁₆ in (1.5 mm) and cut out a disc 9 in (23 cm) diameter.
2 Place this piece on a clean baking tray, moisten the edges, and prick it all over with a fork or docker.
3 Spread over the jam to within 1 in (2.5 cm) from the edge.
4 Repeat using the frangipane filling.
5 Roll out the remaining pastry to approximately ¹⁄₁₀ in (2.5 mm) and cut out a slightly larger disc.
6 Dampen the edge, turn over and lay this piece carefully on top.
7 Decorate the edge and with a sharp knife make curved slits from the centre to within 1 in (2.5 cm) from the edge in the top layer of pastry (Figure 16).
8 Brush over with egg wash and allow it to rest for half an hour.
9 Bake in an even at 420°F (215°C) until it just begins to colour.
10 Sprinkle with icing sugar and return to oven to finish cooking and for the sugar to melt and glaze the top.

Jalousie
(Figures 18 and 19)

Yield same as for Pithivier

8 oz (240 g) mincemeat or jam
or 6 oz (180 g) frangipane (1½ oz (45 g) butter, etc.) (see page 62)

1 Roll out a third of the pastry to a thickness of ¹⁄₁₆ in (1.5 mm) and cut into a strip approximately 10 in × 4 in (25 cm × 10 cm).

2 Place on a clean baking tray, moisten the edges, and prick all over with a fork.
3 Spread on the filling to within 1 in (2.5 mm) from the edge which should be dampened with water.
4 Roll out the reamining pastry ¹⁄₁₀ in (2.5 mm) from the edge which should be dampened with water.
5 Fold the strip in half lengthwise and cut slits about ¼ in (6 mm) apart and to within 1 in (2.5 cm) of the edge.
6 Unfold carefully and place this strip over the other, pressing down the edges to seal.
7 Trim and decorate the edge.
8 Brush over with egg wash and allow a half-hour resting period.
9 Bake in an oven at 420°F (215°C) until it just begins to colour.
10 Sprinkle on icing sugar, return to the oven, and bake to a golden brown with a sugar glazed top.

Note: Alternatively, castor sugar could be sprinkled on prior to baking instead of using icing sugar.

Cream horns
(Figures 14 and 17)

Yield 8

8 oz (240 g) puff pastry
1 oz (30 g) jam
1 oz (30 g) sugar
¼ pt (1.5 dl) fresh cream

1 Roll out the puff pastry to ¹⁄₁₆ in (1.5 mm) in thickness and 24 in (60 cm) long.
2 Cut into strips 1 in (2.5 cm) wide.
3 Dampen with water.
4 Wrap the strip carefully round a clean cream horn mould so that each strip overlaps half the other. Start at the point and work towards the open end.
5 Wash top with egg whites or water and dip into castor sugar.
6 Place on a clean baking tray and allow at least a half-hour resting period.
7 Bake in an oven at 420°F (215°C) to a golden brown colour.
8 Remove the moulds whilst the horns are still warm by first giving them a slight twist.
9 Pipe in a small bulb of jam.
10 Using a savoy bag with a star tube, fill the horn with suitably flavoured and sweetened whipped fresh cream. Finish neatly with a little rosette and decorate with a cherry.

Fruit slice – Bande aux fruits or Tranche aux fruits

Yield 8 slices

8 oz (240 g) puff pastry, leaving 2 oz (60 g) scrap
1 oz (30 g) sugar
8 oz–1 lb (240–480 g) fruit
1 oz (30 g) apricot glaze (see page 289).

1 Roll out the puff pastry ¹⁄₁₆ in (1.5 mm) thick and about 14 in (35 cm) in length.

2 Cut a strip approximately 4½ in (12 cm) wide.
3 Dampen each edge with water and lay on a strip of similar thickness ¾ in (2 cm) wide.
4 Press these strips down firmly and decorate with the back of a knife.
5 Prick the base of the slice all over with a fork or docker and let it rest for at least half an hour.
6 According to the type of fruit used either:
  (a) Put the fruit, for example, apple, on the slice and bake together in an oven at 420°F (215°C), or
  (b) Bake the slice without the fruit in an oven at 440°F (226°C). Afterwards finish off with pastry cream and fruit or just the fruit itself.
7 Cover with a suitable glaze.
8 Cut into slices and serve as for flans.

Note: The fruit content is variable depending on the type of fruit used, and whether it is supplemented with pastry cream.

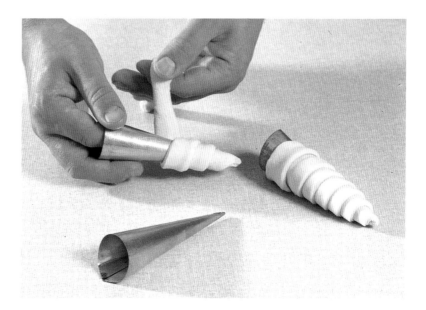

Figure 17   *Cream horns. Showing method of wrapping paste around the tin*

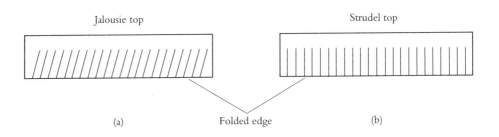

Figure 18   *Cutting tops for jalousie and strudel*

Varieties using all scrap pastry

Palmiers
(Figures 14 and 15)

Yield 8, sandwiched in pairs

8 oz (240 g) scrap pastry
¼ pt (1.5 dl) fresh cream
1½ oz (45 g) castor sugar
1 oz (30 g) jam

1 Roll out the pastry to ⅛ in (3 mm) in thickness and to at least 18 in (45 cm) in length.
2 Wash the surface with water and sprinkle liberally with castor sugar.
3 Starting at each end and folding in three results in six folds altogether, giving a strip approximately ½ in (12 mm) thick and 2½ in (6 cm) wide.
4 Cut this strip into slices ⅜ in (1 cm) thick and lay with the folds showing, on a well greased baking tray. Space about 3 in (8 cm) apart.
5 Allow to rest for at least half an hour.
6 Bake in an oven at 450°F (233°C) until just tinged with colour.
7 Turn over with a palette knife and finish off by baking to a golden brown colour with a glaze of caramelized sugar.
8 When cold, sandwich two palmiers with a little jam and a bulb of sweetened, whipped, fresh cream.

Fleurons
(Figure 14)

These are cut out of scrap pastry rolled to a thickness of approximately ⅛ in (3 mm) and cut into crescents with a fluted 2 in

Figure 19

Top left:	apple strudel	Top right:	gâteau mille feuilles
Bottom left:	jalousie	Bottom right:	gâteau Pithivier

(5 cm) cutter. The decorative finish on the ones shown in Figure 14 is made by first egg washing and then scraping over with a comb scraper. Allow to rest for 30 minutes and bake at approximately 420°F (215°C) until golden brown.

Other shapes may be made by the use of special cutters, for example seahorse (see Figure 1 on page 2).

Apple strudel (German)
(Figure 19)

Yield 8 slices

8 oz (240 g) puff pastry
1 lb (480 g) apples
1–2 oz (30–60 g) sultanas
1½ oz (45 g) sugar
2–3 oz (60–90 g) strip of sponge
2 oz (60 g) apricot purée
2 oz (60 g) water icing

1 Roll well-rested puff pastry very thinly to a rectangle 12 in (30 cm) long and approximately 9 in (22.5 cm) wide.
2 Cut a strip 4 in (10 cm) wide and place this on a clean baking tray.
3 Along the centre of this strip, place a 2 in (5 cm) wide strip of sponge.
4 Wash, peel, and core the apples. Chop very finely.
5 Mix in the sultanas and sugar.
6 Place this mixing on top of the sponge. It should form a mound about 2 in (5 cm) in height. Egg wash the edges of the puff pastry.
7 With the remaining puff pastry, cut a strip about 5 in (12.5 cm) in width. Fold this in half lengthwise and cut slits from the folded edge at ¼ in (6 mm) intervals. See Figure 18.
8 Keeping this strip folded, carefully lay it over one half of the filling and unfold it over the other half.
9 Press each side to make a perfect seal.
10 Egg wash and bake in an oven at 380°F (193°C).
11 When baked and whilst still hot, brush over with hot apricot purée and then water icing.
12 When cold, cut into slices approximately 1½ in (4 cm) in width.

Notes:
1 Instead of fresh apples, stewed or tinned apples may be used. In the latter case only 12 oz (360 g) will be required.
2 The purpose of the sponge strip in the base of these slices is to soak up the juice which will be formed from the mixture. Alternatively, bread or cake crumbs could be added to the filling and the sponge strip omitted.

Other varieties. Other fruits, such as cherries, apricots, pears, etc., could be used instead of apples.

Note:
For puff pastry bases for various gâteaux see Chapter 8.

4 *Sponge goods*

When eggs are beaten or whisked a considerable quantity of air becomes incorporated in the form of bubbles which constitute a foam. The ability of egg to hold air in this way is mainly due to the protein albumen present in the white. When this is agitated, partial coagulation occurs which forms a semi-rigid membrane around each air cell. At the same time as becoming thus aerated, the white also becomes stiffer (which is what one would expect if the egg becomes partially coagulated).

In sponge making, the egg is whisked with sugar until thick and light and the flour carefully incorporated to prevent the light structure from breaking down. Aeration of the sponge is achieved solely by the air trapped by the egg in the beating process.

Detailed method of making sponges

1 Sterilize the mixing bowl and whisk in boiling water to remove any trace of fat or oil. The presence of fat will interfere with the whisking of the egg and will prevent a perfect sponge from being made.
2 Weigh the ingredients.
3 Mix the egg and sugar and warm to approximately 90°F (32°C) by stirring over warm water (*not very hot water* as this might cook the egg). An alternative way to warm the sponge is to place the sugar on a tray and heat it in the oven prior to adding it to the egg.
4 Whisk the egg/sugar mixture until it becomes thick like the consistency of thick cream. This stage can be accurately judged only by experience. It should be thick enough to leave the marks of the whisk for a few seconds after it is withdrawn.
5 While the egg and sugar are whisking, prepare the baking pan or sheet, either with paper (as for Swiss rolls) or with grease and flour and sugar for some varieties.
6 Whisk in any colour, essence, glycerine, or water.
7 Blend in sieved flour with the hand. This must be done carefully so as not to break down the very light structure which has been built up by the whisking process. It is best to use the hand with fingers outstretched, gently lifting the flour through the sponge and turning the bowl.

8 Deposit the sponge in the prepared baking pan and bake at the correct time according to the variety made.

Note: special stabilizers are now on the market which help to keep the sponge from breaking down.

Varieties

Chocolate and almond sponges

The following recipes can be made into either chocolate or almond sponge as follows:

Chocolate   Delete 1 oz (30 g) flour and add 1 oz (30 g) cocoa powder ⎫
Almond   Delete 1 oz (30 g) flour and add 1 oz (30 g) ground almonds ⎬ Sieve well into flour ⎭

Plain sponge sandwich
(Figure 20)

Yield 2 × 6 in (15 cm) round pans

5 oz (150 g) eggs
5 oz (150 g) castor sugar
5 oz (150 g) flour (soft)

1 Prepare sponge mixture as previously described.
2 Prepare two 6 in (15 cm) sandwich pans with a coating of fat and dust with flour. Alternatively grease sides only, placing a disc of paper in the base which is removed after baking.
3 Deposit in the two sandwich pans and bake in an oven at approximately 400°F (240°C) for 25–30 minutes. (To test whether they are done, press the centre of the sponge which should be firm.)
4 When baked, turn the sponges out of the pans onto a cooling wire.
5 When cold, sandwich with jam and, if required, cream.
6 The top may be iced with fondant, water icing, or chocolate, or dusted with icing sugar.

The following provides an attractive alternative finish – cut about ½ in (12 mm) off the top of the sponge and cut into 6. Dust three of these with icing sugar and the other half with a mixture of icing sugar and cocoa powder. Pipe cream on the top of the remaining sponge and fashion in a dome shape. Replace the cut pieces alternately.

Enriched sponge sandwich

As for Plain sponge sandwich but with the addition of:

1–1½ oz (30–45 g) egg yolk (2 to 3)

This egg yolk should be added and beaten with the egg.
Enriched sponges are more suitable for gâteaux because the texture is firmer and the sponge slice will not crumble when cut.

Also sponge drops and fingers are more satisfactory when made with this mixing.

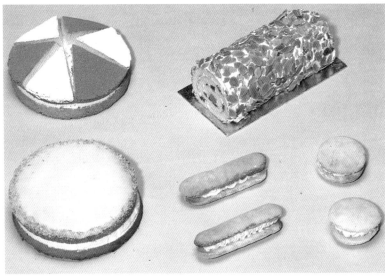

Figure 20 *Sponge goods.*

Description from left to right:
Top row: 1 Sandwich with top dressed in icing sugar and cocoa powder
            2 Swiss roll using buttercream with cherries for the filling and dressed with
              roasted flaked almonds
Bottom row: 1 Sandwich with top iced in fondant
            2 Sponge fingers
            3 Sponge drops

Swiss roll

Yield 3

10 oz (300 g) eggs
7½ oz (225 g) sugar
5 oz (150 g) flour (soft)
½ oz (15 g) glycerine

For chocolate and almond sponges see notes on page 82.

1 Prepare a baking sheet by lining with greaseproof paper.
2 Make a sponge as previously described.
3 Deposit on the lined baking tray and spread level. The area which this amount should cover is approximately 18 in × 15 in (45 cm × 38 cm).
4 Bake in a hot oven at 460°F (238°C) for approximately 4 minutes.
5 Remove from oven when baked and turn upside down on a clean cloth. It is best if it is placed on several layers of cloth or kitchen paper.
6 Leave with the baking tin on top. The steam should now be trapped in the layers of cloth or kitchen paper and eventually moisten the roll.
7 When absolutely cold, remove the tray and the greaseproof paper.
8 Spread on a layer of jam, curd, or cream, and with the aid of the cloth roll up.
9 Cut either into slices or in approximately 6½ in (17 cm) lengths.

Individual Swiss rolls   Yield 18

1 Proceed as for ordinary Swiss rolls but spread the mixture much more thinly on the tray to cover an area of 18 in × 19 in (45 cm × 48 cm).
2 Spread with jam, curd, or cream.
3 Cut into squares approximately 3 in (7.5 cm) square.
4 Roll up each square into a small Swiss roll.
5 These can be dusted with icing sugar or covered.

Swiss roll varieties
(Figure 20)

1 After spreading the roll sprinkle on a few washed sultanas or chopped cherries, then bake. Finish off in the usual way.
2 Make a raspberry, strawberry, or similar fruit flavoured roll by adding the appropriate flavour and colour to the sponge using the same flavour for the buttercream. This may also contain chopped fruit if desired.
3 Cover the roll first in a layer of boiling purée and then ice with a covering of warmed, appropriately flavoured and coloured fondant. Decorate using cherries, angelica, etc.
4 Cover the roll first with boiling apricot purée. Roll out a sheet of either almond, coconut, or sugar paste, trim to size, and cover the roll. The paste may be textured with a roller prior to covering. Decorate if desired.
5 Cover the roll in buttercream and mask with desiccated coconut or nibbed almonds, either plain or roasted.

Note: Varieties 3, 4 and 5 above, together with a suitable centre, may be cut up into slices and used as afternoon tea fancies.

Chocolate log
(Figure 60 page 224)

Make a chocolate roll, using a buttercream filling (see page 285). After cutting into the required length, the roll may be finished in three ways.

Method 1

1 Mask each end with a white buttercream and into this pipe a spiral or circles of chocolate cream to simulate the end grain.
2 Using a savoy bag fitted with a star tube, pipe lines of chocolate buttercream lengthwise, completely covering the surface. Alternatively a comb scraper may be used.

Method 2

1 Cover the roll with boiling apricot jam and chocolate coloured paste. Mark with a fork.
2 For the ends, roll out a piece of paste into a long strip. Cover with chocolate and, when set, roll up like a Swiss roll. Cut thin slices off this and roll out to cover the ends to which they are attached, using purée.

Method 3

1 Cover with chocolate.
2 Mask each end with either the cream (Method 1) or paste (Method 2).

Butter sponge – Genoise

5 oz (150 g) eggs
5 oz (150 g) castor sugar
5 oz (150 g) flour (soft)
1 oz (30 g) melted butter

For chocolate and almond sponges see page 82.

1 Make a sponge of the egg and sugar as previously described.
2 Add the flour and start to blend it into the sponge. When almost mixed, add the melted butter and finish mixing.
3 Deposit in prepared pans and bake as for sandwiches.

Notes:

1 These are difficult to make successfully because the butter tends to break down the structure of the sponge. For success keep the sponge warm so that the butter does not set before the mixture is deposited in the tin.
2 The proportion of added butter may be increased to 2 oz (60 g), giving a closer crumb structure but better keeping, cutting, and eating qualities. Greater care will be required in the mixing process to prevent a breakdown of the sponge.

Sponge drops: sponge fingers – Biscuits à la cuillere
(Figure 20)

Yield 48 singles, size 3 in × ½ in (7.5 cm × 1.25 cm) tube

Use either the plain sandwich or enriched sandwich recipe.

1 Prepare a baking tray with a sheet of greaseproof or silicone paper.
2 Make the sponge mixing and transfer it to a clean savoy bag fitted with a ½ in (12 mm) plain tube.
3 Keeping the size uniform, pipe either fingers or drops onto greaseproof or silicone paper on a clean table top. Use separate sheets for the drops and fingers.
4 When the whole tray has been piped, cover liberally with castor sugar.
5 Remove excess sugar by picking up the papered sheet on which they have just been piped, holding it vertically, then place it on a baking tray.
6 Bake immediately in an oven at 450°F (232°C) for approximately 4 minutes. The colour should be a light brown all over.

Note: Perfect sponge drops and fingers are difficult to make. The best recipe to use is the enriched sponge since this gives stability to the sponge which is an asset for this type of goods.
    The main fault which occurs with these goods is as follows:
    Mixture runs flat when piped, giving flat and mis-shapen drops and fingers with cracked surfaces.

Cause

1 Mixture was overbeaten and broken down when flour was mixed in.
2 Oven temperature too cool.
3 Goods left too long before baking.

Varieties using sponge drops and fingers

1 Sandwich together with jam or cream (buttercream or fresh) and serve in paper cases.
2 Before sandwiching together, dip half the top in chocolate.
3 Sandwich with apricot jam and dip the whole drop or finger in boiling apricot purée. Wipe off surplus with a brush and roll in desiccated coconut either plain or roasted. Instead of apricot, raspberry purée may be used.
4 Charlotte Russe – see Chapter 15.
5 Ice-cream dishes – see Chapter 22.

Sponge flans

Use basic or enriched sponge recipe.
    Deposit the sponge mixture in greased and floured flan moulds.
    When baked these moulds may be filled with various fruit fillings and make quite an acceptable sweet if served with fresh cream.

Victoria sponge sandwich

Yield 1 sandwich

4 oz (120 g) butter
4 oz (120 g) sugar
4 oz (120 g) eggs
2 oz (60 g) flour (soft)
2 oz (60 g) scone flour (see page 52)

    Although this is strictly a cake, it is included in this chapter to avoid confusion.

1 Sugar batter method of cake-making (see page 98).
2 Deposit in two greased and floured 6-in (15-cm) sandwich pans.
3 Bake at 360°F (182°C) for approximately 25 minutes.
4 When cool, sandwich together as described under sponge sandwiches (see page 82).

Othellos (also Desdemonas, Jagos, and Rosalinds)
(Figure 21)

Yield 12 doubles (24 halves)

A
3 egg yolks
½ oz (15 g) sugar
1½ oz (45 g) flour

B
4 oz (120 g) egg whites
1½ oz (45 g) castor sugar

Figure 21   *Othellos, Desdemonas, Jagos and Rosalinds. Method of enrobing the sponge with fondant*

C
1½ oz (45 g) soft flour

For decoration
3 oz (90 g) jam
6 oz (180 g) fondant
6 oz (180 g) lightly beaten buttercream or custard or ¼ pt (1.5 dl) fresh cream

1 Mix ingredients in A to a smooth paste.
2 Whisk ingredients in B to a stiff meringue.
3 Carefully blend the flour C into the meringue and then blend into the paste.
4 Transfer mixing to a savoy bag fitted with a ½-in (12-mm) tube.
5 Pipe small bulbs onto a well-greased and floured baking tray, size 1¼–1½ in (3–4 cm).
6 Bake in a hot oven at 460°F (238°C) for approximately 8 minutes.
7 When cold, scoop out the centre and sandwich together with a good quality cream or custard. Also remove the peak so that they will stand correctly.
8 Brush over or dip into boiling apricot purée and coat with an appropriately flavoured and coloured fondant.
9 Finish by piping a spiral of fondant and add a piece of crystallized flower petal, cherry, or nut.

Othellos

This is the name given to the variety which is finished with chocolate custard cream and chocolate fondant.

Desdemonas

These are Othello bases sandwiched with vanilla flavoured whipped dairy cream and finished with white fondant, flavoured with kirsch.

Jagos

The same as Othellos except that coffee flavour is used.

Rosalinds

The same as Desdemonas except that a rose flavoured cream and fondant is used.

5 *Meringue goods*

Basic recipe

5 oz (150 g) egg whites
10 oz (300 g) castor sugar

1 Scald all utensils with boiling water to eliminate grease.
2 Whisk egg whites to a stiff snow.
3 Continue whisking and add ⅔ of the sugar.
4 Continue whisking until the meringue is very stiff.
5 Stir in the remaining sugar with a spatula.

Note: The whisking of meringue is best done on a machine.

Shells
(Figure 22)

Yield from basic recipe 30 (15 shells)

1 Pipe out meringue into oval shells on greaseproof paper using a ½-in (12-mm) piping tube and savoy bag.
2 Bake meringue in an oven at 250°F (121°C) for approximately ½ hour leaving door of oven slightly ajar to allow the steam to escape.
3 The shells should be removed from the oven once they are slightly fawn in colour and set sufficiently to allow them to be removed from the tray.
4 Remove shells carefully, press in the base with a clean thumb to leave a hollow to receive cream.
5 Stack shells in a tray and store in a warm, dry place until required.
6 Finish off with fresh cream, piping it between two shells placed on their sides in a paper case. The cream may be slightly sweetened and flavoured with liqueurs. Also the meringue may be coloured and flavoured if desired.

Hot meringue

5 oz (150 g) egg whites
14 oz (420 g) castor sugar
Colour and flavour

1 Place sugar on a papered tray and warm in the oven.
2 Whisk the whites to a stiff snow.
3 Add the heated sugar to the whisking whites.
4 Whisk the meringue until very stiff.
5 Colour and flavour as desired.

Figure 22   *Meringues*

Top row: Shells
Bottom row: With fruit

Fancy meringues
(Figure 23)

1 Using a star tube, pipe out a variety of fancy shells on greaseproof or silicone paper. Decorate with glacé fruits, coloured nuts, vermicelli, etc.
2 Bake as for shells.
3 Remove from the paper and store in a dry place until required.

Note: Some of these shapes may be dipped in chocolate or have chocolate piped on them prior to serving. These fancy meringues may be served either on their own if they are flavoured or with ice-cream and/or fruit.

Figure 23   *Fancy meringues. Description in text*

Meringue cases with fruit
(Figure 22)

1 Place meringue shells upside down in a paper case.
2 Pipe on a bulb of whipped fresh sweetened cream.
3 Place on pieces of well-drained fruit.

Figure 24   *Vacherins. Piping bases for individual vacherins and showing tops and bases for larger varieties*

Left hand side
Figure 25   *Vacherins. Piping a meringue dahlia for a top*

Right hand side
Figure 26   *Vacherins. Spraying colour on to a meringue dahlia top*

Vacherins for 8 covers
(Figure 27)

2½ oz (75 g) egg whites
5 oz (150 g) castor sugar

1 Make up the meringue as described for shells.
2 Draw shapes with pencil on greaseproof or silicone paper. For round shapes, circle needs to be approximately 7 to 8 in (20 cm). Other shapes should be of approximately the same area.
3 Pipe outline using a savoy bag with a ½-in (12-mm) plain tube.

For a base and cover, fill in the outline. For the rings, pipe a few extra lines criss-cross inside the outline for strength. See Figure 24.

4 Bake off as previously described under Shells.

5 Remove from the paper and thoroughly dry out in a warm atmosphere.

6 Assemble the meringue rings on the base using a little unbaked meringue to stick the pieces together.

7 Fill the case either during the construction or afterwards with fresh cream and fruit. Cubes of sponge soaked in liqueur-flavoured syrup may also be used.

8 The top may be of meringue and piped into a decorative shape (Figure 25) or decorated with cream and small piped meringue shapes with glacé fruits or other decor. Chocolate may also be used as a decorating medium. The sides too may be masked with cream.

Pavlova
(Figure 27)

This is a type of sweet dish consisting of a meringue base topped with whipped cream and fruit, and was named in honour of the Russian ballerina Anna Pavlova.

It is now becoming increasingly popular and various types are to be found as a deep-frozen sweet dish in many supermarkets. The meringues shown in Figure 27 were done as follows.

Yield 2 (8 covers each)

Basic meringue recipe (page 89)
½ pt (3 dl) whipping cream
Fresh or tinned fruit

1 Place two 7 in (18 cm) flan hoops on to silicone or greaseproof paper and use the same to line them with a 1 in (2.5 cm) band, using a spot of jam or adhesive to keep them in place.

2 Make the meringue and deposit half in each of the hoops.

3 Using a scraper spread the meringue to the sides leaving a small hollow in the centre.

4 Bake in an oven at 240°F (121°C) for about 45 minutes or until the meringue is cooked to a light fawn colour. Remove the bands when cold.

5 The slight hollow in the meringue is now filled with fruit and whipped cream.

6 The pavlova is finished with a dome of fresh whipped cream which is decorated with various fresh and tinned fruits.

Italian meringue

This meringue is partially cooked and is used in the making of goods which are decorated with meringue flashed off in the oven, for example baked Alaska ice-cream. It can also be used for piping fancy shapes, since it is more stable than the other types of meringue.

Yield for fancy meringues 50

5 oz (150 g) egg whites
10 oz (300 g) sugar
3 oz (90 g) water
Pinch of cream of tartar

Colour and flavour according to requirements.

1 Place the sugar, water, and cream of tartar in a copper saucepan and, observing sugar boiling precautions (see page 264), heat to 245°F (118°C).
2 Meanwhile beat the egg whites to a stiff snow.
3 Keeping the egg whites whisking, add the boiled syrup in a steady stream.
4 Continue whisking until the meringue is firm.
5 Lastly, add the colour and flavour according to requirements.

Fruit meringue

Add up to 5 oz (150 g) of fruit pulp to the Italian meringue recipe at Stage (5).

The fruit pulp may be apple, raspberry, strawberry, etc.

Piped meringue shapes

Meringue is an ideal medium with which to pipe out shapes which can then be baked crisp and assembled. Animals, flowers, and many other shapes can be imitated in this way. One of the easiest shapes and one which can form a suitable decoration in various sweets is mushroom which is described as follows:

1 Make a basic meringue.
2 Pipe out very small bulbs using a ¼-in (0.5-cm) tube on greaseproof paper and give a light dusting of cocoa powder.
3 With the same tube, pipe out stems approximately ¾ in (1.5 cm) in length.
4 Bake off in oven approximately 250°F (121°C).
5 When dry, remove from the paper.
6 When baked dig a hole in the underside of the bulb with a knife and cover with liquid chocolate. Push in the pointed end of the stem to form the mushroom shape.

Meringue and ice-cream – Meringue glacé chantilly

For each portion allow two half meringue shells (see page 89).
Sandwich the two meringue shells with a scoop of ice-cream and decorate with Chantilly cream.

Note: The ice-cream may be of various flavours and contain fruit. The decoration could include fruits, nuts, or chocolate pieces (see Chapter 22).

Figure 27
Top: Pavlovas
Bottom: Vacherins

Figure 28   *Individual vacherins. Descriptions in text*

Individual vacherins

Yield from previous recipe: with tops 8, without tops 12
These are made in the same way as the larger varieties but the size should not exceed 3 in (7.5 cm) in diameter. Figure 24 shows the rings and bases being piped.
The varieties described in Figure 28 are as follows.

Top row (left to right)

1 Chocolate flower formed from chocolate cutouts.
2 Piped meringue top with chocolate spun over.
3 Piped meringue dahlia sprayed pink (see Figure 26).

Bottom row (left to right)

1 Ring of pineapple with a centre of angelica.
2 Orange segments arranged as a flower with a cherry centre.
3 A chocolate disc. For special occasions this can be personalized by piping on an inscription or a stencilled design.

6 Cakes

Cake faults

Before dealing with some basic cake recipes, here is a list of common faults and their diagnoses.

Fault – cake sinking in the centre

Causes

1 *Too much aeration.* This may be caused by:
   (a) Too much sugar used in the recipe. This can be detected by excessive crust colour and a sticky seam running in the shape of a U.
   (b) Too much baking powder. Difficult to detect because it can be confused with (c).
   (c) Overbeating of fat/sugar/egg batter prior to adding flour.
2 *Undercooked.* This can easily be detected by the presence of a wet seam just below the surface of the *top* crust.
3 *Knocking in oven prior to cakes being set.* If during cooking when all the ingredients are in a fluid state, a cake gets a knock or disturbance (such as a draught of cold air) some collapse may take place which will result in the centre of the cake caving in.
4 *Too much liquid.* This is easy to detect because, firstly the sides will tend to cave in as well as the top, and if the cake is cut a seam will be discovered immediately *above* the *bottom* crust. Cakes containing too much liquid do not show this fault until they are removed from the oven. During baking, the excess moisture is in the form of steam and actually contributes to the aeration of the cake. On cooling, this steam condenses into water which sinks to the bottom of the cake, collapsing the texture by so doing.

Fault – peaked tops

Causes

1 *Flour used was too strong.* For cakemaking, a weak flour with a low gluten (protein) content is required. If a strong flour is used, the cake will be tough, giving rise to a peaked top which looks unsightly.
2 *Mixing was toughened.* The flour of a cake should be only just mixed in. Overmixing will cause the batter to become tough as

the gluten of flour is being developed. Not only will a tough batter produce peaked tops but also a tough and coarse crumb, detracting from its eating qualities.

3 *Too hot an oven with insufficient steam.* The ideal baking condition for a cake is to have a quantity of steam present which will delay the formation of a crust until the cake has become fully aerated and set. If an ovenful of cakes are baked, there is usually sufficient steam generated from the cakes themselves for this purpose, but for small quantities a tray of water should be inserted to get this required steam. A very hot oven will form a crust on the cake too soon and this will in turn cause the cake to rise in the centre only, giving the characteristic peak.

Fault – small volume with bound appearance

Causes

This is caused by insufficient aeration due to:

1 Insufficient beating of the batter.
2 Insufficient sugar used in the recipe.
3 Insufficient baking powder used in the recipe. Such cakes will have a close crumb structure and be tough to eat.

Fault – fruit sinking in fruit cakes

Causes

1 Cake mixing is too soft to carry the weight of fruit. This may be due to:
   (a) Cake mixing being too light because of overbeating (fat/sugar/egg).
   (b) Excessive sugar used.
   (c) Excessive baking powder used.
   (d) Insufficient toughening of batter.
   (e) Use of too weak a flour. Slight toughening of the batter is sometimes necessary to strengthen the crumb and thus make it possible to support the fruit.
2 Fruit was washed and insufficiently dried before being incorporated into the cake batter.
3 Baking temperature was too low. See following note on Baking.

Baking

The general rule is that cakes should be baked as quickly as possible consistent with their being properly cooked through without adverse discoloration of the crust. The following are the factors which affect the baking temperature of cakes.

Steam

As previously mentioned a humid atmosphere is essential in order to achieve a flat top on a cake and to ensure that thorough baking is carried out with a pleasing crust colour. A pan of water inserted in the oven is usually sufficient for this purpose.

Richness

The more sugar a cake contains, the cooler the oven temperature and the longer the cooking time that is required. This is because the richer the cake, the more crust colour is formed.

Shape and size

The overriding consideration to be given here is the penetration of heat into the cake mass. It follows from this that the smaller the cake the shorter the baking time, and then the higher the baking temperature. Conversely, large cakes require a lower baking temperature with a longer baking time. However, it is not always appreciated that shape plays an important part. Since it is the penetration of heat that counts, a thin slab of cake cooks very much more rapidly than the same weight but say, double the thickness. The range of temperatures over which cakes may be baked is very wide, ranging from 350°F (177°C) for wedding cakes to 450°C (232°C) for very small fairy cakes.

Additions

Substances like sugar or almonds added to the surface of a cake act as improving the richness of a cake, and baking temperature should be reduced by 10–20°F (5.5–11°C) to compensate.

Certain substances like glucose, invert sugar, and honey take on colour at a much lower temperature than sugar. If such substances are added (for example, for their cake moistening properties), the baking temperature also needs to be lower.

Preparation of dried fruit for fruit cakes

The moist eating and keeping qualities of cake containing dried fruit depend to a large extent on the amount of moisture retained by the fruit in the cake. To achieve the maximum retention of moisture by the fruit, proper preparation is essential. The fruit should be sorted, washed, and well-drained before use (see page 30).

Essences, fruit juices, spirits, etc. may be mixed into the fruit, preferably some time prior to their being used.

The fruit is always added last after the flour has been mixed in.

Choice of ingredients

Flour

Always use a soft flour but if this is not possible replace a proportion with cornflour.

Fat

Since the aeration of a good quality cake is partly achieved by the trapping of air by the action of beating the fat, one with good creaming qualities is essential. Unfortunately, both butter and normal lard (special processed lards with good creaming qualities are now available) suffer in this respect. In most recipes where butter is used a small quantity of shortening should be incorporated to help overcome this defect.

Sugar

Fine grain castor is best so that it will readily dissolve in the batter.

Cake making methods

To achieve the best possible results, a temperature of approximately 70°F (21°C) should be aimed at and the materials used should be brought to this temperature prior to mixing.

Sugar batter method

1 The fat, margarine, or butter is first beaten to a light foam with the sugar. With fat and margarine, this can be effected in about 4 minutes but butter is difficult to cream and will require at least three times as long. Colour and essences should be added at this stage.
2 The egg is now added and beaten in. If a machine is employed, the egg can be added in a steady stream over a period of about 2 minutes. If mixing is done by hand, add the egg in about four portions, beating each well in.
3 Add the flour and carefully mix it into the batter. The aim should be to get a clear smooth batter without lumps and yet not toughened.
4 Lastly, add any liquid, for example milk, fruit, nuts, etc., and blend into the batter carefully to ensure even distribution.

Flour batter method

1 Mix the sugar with the egg and whisk to a half sponge. Add any colour or essence at this stage.
2 Cream the fat (margarine or butter) with an equal proportion of flour.
3 Add (1) to (2) in about four portions, blending each portion of the half sponge well into the fat/flour cream.
4 Blend into the batter the remainder of the flour, so that a smooth mixing free of lumps will result.
5 Lastly, add any other materials such as milk, fruit, nuts, etc., and blend in carefully to ensure even distribution.

Note: Dry ingredients like cocoa, baking powder, and ground almonds, are always added with the flour.

Fruit cakes

Yield one 6-in (15-cm) cake

3 oz (90 g) butter
1 oz (30 g) white cooking fat (not lard)

4 oz (120 g) castor sugar
5 oz (150 g) eggs
5 oz (150 g) flour
1 oz (30 g) scone flour (see page 52)
5 oz (150 g) fruit (see below)
¼ (7.5 g) glycerine (see page 48)

Fruit	Mixed fruit	Sultana	Currant	Cherry
Currants	2 oz (60 g)	–	4 oz (120 g)	–
Sultanas	1½ oz (45 g)	4 oz (120 g)	–	–
Cherries	½ oz (15 g)	–	–	9 oz (270 g)
Peel	1 oz (30 g)	1 oz (30 g)	1 oz (30 g)	–

The above quantities (except Cherry) are for lightly fruited cakes. For medium increase by 50%, and for heavily fruited cakes double these quantities.

1 Prepare the cake hoops (see Note 1 below).
2 Make the cake on the sugar batter method.
3 Deposit the above mixing in 6-in (15-cm) papered hoops (see Note 1 below).
4 Bake at 360°F (182°C) for approximately 1¼ hours until thoroughly cooked. Steam in the oven would be an advantage.

Notes:
1 *Preparation of cake hoops.* Cakes baked in hoops need the added protection of paper against the heat of the oven. Several thicknesses of paper should be placed on a tray and covered with greaseproof or silicone paper before the hoops are placed upon the tray. The sides of the hoops should also be lined with paper, the final layer being greaseproof or silicone. Circles of paper can be cut to fit into the bottom of the hoops

Unless there is plenty of steam in the oven, it is also advisable to cover the top of the cake with a sheet of paper. If the paper sides are extended some way above the level of the cake, this sheet of paper can lie on top without touching the cake.
2 *Size and weights.* These apply to lightly fruited cakes and madeira cakes. For heavily fruited cakes these weights need to be increased.

Approximate weight of batter	Size of hoops
1 lb 2 oz (540 g)	5½ in (14 cm)
1 lb 8 oz (720 g)	6 in (15 cm)
2 lb 4 oz (1080 g)	7 in (17.5 cm)
3 lb 6 oz (1620 g)	8 in (20 cm)
4 lb 8 oz (2160 g)	9 in (23 cm)
5 lb 6 oz (2580 g)	10 in (25.5 cm)

Madeira cakes

Yield one 6-in (15-cm) cake

4 oz (120 g) butter
2 oz (60 g) cooking fat (not lard)
6 oz (180 g) sugar
½ oz (15 g) glycerine
7½ oz (225 g) eggs

1½ oz (45 g) scone flour (see page 52)
7 oz (210 g) soft flour
Zest of lemon

1 Make using either the sugar or flour batter method.
2 Proceed as for lightly fruited cakes.
3 The top may be decorated with a slice of citron peel.
4 Bake as the lightly fruited cakes.

Note: The butter and fat may be replaced with margarine.

Genoa cakes

Yield one 6- or 7-in (15- or 17.5-cm) cake

Use the Fruit cake recipe with the following amendments:

Fruit
4 oz (120 g) currants
3 oz (90 g) sultanas
4 oz (120 g) cherries
1 oz (30 g) peel

Add Essences: almond, vanilla and lemon, or almond and marachino. Sprinkle top with flake or strip almonds prior to baking.

Dundee cakes

Yield one 6- or 7-in (15- or 17.5-cm) cake

4 oz (120 g) butter
1 oz (30 g) white cooking fat (not lard)
5 oz (150 g) dark brown soft sugar
5 oz (150 g) eggs
4 oz (120 g) flour (soft)
1 oz (30 g) scone flour (see page 52)
½ oz (15 g) ground almonds
2 oz (60 g) currants
5 oz (150 g) sultanas
1 oz (30 g) cherries
1½ oz (45 g) mixed peel
½ oz (15 g) milk
¼ oz (7.5 g) glycerine (see page 48)
Vanilla, almond, and rum essences
2 oz (60 g) split almonds for decoration

Add Blackjack and egg colour to give a bright golden brown crumb.
   Prepare as for fruit cakes, but before baking cover the top with split almonds with the rounded surface facing.

Birthday or Christmas cakes

Yield on 6- or 7-in (15–17.5-cm) cake

3 oz (90 g) butter
1 oz (30 g) white cooking fat (not lard)
4 oz (120 g) dark brown soft sugar
5 oz (150 g) eggs
4 oz (120 g) flour
1 oz (30 g) scone flour (see page 52)

7 oz (210 g) sultanas
7 oz (210 g) currants
2 oz (60 g) cut mixed peel
2 level teaspoonsful mixed spice
¼ oz (7.5 g) glycerine (see page 48)
Blackjack
Almond and vanilla essences

1 Prepare as for fruit cakes.
2 The sizes and weights are the same as for wedding cakes (see page 103).

Notes:
1 Christmas cakes may have the addition of rum.
2 Cherries may be used to replace some of the sultanas if desired.
3 Blackjack should be added to give the cake a rich dark crumb. If too thick, it should be warmed before adding to the batter.

Heavy genoese

4 oz (120 g) butter
1 oz (30 g) white cooking fat (not lard)
5 oz (150 g) eggs
5 oz (150 g) sugar
4 oz (120 g) soft flour
1 oz (30 g) scone flour (see page 52)
¼ oz (7.5 g) glycerine (see page 48)
Vanilla essence

For chocolate. Replace ½ oz (15 g) flour with cocoa powder and add colour.
For almond. Replace ½ oz (15 g) flour with ground almonds.

1 Make using the sugar batter method.
2 Spread the mixing to a depth of approximately ¾ in (2 cm) on a deep sided tray lined with greaseproof or silicone paper. Make sure the mixing is spread level. This quantity of mixing will produce a sheet approximately 8 in (20 cm) square.
3 Bake at 380°F (193°C) for 35–40 minutes.
4 When cool, keep in a moist place for 24 hours prior to its use.

Boiled genoese

This genoese is strongly recommended for cutting up into petits fours or afternoon tea fancies because of the stability of its texture and its good keeping qualities.

5 oz (150 g) eggs
4½ oz (135 g) sugar
4 oz (120 g) flour
4 oz (120 g) butter
½ oz (15 g) glycerine

Chocolate. Replace ½ oz (15 g) flour with cocoa powder and add colour.
Almond. Replace ½ oz (15 g) flour with ground almonds.

1 Heat the egg and sugar to blood heat and whisk to a thick sponge.
2 Melt the butter in a mixing bowl over heat and stir in the flour and glyercine. Remove from the heat and beat mixture to a smooth paste.
3 Add the sponge to the fat and flour mixture in three portions. Mix each addition thoroughly but gently to ensure a smooth batter free from lumps.
4 Pour batter into a four-sided tray for fancies approximately 8 in (20 cm) square and for petits fours approximately 12 × 9 in (30 × 22 cm) and spread level.
5 Bake in an oven at 375°F (191°C) for approximately 40 minutes or until thoroughly baked.
6 When baked, store in a sealed tin until required. This cake will keep in a moist condition for a month if kept wrapped.

Note: It is usual for the genoese to be cut through the centre and sandwiched either with buttercream or jam. The top and bottom skin should also be trimmed off before the sheet is cut into individual pieces.

Wedding cakes

1 lb (480 g) butter
1 lb (480 g) dark brown sugar
1 lb 4 oz (600 g) eggs
1 lb (480 g) flour (browned in the oven)
4 oz (120 g) ground almonds
2½ oz (75 g) nib almonds (roasted)
3 lb (1440 g) currants
1 lb (480 g) sultanas
12 oz (360 g) cut mixed peel
Zest of 1½ lemons
¼ pt (1.5 dl) rum (to rub into baked cake)

1 Make cake on the sugar batter process omitting the rum.
   The flour as well as the nib almonds are roasted in the oven to enhance the flavour and increase the dark colour. If required, caramel colour can be added to make the cake darker.
2 Bake the cake in hoops or tins which are well protected from the heat with several layers of paper. A sheet of clean paper can also cover the top during baking, and some steam or water in the oven would be advantageous. When the correct amount of batter has been placed in the hoop it should be flattened into a slight hollow with the back of a wet hand. The temperature should not exceed 350°F (177°C) for a medium sized cake, dropping to 330°F (165°C) for a large one. Some indications of weight of cakes in relation to size of hoops follow:

Round cakes

Hoop size (in)	(cm)	(lb	oz)	Cake weight (grammes to nearest 5 g)	Board size (in)	(cm)	Oven time (hours)
5	13	1	8	680	7	18	2–2½
6	15	2	4	1020	8	20	2–2½
7	18	3	0	1360	9	23	2½–3
8	20	4	0	1810	10	25	2½–3
9	23	5	0	2265	12	30	3–3½
10	25	6	8	2950	13	33	3½
11	28	8	8	3855	14	36	3½
12	30	9	8	4310	15	38	3½

Square cakes

Frame size (in)	(cm)	(lb	oz)	Cake weight (grammes to nearest 5 g)	Board size (in) (cm)	Oven time (hours)
5	13	1	15	890	Same as for Round cakes	Same as for Round cakes
6	15	2	14	1305		
7	18	3	13	1730		
8	20	5	1	2295		
9	23	6	5	2865		
10	25	8	4	3740		
11	28	10	13	4905		
12	30	12	1	5470		

The weights above are only approximate and may be varied according to the thickness of cake required.

3 Store the cakes for at least 6 weeks prior to the reception. Keep wrapped in greaseproof or silicone paper in an airtight tin. During this period the rum should be added by pouring onto the surface of the cake and allowing it to soak well in. Apply the rum in two stages, at 14-day and 28-day intervals. The amount stated can be increased to ½ pt (3 lt) if a prolonged storage is given. Of course, it can be omitted altogether but the cake will not be so matured nor taste so rich.

4 After the maturing process, the cake is now ready for marzipanning and icing.

The icing of cakes is so specialized and there are so many publications now devoted to this subject that it is thought inappropriate to include details here which would of necessity be incomplete.

Scones

Notes on scones

Flour

A medium strength flour should be used. If this is not available, it is recommended that a blend of flour should be used from equal quantities of a strong bread-making flour and a soft cake flour, thoroughly sieved together.

Baking powder

Most proprietary brands are made from a phosphoric acid derivative with sodium bicarbonate (see page 36). Such powders used in the proportions of a scone mixing produce an unpleasant 'bite' or after-taste. Their use has the advantage that the scone mixing can be toughened during the mixing stage to develop a good texture, and then allowed to relax for up to an hour before it is needed to be baked, thus producing a scone with a good appearance.

For the discriminating customer who is more concerned with flavour and taste, the author strongly recommends the use of a cream of tartar baking powder (see page 35), since this leaves no objectionable after-taste. However, if a cream of tartar baking powder is used, the following rules should be observed:

1 Do not toughen the mixing but only mix sufficiently for it to be free of lumps.
2 Bake off as soon as possible after the goods have been egg washed.

Scone rounds

Yield two rounds (8 scones)

A
1 oz (30 g) medium flour
7 oz (210 g) scone flour (see page 52)
2 level teaspoonsful salt

B
1½ oz (45 g) nut oil
1½ oz (45 g) sugar
4½ oz (135 g) milk
½ oz (15 g) egg whites

1 Sieve thoroughly the ingredients of A and make a bay (well).
2 Thoroughly whisk the ingredients of B to make an emulsion.
3 Pour the emulsion into the bay and mix to a dough.
4 Add the sultanas which have been previously picked and washed.
5 Mix to a clear dough free of lumps.
6 Divide the dough into two and mould round.
7 Flatten the pieces slightly with a rolling pin and transfer to a clean baking sheet.
8 With a knife or scraper, cut the piece into four (like a cross).
9 Separate the four segments on the tray so that there is a gap of approximately ¼ in (0.5 cm) between them.
10 Egg wash the tops of each segment.
11 Bake in an oven at 450°F (232°C) for approximately 15–20 minutes.

Alternative method of mixing using butter, margarine, or cooking fat instead of oil: Rubbing-in method

1 Sieve ingredients of A.
2 Rub the fat into the flour until it is the consistency of ground almonds with no lumps of fat remaining.
3 Make a bay (well).
4 Dissolve the sugar in the liquids and pour into the well.
5 Mix to a clear dough.
6 Proceed as for (4) above in previous recipe.

Tea scones

Yield 18

1 oz (30 g) medium flour
7 oz (210 g) scone flour
2 oz (60 g) butter
1 ¾ oz (55 g) sugar
½ oz (15 g) eggs
4¾ oz (145 g) milk

Creaming method

1 Sieve the flours.
2 Beat the sugar and butter to a light cream.
3 Add the egg and beat in.
4 Add half the milk to the creamed butter, etc.
5 Add the sieved flour and half mix in.
6 Add the remainder of the milk and mix to a clear and smooth dough.
7 Roll the dough to approximately ½ in (1.25 cm) thick.
8 With a 2-in (5-cm) round cutter, cut out pieces and place on a clean baking sheet.
9 Egg wash.
10 Bake at 440°F (226°C) for approximately 15 minutes.
11 When baked and cool, these scones may be split and served with butter, fresh cream, and/or jam.

Varieties

Sultana or currant scones

Add 2½–3 oz (75–90 g) of the fruit to either of the recipes given.

Fried scones

Use Scone rounds recipe.

1 Roll out the dough to ½ in (1.25 cm) in thickness.
2 Cut into strips 2½ in (6 cm) wide, and then into fingers approximately ½ in (1.25 cm) wide.
3 Drop into boiling fat. When one side is cooked, turn over to cook the other side.

4 When cooked, drain and roll in cinnamon flavoured sugar.
5 The fingers may be split and filled with fresh cream and jam, etc.
   Round and triangular shapes may also be made and finished off in the same way.

Turnover scones

Use either recipe.

1 Divide scone mixing into two and mould round.
2 Roll out the pieces to approximately 8 in (20 cm) and cut into four.
3 Place the pieces on a clean baking sheet.
4 Bake in an oven at 450°F (232°C).
5 Using a palette knife turn the pieces over as soon as they can be moved without damaging them.
6 Return to the oven to finish baking.

Farmhouse scones

Use either recipe.
   Dust heavily with flour instead of egg washing.

Treacle scones

Use either recipe.
   Replace the sugar with black treacle. Bake at 430°F (221°C).

Wholemeal or brown scones

Use the Tea scone recipe.
   Replace the white flour with wholemeal or brown flour. Increase the milk to 5¼ oz (160 g).

Hotplate scones

Use either recipe.
   Bake the scones on a hotplate, turning them over half way through cooking.

Coconut scones

Use either recipe.
   Add ½ oz (15 g) fine desiccated coconut.
   Proceed as for Turnover scones (1) and (2) but cut each round into six.
   Wash with egg and dip into medium desiccated coconut.
   Bake at 430°F (221°C).

Oatmeal scones

Use either recipe.
   Replace half the flour with oatmeal.

Potato scones

Use Scone rounds recipe.
   Omit the sugar.
   Replace up to half of the flour with mashed potatoes.

Other small cakes

Viennese biscuits

Yield 8

4 oz (120 g) butter
5 oz (150 g) soft flour
1 oz (30 g) icing sugar
1 oz (30 g) eggs

   These may be decorated and served for afternoon tea fancies.

Tarts

1 Beat butter and sugar together until light and fluffy.
2 Beat in the egg.
3 Add the flour and mix to a smooth paste.
4 Using a savoy bag and a star tube, pipe the mixture into greaseproof paper cases in the form of a whirl but leaving a shallow depression in the centre.
5 Bake at 400°F (204°C) until golden brown in colour.
6 When cold, dust with icing sugar and finish off with a spot of raspberry jam in the centre.

Piped shapes

1 Proceed as (1), (2), and (3) but pipe the mixture into rosettes, fingers, shells, etc. A glacé cherry may be used for decoration.
2 Bake at the same temperature.
3 When cold dip half the shape into chocolate or spin it over. The shapes may be sandwiched with a suitable cream.

Cup cakes

Yield 18

4 oz (120 g) butter
4 oz (120 g) sugar
6 oz (180 g) eggs
4 oz (120 g) flour
2 oz (60 g) scone flour (see page 52)

1 Prepare a tray of deep custard tart pans in which are placed greaseproof paper cases.

2 Make on the sugar batter method.
3 Transfer to a savoy bag with a ½-in (1.25-cm) tube and pipe a quantity of the mixing into each paper case to within ½ in (1.25 cm) of the top. For decoration a glacé cherry or sprinkling of currants may be added.
4 Bake in an oven at 400°F (204°C) for approximately 15–20 minutes.

Note: These can form the bases for afternoon tea fancies by omitting the cherry or currants added as decoration. Suitable finishes for afternoon tea fancies are shown in Figure 45 on page 143.

Queen cakes

Yield 18

3 oz (90 g) butter
1 oz (30 g) white cooking fat
4¼ oz (130 g) sugar
5 oz (150 g) eggs
5 oz (150 g) flour
1 oz (30 g) scone flour (see page 52)
2 oz (60 g) currants (optional)

Chopped cherries, flaked almonds, or currants for decoration

1 Make on the sugar batter method.
2 Place batter in a savoy tube with ⅝-in (1.5-cm) plain tube.
3 Prepare clean queen cake tins with an even coating of grease. Sprinkle in chopped cherries, flaked almonds, and currants to make three varieties.
4 Pipe the mixture into the tins to within ½ in (1.25 cm) of the top.
5 Bake in an oven at 400°F (204°C) for approximately 20 minutes.
6 When baked, turn out of the tin and present them upside down with the decoration showing.

7 Chou pastries

Chou paste – Pâté à choux

Yield eclairs, 16; cream buns, 16; profiteroles, 32

2 oz (60 g) butter
5 oz (150 g) water
2 level teaspoonsful sugar
4 oz (120 g) strong flour
8 oz (240 g) (approximate) eggs

1 Heat the butter, water, and sugar in a saucepan until boiling.
2 Remove from the heat.
3 Using a spatula, stir in the flour.
4 Re-cook and stir mixture until it leaves the sides of the pan.
5 Remove from the heat and allow mixture to cool.
6 Beat in the egg, a little at a time.
7 The paste should be soft but retain its shape if piped.

Note: The quantity of egg depends upon the strength of the flour: the stronger it is the more eggs are required.

Varieties using chou paste

Éclairs

(Figure 29)

Yield 16

Chou Paste recipe
2 oz (60 g) fondant (flavoured and coloured)
½ pt (3 dl) whipped cream

1 Pipe out the chou paste into finger shapes on a clean baking sheet, approximately 4 in (10 cm) long using a savoy bag fitted with a ½-in (1.25-cm) plain tube.
2 Bake in an oven at 420°F (215°C) for approximately 15 minutes, until brown and set.
3 When baked and cold, split open with a knife.
4 Fill with whipped, sweetened fresh dairy cream.
5 Dip either the top or the base of the eclair in:
   (a) Chocolate couverture.
   (b) Chocolate flavoured fondant icing.
   (c) Chocolate icing (see page 239).
6 Allow to set and then serve.

Note: The base of the éclair is flat and therefore makes an easier surface to coat with icing. Flavours other than chocolate may be used, for example coffee–Éclairs au café.

Cream buns

Chou paste recipe

½ pt (3 dl) whipped cream

1 Using a savoy bag with a ½-in (1.25-cm) star tube, pipe out rosettes or bulbs, either in a special cream bun tin or on a baking tray.
2 The cream bun tin is fitted with a lid in order to prevent steam from escaping from the goods whilst they are being baked. If a baking tray is used, the cream buns will need to be covered with inverted bread tins for the same purpose.
3 After covering the cream buns, bake in a hot oven at 450°F (232°C) for approximately 20 minutes or until they are brown and set. Since these goods are baked under cover, the covers have to be removed to ascertain whether they are ready to be withdrawn from the oven. *Beware of steam!*.
4 When baked, remove the covers and allow to cool.
5 Split open with a knife.
6 Fill with whipped fresh dairy cream which may be sweetened if desired.
7 Dust with icing sugar and serve.

Petit cream buns – Petits choux à la crème

These are made for profiteroles, croquembouche, and gâteau St-Honoré. They are made by piping out small bulbs with a savoy bag fitted with a ⅜-in (1-cm) tube.

Rognons

Same as eclairs except that the paste is piped into a kidney shape. They are iced in coffee fondant and may be dipped in roasted flaked almonds to finish.

Horseshoes and rings
(Figure 29)

Pipe the chou paste into the shapes described and finish off in the same way as eclairs.

Swans
(Figure 29)

1 Use the eclair recipe to pipe out ovals onto a slightly greased or silicone papered tray using a savoy bag with ½ in (12 mm) tube.
2 Transfer the paste to a ¼ in (6 mm) tube and pipe the neck and heads. These should resemble the figure 2. Pipe the neck at the base and finish by the head so that when the tube is pulled away the beak is formed. Bake the bodies as for eclairs but a much cooler oven is required for the necks.
3 When cold, cut right through the body and cut the top in half lengthwise.
4 Pipe fresh cream on the base, set in the neck and head and arrange the two half top sections to resemble the wings.

Figure 29   *Chou paste varieties. Eclairs horseshoes and swans*

Chou paste fritters – Beignets soufflés

Yield 8 covers

Chou paste recipe
5 oz (150 g) apricot sauce (see page 187)

1 Using a spoon and finger, break pieces of chou paste about the size of a walnut and drop them into hot fat.
2 Cook for approximately 10–15 minutes until brown.
3 Remove, drain well, and sprinkle liberally with icing sugar.
4 Dress on a doily on a flat silver tray.
5 Serve separately with a sauceboat of hot apricot sauce.

Profiteroles and chocolate sauce – Profiteroles au chocolat

Yield 8 covers

Chou Paste recipe
½ pt (3 dl) cream Chantilly (see page 189)
Chocolate sauce (see page 186)

1 Pipe out petit cream buns about half the size of the ones already described.
2 After baking, split and fill with sweetened whipped fresh dairy cream.
3 Dredge with icing sugar and dress neatly on a doily or a flat silver dish.
4 Serve with a sauceboat of cold chocolate sauce.

Savoury choux pastries

See Chapter 12.

8 *Torten and gâteaux*

Torten

On the Continent, especially in Germany and Switzerland, a slice of torten has become a popular after-dinner sweet, as well as a pastry to be eaten with coffee or tea.

There are many interpretations. In some cases any large decorated gâteau is called a torte, but the generally accepted view, is that of a large gâteau already divided into a number of wedge-shaped slices which are individually decorated.

There is a wide variety in the 'make-up' of a torte but basically it is made from a sponge, usually soaked with liqueur-flavoured syrup with buttercream or fresh cream and mounted on a disc or either sweetpaste or japonaise.

The sponge may be in three or more layers sandwiched with cream or a suitable alternative. If fruit is to be incorporated, two layers with fruit between suffice.

Marzipan, chocolate, nuts, or fruits may all be used, either incorporated in the interior of the torte or used as decoration.

Because the torte is usually sold as a slice, it is important that the interior should look attractive as well as the exterior. If fruits are to be used, these should be put in whole or in slices so that they are clearly visible when the torte is cut.

Various sections of torten are shown in Figure 30.

Quantities of materials for one 10-in (25-cm) torte

16 portions

1 sponge base approximately 12 oz (360 g) (see page 85)
4 oz (120 g) raspberry jam
1 jap or sweetpaste disc (see page 145 or 53)
1 A 2 tin of fruit (approximately 1¼ lb)
½ pt (300 g) syrup
2–4 oz (60–120 g) liqueur
1½ lb (720 g) buttercream (see page 285)
or 1 pt (6 dl) whipped double fresh cream)
2 oz (60 g) golden syrup (to sweeten fruit juice if required)
2 oz (60 g) browned nib or flaked almonds or browned desiccated coconut

Size of torte

This is largely at the discretion of the patissier but the height should not exceed 2½ in (6.5 cm). The diameter may vary between 8 and 12 in (20–30 cm) according to the number of slices required.

An 8-in (20-cm) torte will produce 12 large or 16 small slices, while a 12-in (30-cm) torte will produce 24 slices.

Method

The following is a step-by-step method of assembling a torte.

1 Select the size of board. A cake board or plate at least 2 in (5 cm) larger in diameter than the torte on which it should be mounted is needed. A disc of thick waxed card of silvered strawboard the same size as the torte is also necessary.
2 Place the circle of waxed card on top of the cake board and on this card place a disc of either sweetpaste or japonaise.
3 On the sweetpaste or japonaise, spread a good quality jam, for example raspberry, or cover with chocolate.
4 Place a disc of sponge on the jammed base and saturate with a suitably flavoured syrup (see page 257). This may be done with either a spray or a brush.
5 Spread this first layer of sponge with good quality, flavoured buttercream or fresh cream, and then distribute the fruit evenly.
6 Spread on another layer of cream and then place on the second sponge disc.
7 Saturate this sponge layer also with the flavoured syrup.
8 Trim sides with a sharp knife to allow approximately $\frac{3}{16}$ in (0.5 cm) clearance between the edge of the waxed card and sides of the torte. Also gently press the top level with a cake board.
9 Coat the top and sides with cream and finish off as follows:
   (a) *Side coat.* Use a celluloid or plastic scraper (a plastic set square is an ideal tool). Coat the side by holding it against the edge of the waxed card or strawboard, at the same time turning the torte on a turntable. The card acts as a template in this connection and will produce a perfect symmetrical shape.
   (b) *Top coat.* Using a long-bladed knife, the top is levelled by sweeping the knife from the outside edge to the centre, from about four positions of the turntable. After practice a level and smooth top may be achieved with a clear unbroken edge.
      An alternative method is to coat the top first by sweeping over with a knife or straight edge and cutting off with a palette knife as the sides are coated.
      If the whole side is to be masked afterwards, less care is required to obtain a perfect edge. In this case the main effort should be directed to obtaining a perfectly smooth and level top coat.
10 By means of the card under the torte, it may now be picked up and a suitable dressing of nuts or coralettes applied as decoration either to the lower part of the sides or to the complete side.

11 The top is marked into an appropriate number of divisions by means of a torten marker.
12 Decoration may now be applied, first by placing coralettes in the centre using a shield, then decorating each segment using buttercream, nuts, fruit, etc.
13 Store in a cool place, preferably in a refrigerator especially if fresh cream is used.

Flavours

Most Continental torten are flavoured with liqueurs in combination with fruit or nuts. The following chart shows some useful combinations:

Fruit, etc.	*Liqueurs*
Apricot	Apricot brandy
Peach	Peach brandy
Cherry	Kirsch, Cherry brandy, Maraschino
Pineapple	Kirsch
Orange	Grand Marnier, Curaçao
Ganache	Rum, Brandy
Chocolate	Rum
Praline	Rum
Coffee	Tia Maria, Rum, Brandy

Lemon is so strongly flavoured that it is unnecessary to add any liqueur.

The syrup for such torten should be strongly flavoured with the juice of the fruit itself. If tinned fruit is used, the juice should also be employed for the syrup with which to soak the sponge. However, if a liqueur is used the sweetness may have to be adjusted by adding golden syrup or sugar (icing).

Varieties

Pineapple torte
(Figures 31 and 30(c))

Proceed as previously described using either fresh or tinned pineapple pieces in the interior make up and soaking the sponge with a mixture of equal quantities of pineapple juice and syrup. Instead of incorporating whole pieces of pineapple, it may be finely chopped and incorporated in with the buttercream.

Side decoration. This may be either roasted chopped almonds or coconut.

Top decoration. Use confiture pineapple (page 253) cut into wedges and placed in a split glacé cherry to form a flower figure. Lines of buttercream are piped on each segment and on these are placed the flower and a piece of angelica cut into a diamond. The centre is filled with chopped roasted nuts, sieved japonaise crumbs, roasted desiccated coconut, or a ring of pineapple.

Orange torte
(Figure 31)

Proceed as previously described using tinned oranges or peeled and skinned segments of fresh oranges in the interior make up. Flavour the syrup with the orange juice (from tinned oranges) and

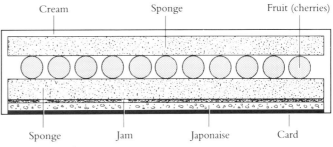

Cream   Sponge   Fruit (cherries)

Sponge   Jam   Japonaise   Card

(a) Containing fruit

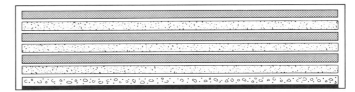

(b) Made from layers of sponge or japonaise

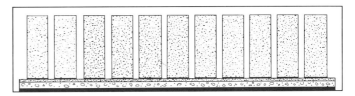

(c) Made from strips of sponge formed into a large roll

Figure 30 *Torten sections*

Figure 31 *Torten and Gâteaux*

Top left: Ganache
Top right: Orange
Bottom left: Black forest (showing section (a) in Figure 30)
Bottom right: Pineapple (showing section (c) in Figure 30)

the appropriate liqueur. Also add sufficient liqueur to the cream to flavour.

Side decoration. As previous torte.

Top decoration. Pipe a rosette of cream on each segment and on this place a glazed segment of orange. The glazing is done by dipping the orange segments into boiling apricot purée or sugar. The centre is finished off with a slice cut from the centre of a large orange.

Apricot torte
(Figure 32)

This is made in a similar way to the other fruit torten except that the character of the fruit used should be clearly shown in the cut section. Figure 32 shows how this can be achieved so that when the torte is cut as indicated, the shape of the fruit is clearly shown. The board on which the torte is assembled must also be marked as to the position of the fruit so that when cut the apricot is cut into two equal halves. A glazed half apricot should be used for a centrepiece and the torte finished in the same way as the Peach torte in Figure 34.

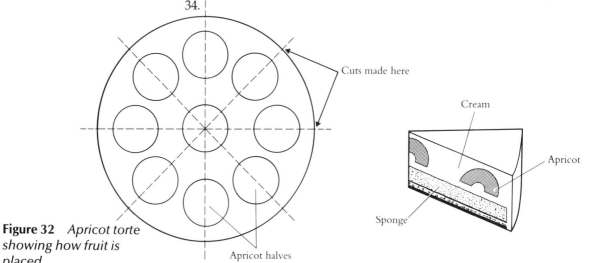

Figure 32 *Apricot torte showing how fruit is placed*

Peach torte
(Figure 34)

This is made in the same way as the Apricot torte except that peaches are used. However because this fruit is much larger the halves need to be trimmed to fit into the torte ring and the centre half omitted. For decoration, a half glazed peach is placed in the centre with angelica diamonds. Marzipan moulded into peach shapes and sprayed (see page 244) adorn each segment.

Praline torte
(Figure 34)

Proceed as previously described using rum flavoured syrup with which to soak the sponge, and a praline and rum flavoured cream. Since no fruit is to be placed inside this torte, three layers of sponge should be used.

Note: Praline is made from croquant (page 257) crushed and milled into a smooth paste. Unless it is added to the cream carefully, lumps can be formed. The praline should be first broken down to a smooth semi-fluid paste with a little of the cream and then added to the rest. If it is very hard, heat should be applied to soften it first.

Side decoration. Roasted almonds either crushed, nibbed, or flaked should be used.
Top decoration. On a piped line of white cream (without the addition of praline) place an unblanched almond. The centre is covered with roasted almond nibs, or coloured nibs with chocolate coralettes.

Chocolate ganache torte
(Figure 31)

Proceed as previously described using a mixture of cream and ganache flavoured with rum. The syrup used to soak the sponge is also flavoured with rum. Use three layers of sponge as in the previous torte.

Side decoration. Use chocolate coralettes or a mixture of chocolate coralettes and green almond decor.
Top decoration. On each segment, pipe a rosette of white cream and place on filigree chocolate flowers (see Chapter 18). In the centre place a truffle ball made from cake crumbs bound with a little apricot purée, dipped into melted chocolate and coralettes. Dust this ball with icing sugar first and set it off with a surround of angelica diamonds. Alternatively cover with chocolate coralettes.

Method of coating using fresh cream, wine cream and bavarois (see Figure 33)

Allow at least ¼ in (6 mm) of space between the inside of the torte ring and the filling. The interior sponge can also be trimmed smaller than the ring to allow for this clearance.

Cover the sponge and filling with the torte ring and fill with the cream spreading it carefully to prevent air pockets forming. Using a straight knife spread the cream level using the ring as a template. Place in the refrigerator or deep freeze with its ring.

To remove the fresh cream filled torte from its ring it is usually only necessary to leave it for a few minutes in the warm kitchen before its ring can be lifted off.

For creams containing gelatine and placed in the refrigerator, the ring would have to be released with the use of a thin bladed knife, if it is deep frozen the blow torch is usually used or the ring can be rotated against a low flame to release the cream from its ring.

Undecorated torte can be stacked on top of each other merely separated with a disc of silicone paper and a strawboard. They can thus be removed and decorated when required.

Wine cream torte

Same ingredients as Fresh cream torte except that wine cream (see page 288) is used instead of fresh.

1 Same as (1)–(4) on page 113.
2 After the fruit has been added, place on a hoop the same size as the torte.

3 Pour the wine cream into the hoop when cool but before it sets; fill to the appropriate depth sufficient to cover the fruit. Release from the hoop as described on page 117.
4 Mask the sides with roasted almonds.
5 Mark the top into the desired number of portions.
6 Decorate each portion with the fruit covered with an appropriate glaze (see pages 289–91).

Fruit torte (alternative method)

The torte previously described contains fruit but it is totally enclosed by the buttercream or fresh fruit filling. Some fruits, such as fresh strawberries, look so attractive that the whole of the top of the torte may be covered with them, suitably glazed. The method for such a torte is as follows.

Fresh strawberry torte

1 Prepare a base of japonaise or sweetpaste and sponge ½–¾ in (1.25–2 cm) thick as already described.
2 Sprinkle the sponge with liqueur syrup, that is, Kirsch or Maraschino.
3 Spread on a layer of good quality buttercream or whipped fresh cream flavoured with liqueur.
4 Select strawberries of uniform size, remove the stalks, and place them upside down on top of the cream layer to cover it completely.
5 Brush over a red glaze (page 290).
6 Finish by masking the sides with cream and roasted flake almonds.

A variety of fruit torte may be made in this way with fruits used either on their own or mixed. With the latter many attractive decorative patterns may be made, not unlike fruit flans.

Figure 33   *Method of coating using fresh cream, etc. Also shown is the use of a torte marker and shield used to aid the decoration of the centre. The torch used for the release of deep frozen torten from their rings is shown in the foreground*

Figure 34   *Torten and gâteaux*

Top left: Florentine
Top right: Praline (with sides coated with comb scraper)
Bottom left: Peach.
Bottom right: Dobos (showing section (b) in Figure 30, page 115)

Dairy cream cheese torte
(Figure 35)

1 sponge 9 in (23 cm) by ¾ in (2 cm) thick

8 oz (240 g) cheese curd (cream cheese)
2 oz (60 g) sugar
7 oz (210 g) lemon curd
¾ oz (22.5 g) gelatine (leaf) (see page 48)
½ pt (3 dl) whipped cream
3 oz (90 g) sultanas (soaked in rum)
1 oz (30 g) rum
2 oz (60 g) syrup
1 oz (30 g) icing sugar (for decoration)
1 oz (30 g) whipped cream (for decoration)
Roasted nib almonds (for decoration)

1 Split the sponge into two discs one ½ in (12 mm) and the other ¼ in (6 mm) thick.
2 Place the ½ in (2 mm) thick sponge in a 9-in (23-cm) torten ring.
3 Sprinkle the sponge liberally with rum syrup. (First soak the sultanas in rum, drain, and mix the remainder of the rum with the syrup).
4 Spread on top of the sponge the cheese filling which is made as follows:
   (a) Soak the gelatine in water until pliable and then melt over heat.

Figure 35   *Torten and Gateaux*

Top left: Fudge
Top right: Dairy cream cheese
Bottom left: Macmahon
Bottom right: Kirsch

Black forest torte
(Figures 31 and 30(a))

This classical torte may be made as follows:

1 Lay a disc of chocolate sponge inside the torte ring and cover with a compote of black cherries.
2 Fill to within ½ in (12 mm) of the top with whipped cream which has been flavoured with Kirsch liqueur syrup.
3 Place another disc of chocolate sponge trimmed smaller and press down to within ¼ inch (6 mm) of the top.
4 Sprinkle this chocolate sponge liberally with Kirsch liqueur syrup.
5 Fill with Kirsch flavoured whipped cream and level off. This can now be refrigerated with its ring and released as already described on page 117.
6 Mark into segments and decorate with a rosette of cream and a cherry. Place chocolate curls or shavings in the centre.

French decorated torten
(Figures 36 and 37)

Special stencils are first used to make a pattern on to a strip of sponge which forms the outside wall of the torte. These are shown in Figure 2 (page 3). The stencil is laid on to silicone paper and a coloured langue du chat mixing is spread with a narrow scraper to form several patterns on to the paper at a width approximately ¼ in (6 mm) below the height of the torten ring (see Figure 36). The stencilled sheets of silicone paper are then transferred to a deep freeze. Once frozen they are then transferred to a baking tray and a dobos sponge mixing (see page 120) is spread over and the whole baked and then allowed to rest to soften.

Figure 36 *French torten and gateaux. Stencilling langue de chat mixing on to silicone paper in preparation for the sides of torten. In the foreground are the finished stencilled strips of sponge*

Figure 37 *French torten and gâteaux. Description in text*

Assembly of the torte

1 Prepare a base of sweetpastry, jap or sponge inside the torte ring.
2 Cut between each design a strip of the stencilled sponge and cut it to fit the inside wall of the torte ring.
3 Fill to the top of the ring with a filling such as sponge and cream, or bavarois which needs to be refrigerated.
4 The top of either sponge or bavarois is covered in the fruit mirror glaze (see page 291).

   The torte completed in this fashion is shown on the *right* in Figure 37. A simple pulled sugar rose and leaves form the only top decoration.

Chocolate torte
(Figure 37 *left*)

1 Chocolate sponge is sandwiched with a suitable cream and assembled on a jap or sweetpaste base in the usual way.
2 The torte is covered either with chocolate or a suitable chocolate icing, see page 239.

3 Chocolate is spread on to silicone paper and when nearly set cut into squares or other shapes. When completely set these are attached with chocolate to the sides of the torte.
4 Top decoration is formed from chocolate roses (see page 238) with pieces of broken chocolate.
5 Finally it is dusted with cocoa powder.

French small (petits) gâteaux
(Figure 38)

Other shapes, other than round, may be made in special moulds and these are explained here.

Six sided

The mould is lined with the stencilled sponge and filled as already described. Coffee flavoured mirror glaze (see page 291) is first brushed on to create a marbled effect. Over this is spread the clear glaze. A cluster of chocolate flakes (see page 238) is then deposited on top.

Round

Here small swiss rolls are used to line the sides of the ring before being filled with bavarois. The top is covered in the clear glaze and a glazed half strawberry completes the decoration.

Heart

Made in the same way as Figure 37 (*right*).
    A simple marzipan flower (see page 247) completes the design.

Figure 38 *French petits gâteaux. Description in text.*

Checkerboard torte
(Figure 39)

For this sponge, two alternative colours are required, for example white and chocolate, and split into three to make two tortes as follows. The sponge layers are cut into two discs as shown and the appropriate sections interchanged before sandwiching with cream.

Gâteaux

The dividing line between gâteaux and torten is very fine and, in fact, in some cases, one is indistinguishable from the other. Each means a large decorated cake, the name gâteaux being the French term and the word torte being the German. In Switzerland especially, the name of torte is given to many types of large decorated cakes which are not divided into slices (see Kirsch torte and Fruit torte). The definition that a torte should be divided into portions in the decoration is the accepted British interpretation; but if classical cakes like Kirsch torte are being sold it is best to retain the descriptive name of the country of its origin.

Except for specialities, the make up of most gâteaux is similar to torten. It usually consists of an enriched sponge or butter sponge (page 85) sandwiched with buttercream, fresh cream, ganache, curd, jam, with or without fruit, liqueur, chocolate, nuts, etc. Buttercream, fresh cream, fondant, or other suitable icing is then used to cover the sponge which may be masked in nuts and suitably decorated. Gâteaux may be named according to the type of mixings and the flavours used. For example, if meringue is used, this could be named with the fruit or flavour used, for example Strawberry meringue gâteaux. Usually, however, the gâteau is named according to the main flavour used, whether it is fruit, liqueur, chocolate, praline, coffee, etc.

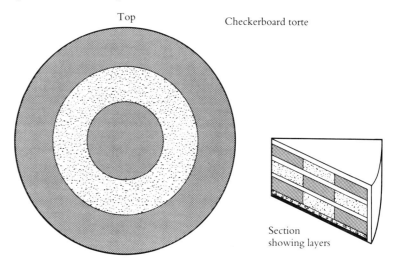

Top   Checkerboard torte

Section showing layers

Figure 39 *Checkerboard torte*

**Gâteau millefeuilles –
Gâteau of a thousand leaves**
(Figure 19 page 79)

Yield 8 in (20 cm) suitable for cutting into 8 portions

12 oz (360 g) puff pastry trimmings
2 oz (60 g) jam
½ pt (3 dl) pastrycream or fresh cream
4 oz (120 g) fondant or water icing
1 oz (30 g) browned almonds

1 Roll out the paste very thinly and cut three discs of approximately 9 in (23 cm) diameter. This will shrink to approximately 8 in (20 cm) in baking.

2 Prick each piece all over with a fork or a docker and allow to rest for at least half an hour.
3 Bake in a hot oven at 450°F (232°C) until crisp and brown in colour.
4 When cold, trim each piece to a perfect round shape and select the best for the top.
5 Sandwich the pieces together with the cream and jam. Place the top disc on upside down to present a good surface.
6 Prepare the fondant with syrup to a thin spreading consistency.
7 Prepare a little of the icing in two colours, for example chocolate and pink, and fill a paper cornet with each.
8 Pour and spread on the icing evenly over the top and immediately pipe alternate lines about ½ in (12 mm) apart of chocolate and pink fondant from the paper cornets.
9 Using the back of a knife and wiping between each stroke, pull the knife across the piped lines at approximately 1 in (2.5 cm) intervals.
10 Turn the gâteau round and repeat pulling the knife in the opposite direction between the first strokes.

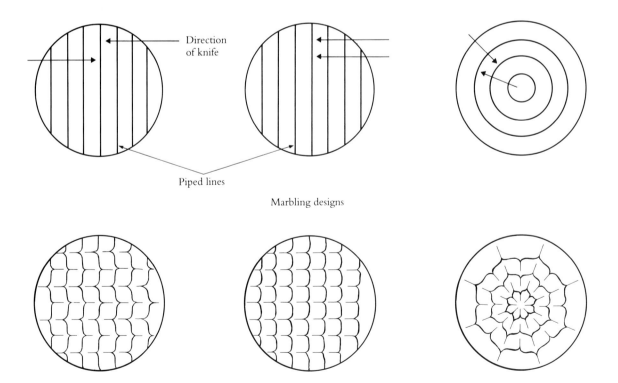

Figure 40 *Marbling or feathering*

11 Allow to set and trim off the edge.

12 Coat the edge with cream and mask with the browned almonds.

Note: The operation described under (8)–(10) is called marbling or feathering and is illustrated in Figure 40. To get the best results, speed is essential and the icing should not be either too warm or too stiff in consistency.

Millefeuille slices

These are done similarly by sandwiching three strips of baked puff pastry approximately 4 in (10 cm) wide, icing and marbling the top and cutting into slices.

Nougat gâteau

Yield 8 in (20 cm) suitable for cutting into 8 portions

12 oz (360 g) puff pastry trimmings
2 oz (60 g) icing sugar
½ pt (3 dl) whipped fresh cream
6 oz (180 g) nougat nibs (see page 257)

1 Roll out the paste very thinly and cut three discs of approximately 9 in (23 cm) diameter. These will shrink to about 8 in (20 cm) in the baking.

2 Prick each piece with a fork or docker and allow to rest approximately half an hour.

3 Dust each piece liberally with icing sugar.

4 Bake in a hot oven at 450°F (232°C) until brown and crisp. (Some of the sugar will caramelize into a brown glaze.)

5 Keep a little of the whipped cream aside to coat the sides. Mix the remainder with 4 oz (120 g) of crushed nougat nibs.

6 Trim the puff pastry discs all to the same size and an even round shape and select the best for the top.

7 Sandwich together using the nougat cream, placing the selected disc upside down on top.

8 Mask the sides with the whipped cream reserved for this purpose and also the rest of the nougat nibs.

9 Dust the top liberally with icing sugar and mark on a diamond pattern with the back of a knife. Finish is similar to Kirsch torte (Figure 35).

Gâteau florentine
(Figure 34)

1 Make an almond sponge in an 8-in (20 cm) torte ring.

2 Split into three and sandwich with buttercream to which a little praline may be added for flavouring.

3 Use buttercream to coat the top and sides and mask with roasted nibbed or flaked almonds.

4 Eight segments of florentine are now placed on top with a rosette of cream. The florentine mixing on page 149 is baked in an 8-in (20 cm) hoop spreading the mixing to the edge to form a perfect circle. When baked this is coated with chocolate and when set cut into the eight segments.

(c) chopped glacépineapple

(d) nibbed green almonds or pistachio nuts

(e) broken crystallized rose petals

(f) browned nib almonds.

13 Arrange these alternately around the top edge of the base.

14 Brush the outside edge with apricot purée and cover with pale roasted flaked almonds.

15 Cover with spun sugar (see page 265) immediately prior to service.

Note: There are many variations of this traditional dish. Besides cream Chantilly and cream St-Honoré, a mixture of pastrycream and fresh cream is often used to fill the centre, and in some recipes no genoese is used. Glacé and sometimes fresh fruits dipped in boiling sugar are also used to decorate the top prior to service.

Figure 41   *Gâteaux St Honoré*

Croquembouche
(Figure 42)

Chou paste (see page 109)
Nougat (see page 257)
Boiled and spun sugar (see page 265)
Crème bavarois (see page 194)
Crème Chantilly (see page 189)

1 Prepare a number of petit cream buns. Vary the size a little so that some are very small and others larger. Thoroughly bake, allow to cool, and fill with crème Chantilly.

2 Meanwhile prepare a conical mould of the size required. This may be made of tin but a temporary one may be made of cardboard. Grease the mould evenly and stand on a greased tin.

3 Boil a sugar syrup to the hard crack degree 310°F (154°C). Remove, plunge pan into cold water to arrest the rise in temperature, and dip each petit cream bun.

4 Place the cream buns side by side against the base of the mould. Once a ring is formed, start on another ring and so on until a pyramid of cream buns has been built up. Use the smallest cream buns for the top and the largest for the base.

Figure 42
Croquembouche

5 Once set, turn upside down and remove the mould and paper lining.
6 The centre of the croquembouche can be filled in a variety of ways:
  (a) cubes of genoese soaked in liqueur-flavoured syrup and cream Chantilly and sometimes fruit.
  (b) alternate layers of bavarois and fruit.
7 Mount the croquembouche on a decorative base made of nougat.
8 Finish off the top with a ball of spun sugar or some figure.

Cheesecake

Yield 8 covers

Base

4 oz (120 g) digestive biscuits
1 oz (30 g) castor sugar
2 oz (60 g) butter

Filling

8 oz (240 g) soft cheese (see Note 1)
3 oz (90 g) castor sugar
5 oz (150 g) soured cream or double fresh cream
2 oz (60 g) water
4 oz (60 g) pasteurized egg (see Note 2)
½ oz (15 g) gelatine
Juice and rind of 1 lemon or orange or juice of some other fruit

Gum arabic solution

¾ oz (22.5 g) powdered gum arabic (see page 48)
4 oz (120 g) water

Bring to the boil to dissolve.

Figure 43   *Petits fours sec*

Rows left to right:
1 Dutch macaroons
2 Sables
3 Engish routs
4 Fancy macaroons
5 Dutch biscuits
6 Parisian routs
7 Toscaner
8 Marquis biscuits

Dutch macaroons
(Figure 43, row 1)

Yield 24 or 48 halves

2½ oz (75 g) ground almonds
½ oz (15 g) castor sugar
5½ oz (165 g) icing sugar
2 oz (60 g) egg whites

1 Mix all ingredients together to a smooth paste and warm.
2 Prepare a clean tray with a sheet of greaseproof paper.
3 Pipe the warm mixture into oval shapes on the greaseproof paper using a savoy bag fitted with ¼-in (6-mm) tube. The mixture should flow quite flat.
4 Let the biscuits lie for at least 6 hours or overnight.
5 Using a razor blade, cut the surface of each shape lengthwise.
6 Bake in a cool oven at 350°F (177°C) until golden brown in colour.
7 Remove from the greaseproof paper by washing the back with water. Alternatively bake on silicone paper.
8 Join the biscuits together with either jam or jelly.

Almond boulée

Yield 24–30

4 oz (120 g) ground almonds
4 oz (120 g) castor sugar
1 oz (30 g) icing sugar
1 oz (30 g) egg whites

1 Mix all ingredients together to a smooth paste: do not overwork.
2 Prepare a tray with grease and dust with flour.
3 Divide and make into small balls.
4 Dip balls in soft royal icing (see below), drain, and roll into the following mediums:
 (a) Nib almonds.
 (b) Flaked almonds.
 (c) Strip almonds.
 (d) Coloured nib almonds.
 (e) Desiccated coconut.
5 Place on a greased and floured or silicone papered baking tray.
6 Let balls lie for at least 6 hours or overnight.
7 Bake in an oven at 350°F (177°C) until golden brown in colour.
 Note: This mixture may be flavoured and appropriately coloured to give a wider variety.

Royal icing for dipping

4 oz (120 g) icing sugar
1 oz (30 g) egg whites

Beat together.

Fancy macaroons
(Figure 43, row 4)

Yield 48

4 oz (120 g) ground almonds
8 oz (240 g) castor sugar
¾ oz (22.5 g) ground rice (see page 48)
2½ oz (75 g) egg whites

1 Mix all ingredients together to a smooth paste.
2 Prepare a tray with ground rice covered with rice paper, or silicone paper.
3 Pipe out biscuits of 1 in (2.5 cm) diameter, using a savoy bag with ⅜ in (9 mm) star tube.
4 Decorate using a wide variety of nuts as follows:
 (a) Split almonds.
 (b) Strip almonds.
 (c) Nib almonds.
 (d) Coloured nib almonds.
 (e) Pistachio nuts.
 (f) Walnuts.
 (g) Hazelnuts.
 (h) Cashew nuts.
5 Bake in an oven at 350°F (177°C) until golden brown in colour.

4 Cut strips ⅜ in (1 cm) wide and join three of these together using water to dampen the surfaces so that white is against chocolate and vice versa.
5 Roll out a piece of white paste ¹⁄₁₆ in (1.5 mm) thick, dampen the surface, and wrap up the composite strip.
6 Cut the strip into slices approximately ⅜ in (1 cm) thick and lay them flat on a clean baking tray.
7 Bake at 400°F (204°C).

Langue du chat biscuits – Cat's tongues

Yield for biscuits approximately 1½ in (4 cm) long piped with a ¼-in (6-mm) tube = 160)

These biscuits may be made in different sizes and in either a finger or round shape. They have several uses as follows:

1 As a decoration for gâteaux, torten, ice bombs, etc.
2 They may be served with ice-cream dishes.
3 Sandwiched with an appropriate buttercream or ganache, they may be made into either afternoon fancies (large shapes) or petits fours secs (small shapes), then either partly dipped into chocolate or left plain.
4 Also used for the decoration of French torten page 123.

> *4 oz (120 g) butter*
> *4 oz (120 g) sugar*
> *3 oz (90 g) egg whites*
> *4½ oz (135 g) soft flour*

1 Prepare a baking tray with a coating of grease.
2 Make the biscuit mixing on the sugar batter method.
3 Transfer mixing to a savoy bag fitted with a ¼-in (6-mm) tube.
4 Pipe out shapes to the size required. As these biscuits flow during baking, allow sufficient space on the tray.
5 Bake in an oven at 420°F (215°C) until the edges of the biscuit are tinged a light golden brown colour.
6 Remove from the baking tray while still warm.

Notes:
1 If the biscuits are removed from the tray as soon as they are baked they are flexible enough to be twisted or curled. These curled biscuits are especially attractive to serve with ice-cream dishes.
2 They may also be half dipped into chocolate as an added decoration.

Marquis
(Figure 43, row 8)

Langue du chat biscuit recipe (see above)
Ganache recipe (see page 239)
Praline (ground nougat) recipe (see page 257)
Chocolate

1 Sandwich two langue du chat biscuits with the following filling: 3 parts ganache and 1 part crushed nougat or praline paste.
2 Either write the word 'Marquis' in chocolate on the top biscuit or dip each end in chocolate couverture.

Sable à la poche
(Figure 43, row 2)

Yield 48 petits fours or 24 afternoon tea fancies

8 oz (240 g) soft flour
6 oz (180 g) butter
4 oz (120 g) castor sugar
1½ oz (45 g) egg yolks

1 Beat the butter and sugar to a cream.
2 Add the egg yolk and beat into the cream.
3 Add the flour and mix to a smooth paste.
4 Transfer to a clean savoy bag fitted with a star tube.
5 Pipe the mixing into rosettes.
6 Decorate with half a cherry.
7 Bake in an oven at 380°F (193°C) until tinged a golden brown colour.

Other mixings from which petits fours varieties may be made can be found in the following chapters: 2 Shortpastry, flans, and tarts; 5 Meringue goods; 6 Cakes; 11 Afternoon tea fancies; 20 Sugar work.

10 *Petits fours glacés*

Genoese base

Yield 96 squares (less for shapes)
   See Genoese recipes (page 101).

Varieties

Fondant dips

(Figure 44, row 4)

1 Cut cake in half and sandwich with a suitable filling, that is, jam, curd, ganache, buttercream, etc.
2 Cover the sheet of genoese with a thin layer of marzipan, using hot apricot purée with which to stick it to the cake.
3 Cut this sheet into a variety of different shapes using the knife and assorted cutters. The shapes should be approximately ¾ in (2 cm) square in area.
4 Dip each shape into hot apricot purée and place approximately ¾ in (2 cm) apart on a wire tray resting on a drip tray.
5 Using a bain marie, warm and reduce fondant with stock syrup to the correct consistency and temperature (approximately 100°F (38°C).
6 Place the fondant in a savoy bag fitted with a ¼-in (6-mm) tube and pipe it over the shapes so that they are completely covered. The surplus fondant in the drip tray can be used again.
7 When the fondant has set, remove the shapes from the tray and place them in paper cups.
8 Decorate using cherries, angelica, chocolate coloured fondant, coloured jelly, or prefabricated decorations.

Note: The variety may be increased further by placing a piece of marzipan or piping a small bulb of buttercream, ganache, etc., on the shape prior to enrobing it with fondant. The use of flavours and colours for the genoese cake, fillings, and fondant, produces an even wider variety.

Battenburg slices

(Figure 44, row 8)

Bake the genoese in two or more colours, for example chocolate and yellow.

Four square

1 Cut two differently coloured sheets into slices ½ in (12 mm) thick.

2 Using a liberal amount of boiling apricot purée, sandwich two different coloured layers together.
3 Cut the laminated sheet into strips ½ in (12 mm) wide.
4 Place these strips on their side, spread with purée, and stick together so that the coloured strips are opposite each other, that is, chocolate adjacent to yellow.
5 Roll out a piece of marzipan, cover with purée, and wrap up the composite strip of genoese.
6 Cut the strip into slices approximately ½ in (12 mm) thick and lay flat in paper cases.
7 Glaze top by spreading over pectin jelly, hot apricot purée or thin fondant.

Fruit glacés
(Figure 44, rows 3 and 6)

8 oz (240 g) cube or granulated sugar
2½ oz (75 g) water

1 Boil ingredients to 310°F (154°C) (hard crack) washing down sides of pan with water to prevent crystallization (see notes on sugar boiling, page 264).
2 Dip the fruit into the boiling syrup and quickly transfer it onto an oiled slab to set.

The following fruits may be used for this purpose:

Dates	– Usually stuffed with marzipan. (Figure 44, row 6).
Grapes	– Cut with scissors but leave on stalk with which to handle fruit. If large, glaze individually but if small, in pairs.
Cherries	– Keep in pairs with stalks attached.
Mandarin oranges	– If tinned, make sure fruit is dried.
Strawberries	– Make sure fruit is dry and keep on stalk for handling the fruit.

Many of the fruits may be stuffed with marzipan, for example: cherries or a petit four made from marzipan and nuts may be used.
Two walnut halves with marzipan sandwiched between.
Two halves of glacé cherry with marzipan sandwiched between.

Because of the hygroscopic nature of boiled sugar, it is essential to store these glacé fruits in a warm dry place. Moist conditions will dissolve the sugar, making the fruits sticky and eventually washing away the sugar from the fruit. It is advisable for these glacé fruits to be made at the last moment before being presented at the function, or keep in a drying cabinet.

Varieties in barquette moulds
(Figure 44, row 1)

1 Spread some suitably flavoured and coloured buttercream in baked sweet paste moulds and fill with either individual small fruits, that is, cherries, grapes, mandarin oranges, etc., or various other fillings.
2 Glaze with fondant.

Rum truffles

(Figure 44, row 2)

1 Make a rum flavoured ganache.
2 Refrigerate and make into small balls using icing sugar as the dusting medium.
3 Dip into chocolate and roll into chocolate coralettes.

Fondants – Glacé fruits – Nougat

See Chapter 20 on sugar work.

Figure 44   *Petits fours glacé*

1 Barquettes	5 Fondant sweets
2 Rum truffles	6 Marzipan stuffed dtates
3 Sugar glazed fruits	7 Nougat sweets
4 Fondant dips	8 Glazed battenburg slices

11 Afternoon tea fancies

Almost any small variety of cake may be served with afternoon tea and thus be termed an afternoon tea fancy. The range is so enormous and decoration so wide that a tome could be written on this aspect of patisserie alone. The author has endeavoured to give a cross-section of decorated fancies which may be produced from a very limited range of cake bases.

Figure 45 *Frangipane fancies. Description in text*

Frangipane fancies

Yield 36 tarts

10 oz (300 g) flour into sweet pastry (see page 53)
Frangipane filling (see page 62)
Decorating materials (buttercream, chocolate, nuts, etc.)

1 Make the sweet pastry.
2 Roll out the paste to ¹⁄₁₆ in (1.5 mm) thick.
3 Cut out with a suitable size cutter and line clean patty pans, pressing the paste into the pan with the thumb. Trim off excess with a small knife. (See Figure 9, page 59, for alternative method.)
4 Into the 36 lined patty tins, pipe some jam, curd, or other filling, such as crushed fruit, sultanas, glacé fruit, or fruit-cream.
5 Pipe the frangipane mixing into the pan and fill to within ¼ in (6 mm) from the top.
6 Bake in an oven at 365°F (185°C) until golden brown in colour.

An explanation of the decoration of these frangipane fancies is now described in Figure 45 (numbered from top to bottom).

First row

1 A round of thin marzipan is cut and three small holes made as shown. The marzipan is attached with purée and the holes filled with jelly or jam.
2 Lay on a ring of pineapple, pipe a whirl of cream in the centre and adorn with a cherry.
3 Pipe a rosette of cream in the centre and cover this with a disc of marzipan into which a cross has been cut.
4 Chop some glacé fruits, for example cherries, pineapple and angelica, add some apricot purée and spread the mixture on top of the tart.

Second row

1 Cut through the top of the cake, remove and cut in half. Pipe a scroll of buttercream each side, replace butterfly fashion and dust with icing sugar.
2 Colour and flavour some buttercream by adding and stirring in some melted chocolate. Using a small star piping tube pipe lines from the edge to the centre until the whole top is covered. Finish with a piece of marzipan to resemble the stalk of this 'mushroom' fancy.
3 Remove a disc of the frangipane cake from the centre with a small cutter. Fill the hole with buttercream and dust top with icing sugar. Replace the top after covering it in red purée.
4 Cut top almost through, raise, and pipe in a scroll of buttercream. Lower the top so that it rests on the cream. Coat top with red purée and sprinkle on some green almond decor.

Third row

1 Cover with chocolate fondant and decorate with three yellow sugar balls (see page 145).
2 Coat top with boiled apricot purée and with pale yellow fondant. Decorate with diamonds of angelica.
3 Cover top with cream piped from a star tube. Spin chocolate over to enhance the decorative effect.
4 Coat top with cream and spread to give a raised centre. Dip into browned desiccated coconut and decorate with an unblanched almond.

Fourth row

1 Using a star tube pipe a line of buttercream along each edge. Fill the centre with chocolate or chocolate buttercream. Sprinkle on some almond nibs for decoration.
2 Cover top with a thin layer of boiled purée. Pipe on three rosettes of buttercream and on these place the chocolate

decoration. These are cut from a sheet of chocolate spread first on paper and set. Alternatively chocolate buttons or drops could be used.

3 Spread over the top some boiled apricot purée. Cover with half cherries and glaze with purée.
4 Cover with a mixture of glace fruits including angelica and glaze with purée.

Sugar balls

Little sugar balls of different colours can easily be made as follows.

1 Spread about ¼ in or 0.5 cm of castor sugar evenly in a shallow tray. Make small indentations close together with the end of a pencil.
2 Make royal icing and soften slightly with water.
3 Transfer to a piping bag with a small tube and pipe small bulbs into each indentation.
4 Cover completely in castor sugar and put aside to set and dry.
5 After 24 hours pass the whole tray's contents through a fine sieve or strainer to remove the coloured balls from the sugar.

Ganache fancies
(Figure 46, right hand row)

Yield 36

8 oz (240 g) flour into sweet pastry (see page 53)
12 oz (360 g) ganache (see page 239)
6 oz (180 g) sultanas
Stock syrup
Rum
Icing sugar

The following is a description of the fancies in Figure 46.

1 Roll out the sweetpaste to ¹⁄₁₆ in (1.5 mm) and cut out, using a round cutter. Line patty pans with the paste, trim, and bake off at 380°F (193°C). See Figure 10, page 59 for alternative method.
2 Soak the sultanas in a mixture of stock syrup and rum for at least 24 hours.
3 Drain the sultanas and place a few in the bottom of the baked unfilled pastry cases.
4 Top up with the ganache and spread level.
5 Decorate with icing sugar, using paper as a mask to get the four different patterns shown on the right of Figure 46.
6 Finish with a small rosette of ganache and either a crystallized mimosa ball or silver dragee.

Note: Instead of sultanas other fruits may be used, for example cherries soaked in a little Kirsch or Cherry brandy make a delicious variation.

Japonaise
(Figure 46, centre rows)

Yield 36–40 individual biscuits = 18–20 fancies

5 oz (150 g) egg whites
5 oz (150 g) castor sugar
5 oz (150 g) ground almonds

1 oz (30 g) cornflour
1½ oz (45 g) castor sugar
Buttercream or ganache
Decorating materials

1 Prepare some trays by brushing on a thick film of vegetable fat and dusting with flour, or with silicone paper.
2 Whisk the egg whites with 5 oz (150 g) castor sugar to a meringue.
3 Mix and sieve the almonds, cornflour, and 1½ oz (45 g) castor sugar.
4 Carefully stir these dry ingredients into the meringue.
5 Place the japonaise mixing into a savoy bag with ⅜ in (1 cm) tube and pipe out the shapes as follows:
   (a) Pipe a spiral to make a flat biscuit approximately 2 in (5 cm) diameter. A cutter may be used to mark out the size on the tray prior to piping.
   (b) Using a large tube approximately ½–⅝ in (1.5 cm) pipe out a ring approximately 2 in (5 cm) diameter.
   (c) Using a ½-in (12-mm) tube, pipe out fingers or ovals.
      Alternatively the mixture may be stencilled onto the tray through special rubber stencils. (see Fig 3(7) page 6).
6 Bake in an oven at 350°F (177°C) for approximately 15 minutes until biscuits are light fawn in colour.
7 Using buttercream or ganache, decorate as follows.

Figure 46   *Fancies*

Right-hand row:	Ganache	
Centre rows:	Japonaise	See text for description
Left-hand row:	Cup cakes	

Flat biscuits

First trim the flat and ring biscuits with the 2-in (5-cm) cutter. Pipe on a bulb of cream, place on another biscuit upside down and press down slightly with the back of a flat tray to get a uniform thickness.

Do a number of these and place them in the refrigerator to set the cream firm. Remove, mask the sides with cream, and roll in either nibbed brown almonds, roasted desiccated coconut, or japonaise crumbs.

The top may be decorated as follows:

1 Coat all over with cream and cover with either of the dressing described.
2 Cover with fondant icing or chocolate.
3 Place on a 2-in (5-cm) disc of marzipan which may be marked with a knife or similarly patterned.

Rings

The ring is sandwiched to the jap base with cream and the sides masked in the manner already described for the flat biscuits. The biscuit may be left showing or decorated with cross-cross lines of chocolate. The centre is then filled with either chopped glacé fruit or a suitable jelly.

Fingers and ovals

Sandwich together with cream piped from a star tube. Lines of chocolate may also be used for a decorative effect (spinning chocolate).

Other varieties

Using either the round or oval base, pipe on a bulb or rosette of well-beaten ganache cream. Chill and coat with chocolate.

In Figure 46 the varieties are explained as follows (centre rows).

Second row (from top to bottom)

1 Covered in textured marzipan (see page 241).
2 Covered in textured marzipan.
3 Finger sandwiched with ganache (see page 239).
4 Finger sandwiched with buttercream and chocolate spun over.

Third row (from top to bottom)

1 Centre of ring filled with crushed pineapple and chocolate spun over.
2 Ring is first dusted with icing sugar and hole filled with coloured jam or jelly.
3 Buttercream coated and masked in toasted desiccated coconut.
4 Buttercream coated and masked in toasted flaked almonds.

Fancy genoese tea fancies
(Figure 47)

Yield from basic ingredients 30 including slices

Genoese
5 oz (150 g) egg into genoese (see page 101)
Buttercream
Red purée
Decorating materials

In Figure 47 the varieties are described in rows from left to right as follows.

First row

Top   The top and sides of a square of genoese are first coated in apricot purée and then wrapped in a strip of pink marzipan the top of which has been cut with a jigger wheel. White fondant is piped into the centre and a cherry and a diamond of angelica added for decoration.

Middle A round of genoese is similarly treated with white marzipan and fondant with a tinted flake almond placed in the centre to simulate a 'night-light'.

Bottom Five thin circles of white marzipan are attached to a round of genoese and white buttercream stars are piped into the centre to simulate a cauliflower.

Second row

Top   Chocolate squares (see page 238) are attached with cream to the sides of a square of genoese. Another chocolate square is placed on a rosette of cream piped on top to form a box.

Middle A round of genoese is dipped into red purée. The sides are masked in desiccated coconut while a rosette of cream and a piece of glacé pineapple decorates the top.

Bottom Similarly made but with a ring of cream filled with red purée and decorated with a sugar ball (see page 145).

Third row

Top   A square of genoese is dipped into red purée and completely covered in desiccated coconut. A cut is made near the top into which a scroll of cream is piped.

Middle Similarly treated with only the sides masked in coconut. A scroll of cream is piped on top with a cherry and a diamond of angelica used for decoration.

Bottom Similarly treated with the top covered with cream piped with a star tube in zigzag fashion. Liquid chocolate is then spun over in the opposite direction and an unblanched almond is placed in the centre.

Fourth row

Top   Two strips of chocolate genoese are sandwiched between glacé pineapple. The sides and top are first coated with apricot purée and then pink fondant. After it is set and cut into slices a jelly filled marzipan flower and an angelica diamond are placed for decoration.

Middle Two strips of genoese are sandwiched with a liberal layer of red purée. After coating top and sides with purée, three ropes of marzipan are laid with green in the centre and pink either side. The whole is now enrobed in chocolate fondant or icing and when set the strip is cut into slices.

Bottom Buttercream is used to layer the two strips as well as the piping of the borders with a star tube. Between these, pink fondant is piped. When set, it is cut into slices and decorated with a piece of cherry and angelica diamond.

Cup cakes
(Figure 46, row 1)

Cup cake bases (see page 107)
Buttercream
Fondant
Icing sugar
Glacé cherries

These can be decorated in a similar way to the frangipane fancies described on page 144.

Florentines
(Figure 48)

Yield 48 petits fours
Yield 24 afternoon tea fancies

3 oz (90 g) butter
3¼ oz (100 g) sugar
1 oz (30 g) chopped cherries
1 oz (30 g) chopped peel
2 oz (60 g) sultanas or other crushed fruit, for example pineapple, ginger, etc.
4½ oz (135 g) flaked or nibbed almonds
1 oz (30 g) fresh cream
Chocolate couverture (for decoration)

1 Melt the butter in a saucepan.
2 Add the sugar and bring to the boil. Remove from the heat.
3 Add the fruit, then the almonds and stir well.
4 Lastly stir in the cream.
5 Deposit the mixture with the aid of a spoon, in small heaps on either:
    (a) A well-greased and floured baking tray.
    (b) A silicone papered tray.

Allow plenty of space between the heaps for spreading during baking.

6 Flatten the heaps as much as possible before baking.

7 Bake in an oven at 360°F (182°C) until they are baked a light golden colour.

8 As soon as they are removed from the oven and whilst still hot, pull the edges of the baked mixing inwards with a circular cutter to form the florentine into a perfect circle.

9 Leave to get quite cold and crisp before removing from the tray.

10 Coat the flat underside of the florentine with tempered chocolate couverture.

Figure 47   *Genoese fancies. Description in text*

Figure 48   *Florentines. Coating the backs of florentines with a comb scraper, with partly finished goods in background and the finished product in the foreground with the petit four florentine mould*

Coating florentines with chocolate (Figure 48)

1 Temper the chocolate and spread it out in a thin sheet on greaseproof or silicone paper.
2 Before the chocolate sets, lay the florentines flat side down on the liquid chocolate.
3 When the chocolate has set, trim the florentines round with an appropriately sized cutter.
4 Remove from the paper.
5 Spread some more chocolate on the already coated side of the florentine and, just before it sets, use a comb scraper to mark on wavy lines (Figure 48).
6 Display the florentines alternately showing the nut side as well as the chocolate side (Figure 48).

Figure 49 *Brandy snaps. Curling a brandy snap round a rod, with examples of other shapes and a basket filled with fruit for a sweet*

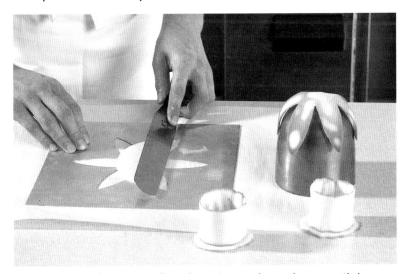

Figure 50 *Tuiles. Spreading the mixture through a stencil the baked example of which is shown to the right of the figure. Stencilled tubs are shown in the foreground*

Notes:

1 An alternative method of giving the florentine its first coating of chocolate, is to spread some chocolate on its underside and place coated side down on the paper. The only disadvantage in this method is that if the florentine has any holes in its surface, the chocolate will pass through to the nut side and so spoil its appearance.
2 The florentine mixing may be spread, baked in sheets, and cut into squares.
3 It may also be baked in rings and cut into segments to form a top decoration of a torte.
4 For an afternoon tea fancy the usual size is approximately 3 in (7.5 cm).
5 For petits fours, the size should be 1½ (4 cm). When making these, fruit and the nuts need to be much more finely chopped.
6 The pieces of florentine left in the chocolate remaining on the greaseproof paper, may be removed by melting the chocolate and passing it through a fine sieve.
7 Moulds are now available with which the chocolate underside of florentines can be made to attach to the nut surface with chocolate. These are shown in Figure 48.

Brandy snaps
(Figure 49)

Yield 36–40

4½ oz (135 g) butter
8 oz (240 g) castor sugar
4 oz (120 g) soft flour
4 oz (120 g) golden syrup
2 level teaspoonsful ground ginger

1 Mix all the ingredients to a smooth paste.
2 Prepare a baking tin by thoroughly cleaning and giving it a liberal dressing of fat.
3 Roll out the paste into a long rope and, with a knife, chop off small pieces of equal size (approximately ½ oz (15 g)).
4 Place these about 5 in (13 cm) apart on the greased tray and flatten them with the hand or a fork.
5 Bake at 340°F (171°C) until they are golden in colour. During baking the paste flows out flat with a holey surface.
6 Once they are baked allow them to cool slightly and then lift them off with a palette knife.
7 While still warm, they may be moulded into a shape; but once cold they are very brittle and easily snap.
8 The brandy snap may be rolled round a wooden rod or a metal cream horn tin (with the top surface showing). They may also be moulded over a fluted tin to form a basket shape.
9 These shapes may then be filled with fresh whipped cream.

Notes

1 Brandy snaps, moulded into shapes, may be used as decorative pieces. For example, each segment of a torte could be decorated with a cornet shape filled with cream.

2 If the brandy snaps have become too cold to mould into shape, warm the tray and they will once again become soft enough to mould.

Tuiles
(Figure 50)

This is a mixing which can be stencilled into different shapes and after baking, moulded into various forms while still hot. It can be used for centrepieces or various novel sweets.

3½ oz (110 g) castor sugar
4¼ oz (130 g) flour
4¼ oz (130 g) butter
4¼ oz (130 g) egg white
Vanilla flavour

1 Cream the sugar, butter and egg whites and blend in the flour.
2 Spread the mixing through a stencil on to a clean greased tray and bake in a hot oven of 400°F (204°C) until the edges become tinged with colour.
3 Remove and mould into shape immediately.

To make the tub shown in the figure, the base and the sides are first stencilled separately. When baked, the side is wrapped round an appropriate size rolling pin to form the shape and then cemented to the base with boiling sugar. The tub is then filled with fresh cream and fruit to make it into a sweet.

Butterfly shapes may be stencilled and after baking moulded as one in flight. These make an added attraction if applied to sweets with cream or ice-cream.

12 *Savoury goods*

Cold savoury paste

14 oz (420 g) flour
6 oz (180 g) lard
¼ oz (7.5 g) salt (see page 48)
3¾ oz (115 g) cold water

1 Mix all the fat with half the flour and cream well together.
2 Add remaining flour and salt dissolved in the water.
3 Mix to a clear paste.

Hot savoury paste

Yield 2 pork pies at approx. 1 lb (480 g) each

10 oz 300 g) flour
5 oz (150 g) lard
2 level teaspoonfuls salt
2½ oz (75 g) boiling water

Method 1

1 Rub lard into the flour.
2 Add the boiling water.
3 Partially mix flour and water until cooler.
4 Finish off to a clear paste by mixing lightly with the hands.

Method 2

1 Rub half the fat into the flour.
2 Melt remainder in the water.
3 Proceed as (3) and (4) above.

Note: Do not use this paste until it is *cold*.

Boiled savoury paste

Use previous recipe.
1 Boil water, salt, and lard.
2 Add flour to the boiling mixture.
3 Mix to a clear smooth paste.
4 Use immediately while still hot.

Hand raised pork pies

Use a boiled or hot paste.

To shape a pork pie case successfully, we need a block of approximately 4 in (10 cm) diameter. Special wooden blocks are available for this purpose but, if not available, the bottom of a large jar may be used.

1 Use approximately 6 oz (180 g) of paste and form a ball.
2 With the heel of the hand, form a cup shape.
3 Reverse and press onto the block.
4 Pressing firmly, rotate the block to raise the paste up its side. Aim at producing a slightly thicker paste at the base with the sides tapering off to the top.
5 Allow the paste to set and remove from the block.
6 Fill with approximately 11 oz (330 g) of meat (see below). Flatten the meat and make sure that there are no air spaces left.
7 Roll out the remaining 2 oz (60 g) of pastry for the lid and cut out to the required size.
8 Wash the top inside edge with egg or water.
9 Place on the lid and press firmly into the sides. Pinch with fingers or nippers to seal.
10 Wash sides and top with egg and apply top decoration, that is, diamonds of paste or shaped as leaves.
11 Bake at 400°F (204°C) for approximately 1 hour.
12 After baking and whilst still hot, puncture the top crust and insert a good stock to which 1 oz (30 g) of gelatine per pint (6 dl) has been added.

Meat filling

Yield sufficient for two 1-lb (480-g) pies

11 oz (330 g) lean pork
5½ oz (165 g) fat pork
2 oz (60 g) rusk or bread
3¾ oz (115 g) cold water
½ oz (15 g) seasoning No. 2.

Seasoning

Recipe 1

2 of salt
1 of pepper

Recipe 2

1 lb (480 g) salt
½ lb (240 g) pepper
¼ oz (7.5 g) ground nutmeg (see page 48)
¼ oz (7.5 g) ground mace (see page 48)

Seasoning used at the rate of ½ oz per 1 lb (15 g per 480 g) of meat gives a spicy flavour that may be too pronounced for some palates. This, of course, may be adjusted to suit individual tastes.

Steak and kidney pie

Paste

4 oz (120 g) cold savoury paste (see page 154)

Filling

1 lb (480 g) lean steak
4 oz (120 g) kidney
1½ oz (45 g) flour
2 level teaspoonsful seasoning no. 1
Pinch of thyme
A little water

1 Cut meat into small cubes.
2 Cover with water and place in oven in a pie dish.
3 When cooked, mix flour with a little water and stir in.
4 Season and then allow to cool.
5 Cover with the paste, making sure that it sticks securely to the top edge of the pie dish, using a little egg wash.
6 Egg wash the top and bake at approximately 425°F (218°C) for approximately 25 minutes.

Veal and ham pie

Use boiled savoury paste and proceed as for the making of pork pies.

Filling

8 oz (240 g) chopped veal
11 oz (330 g) chopped pork
½ oz (15 g) seasoning No. 2
2 oz (60 g) water

Meat and potato pie

Paste

4 oz (120 g) cold savoury paste (see page 154)

Filling

10 oz (300 g) potatoes
2 oz (60 g) onions
4 oz (120 g) lean beef
2½ oz (75 g) water
2 level teaspoonsful seasoning no. 1

1 Cut the meat into cubes and dice the onion.
2 Cover with water, add the seasoning, and place in a pie dish.
3 When cooked, thicken with flour.
4 Partially cook the potatoes and add.
5 Proceed as for steak and kidney pies.

Cornish pasties

8 oz (240 g) savoury paste (see page 154)
4 oz (120 g) steak (minced or finely chopped)
4 oz (120 g) potatoes (minced or finely chopped)
2 oz (60 g) onions (minced or finely chopped)
Salt
Pepper

1 Divide the paste into four and pin each piece to a diameter of approximately 5 in (13 cm).
2 Mix the steak, potatoes, and onions together with a little water and season.
3 Place the filling in the centre of the pastry discs.
4 Wash the edges of the pastry with either water or egg.
5 Draw up each side of the pastry to the centre to cover the filling, pinching them firmly together.
6 Notch the seam with the thumb and finger. Finish moulding it into a boat shape with the fluted seam on top.
7 Egg wash.
8 Bake in an oven at 400°F (204°C) for approximately 30 minutes until the filling is thoroughly cooked.

Note: Other pasties may be made in a similar way using different fillings such as veal, ham, potatoes, and carrots.

Pizza

Yield one 8-in (20-cm) plate

Dough

4 oz (120 g) bread roll dough (see page 173)
½ oz (15 g) butter

Mix well together.

Filling

Finely chopped garlic (to taste)
Tomato (cut in slices)
Salt, pepper, and sweet marjoram
Anchovy fillets
Black olives (stoned)
Oil

1 Divide the dough into two 4-oz (120-g) portions.
2 Mould round and then roll out to cover an 8-in (20-cm) metal plate.
3 Allow the paste to rise slightly.
4 Sprinkle with finely chopped garlic.
5 Cover with the slices of tomato, overlapping.
6 Sprinkle on salt, pepper, and sweet marjoram.
7 Decorate with strips of anchovy and stoned black olives. A criss-cross or star pattern may be formed.
8 Sprinkle with olive or cooking oil.
9 Leave to rise for approximately ½ hour.
10 Bake in an oven of 390°F (199°C) until baked.

Note: Many other varieties may be made using different fillings such as cheese and salami.

Short pastry savouries

A very wide variety of savouries, both hot and cold, may be made from tartlets lined with the savoury short pastry and either baked with a savoury filling or baked blind and a savoury filling inserted afterwards.

Flans may also be made in this way and cut into portions afterwards (see quiche lorraine).

Quiche Lorraine

Yield 1 large flan suitable for 8 covers

8 oz (240 g) savoury short pastry
¾ pt (4½ dl) milk
2 oz (60 g) Gruyère cheese
3 eggs
6 oz (180 g) bacon
Salt and cayenne pepper

1 Roll out the pastry and line a large flan ring.
2 Prick the base with a fork.
3 Place on strips of bacon.
4 Place on thin slices of Gruyère cheese.
5 Whisk the eggs and milk together to form a custard, add the seasoning, and pour this over the cheese and bacon.
6 Place into an oven at 400°F (204°C) until set and brown.

Note: The milk may be replaced with single cream to improve quality.

Individual quiches
(Figure 11, top left)

Special small shallow teflon coated tins are available for individual quiches. They are thinly lined with unsweetened or savoury short pastry and filled with the filling in which the bacon, cheese and any other type of similar ingredient is chopped very small.

Savouries from chou paste

Cheese fritters

Add to the basic chou paste recipe (see page 109)

8 oz (240 g) grated Cheddar cheese

1 Using a spoon and finger, break off pieces of the savoury chou paste and drop into hot fat.
2 Cook until brown.
3 Remove, drain well, and serve immediately.

Note: Instead of a spoon, the mixture may be piped into the hot fat by means of a savoy bag fitted with a ⅛-in (3-mm) plain tube. A pair of oiled scissors can be used to cut off appropriately sized pieces as it emerges from the tube.

Cheese éclairs or cream buns

Basic chou paste recipe (see page 109)

1 Pipe out as for small éclairs or cream buns, but before baking sprinkle on grated parmesan cheese.

2 Bake in the usual way.
3 When cold, split open and pipe in the cheese filling (see below).

Béchamel

Yield 1 quart (12 dl)

1 qt (40 oz) (12 dl) milk
4½ oz (135 g) margarine
4 oz (120 g) flour
1 small onion studded with 2 cloves

1 Add the studded onion to the milk and bring to the boil.
2 Melt the margarine in a saucepan.
3 Add the flour and gently cook the mixture (roux) for a few minutes.
4 Add the warmed milk gradually, thoroughly stirring in each addition to make a smooth sauce.
5 Simmer the sauce gently for 30 minutes to 1 hour.
6 Remove the onion and pass the Béchamel through a conical strainer.

Cheese fillings

Recipe 1

4 oz (120 g) powdered or finely grated cheese
4 oz (120 g) butter
4 oz (120 g) water

1 Beat the cheese and butter together to a light cream.
2 Add the water gradually beating in each addition.

Recipe 2

2½ oz (75 g) Béchamel
1½ oz (45 g) egg yolks
2 oz (60 g) butter
4 oz (120 g) grated cheese
2 oz (60 g) cream
Salt
Cayenne pepper

1 Using hot Béchamel, add first the butter, and when this has been mixed in follow with the egg yolks, cheese, and lastly the cream, mixing in each addition before adding the next ingredient.
2 Season with salt and cayenne.

Savouries from puff paste

Vol-au-vents and bouchées

Various fillings may be used including chicken, ham, cheese, mushrooms, shrimps, salmon, etc.

1 Prepare the puff pastry cases as described in Chapter 3 on Puff pastry (see page 71).

2 Dice the chicken, ham, mushrooms, or salmon. The cheese should be grated and the shrimps left whole.
3 Mix with either Béchamel sauce or Velouté (see below) and a small quantity of fresh double cream.
4 Deposit in the baked cases. Replace the puff pastry top or, alternatively, omit and use an appropriate garnish instead.

Velouté

This is made in the same way as the Béchamel sauce but instead of milk, an appropriate stock is used, e.g. chicken stock for chicken, fish stock for shrimps.

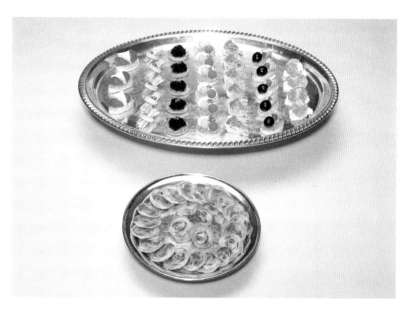

Figure 51   *Canapes.*
Description in text

Cheese straws – paillettes au fromage
(Figure 51, row 2)

4 oz (120 g) well-rested puff pastry
2 oz (60 g) grated cheese
Cayenne pepper

1 Roll out the pastry to about 6 in × 18 in (15 cm × 45 cm).
2 Cover two-thirds with the grated cheese and sprinkle with cayenne.
3 Fold the uncovered one-third portion into the centre of the covered portion and complete as if a single turn is given (English method).
4 Roll out to ⅛ in (3 mm).
5 Cut out four or five discs with a 2-in (5-cm) cutter and remove the centre with a 1½-in (4-cm) cutter to form rings.
6 Cut up the remainder of the puff pastry into strips approximately 3 in × ¼ in (7.5 cm × 6 mm) wide.
7 Twist each of these and place upon a lightly greased baking tray together with the rings.
8 Bake at 450°F (232°C) for approximately 10 minutes, until they are golden brown in colour.
9 Place a bundle of straws inside each circle and serve.

Parmesanes

Base

Puff pastry
Gruyère or Parmesan cheese (grated)

Filling (Garniture à parmesanes)

10 oz (3 dl) milk
1 oz (30 g) cornflour
2 egg yolks
3 oz (90 g) butter
3 oz (90 g) grated Parmesan or Gruyère cheese

Method for making filling

1 Mix the cornflour with about ¼ of the milk.
2 Add the egg yolks and grated cheese and mix.
3 Boil the remainder of the milk.
4 Pour the boiling milk onto the cornflour mixture and stir well to prevent formation of lumps.
5 Return to the heat and allow to boil for a few minutes.
6 Lastly, add the butter and remove from the heat.
7 Store in a cold place until required.

Method for making parmesanes

1 Roll out virgin puff paste to ⅛ in (3 mm) in thickness, cut out rounds of approximately 4 in (10 cm) diameter.
2 Place them on moistened clean baking tins.
3 Place in the centre of each, a small quantity of grated Gruyère cheese.
4 Allow a short resting period and bake off in a hot oven at 480°F (249°C).
5 After they are cooked, split in half, place in some of the filling in the bottom half, and replace the top.

Other varieties

Many other varieties of puff paste savouries may be made as follows:

1 Roll out the puff paste to approximately (½ cm) thick and cut out with a 3½-in (9-cm) fluted cutter.
2 Extend these with a rolling pin to form an oval shape keeping the edges thicker than the centre.
3 Wash with egg and place in the centre a quantity of filling (see below).
4 Fold over to enclose the filling and seal edge.
5 Wash with egg and bake at 390°F (199°C).

Fillings

Cheese, cooked minced meats, vegetables, cooked chicken, scampi, etc.

Note: The crimper shown in Figure 2 (page 3) may be used with advantage to make small savoury pasties.

Canapés

These are very small round, square, rectangle or oval shapes made out of a variety of bases such as bread, biscuit, puff pastry, short pastry, choux pastry, pancakes etc. Bread can be wholemeal, rye or white and either left plain, fried or toasted. It is usually buttered or spread with a savoury paste.

The stages in the making of canapes are thus:

1 Make a number of bases.
2 Cover with a combination of different savoury products.
3 Decorate with a suitable garnish.
4 Glaze with aspic or an alternative.

For ease of handling, cocktail sticks may be inserted so that the customers need not soil their hands.

Figure 51, on page 160, shows an unusual selection of canapes which are now described.

Large tray, rows numbered from left to right

1 Base of cheese puff pastry. Cut small wedges of Brie cheese are placed in the centre and sandwiched between two cut strawberries.
2 Small cheese straws made from very thin puff pastry.
3 Round base made from a buck-wheat pancake (Blinis, see recipe on page 163). When cooked these are trimmed round and covered with caviar.
4 Base of puff pastry covered with cream cheese and garnished with small balls of honeydew melon and water melon.
5 Small wedges cut from the individual quiche described on page 158.
6 Base of puff pastry covered with a mousse made from blue cheese blended with cream and garnished with black grape and a stick of celery.
7 Choux paste flavoured with cheese and paprika, piped very small, deep fried and rolled in Parmesan cheese.

Note: Before baking, the puff pastry is dusted with cayenne pepper.

Small round tray

Anchovy canapés

These are made as follows:

1 Roll out the puff pastry very thinly into a square and transfer to a sheet of clingfilm.
2 Lay strips of dried anchovies lengthwise on to the pastry.
3 Roll up Swiss roll fashion in the same direction as the anchovies.
4 Place in a freezer to chill.
5 Slice very thinly and bake in a hot oven, turning the slice half way through baking.
6 Trim with a round cutter and garnish with parsley.

Blinis (buckwheat pancakes)

A
⅓ oz (10 g) yeast
5 oz (150 g) milk (warm)
½ oz (15 g) flour

B
2½ oz (75 g) flour
10 oz (300 g) milk (warm)
2 egg yolks

C
2 egg whites

1 Mix A and allow to ferment for ¾ hour in a covered bowl in a warm place at approximately 85°F (29°C).
2 Add B to A and beat into a batter. Allow to stand for 30 minutes.
3 Beat C to a stiff snow and fold into the batter.
4 Cook on a hot griddle to make pancakes approximately 3–4 in (10 cm) diameter.

Some other ideas for varieties

Liver

1 A slice of goose liver, garnished with a disc of truffle in the centre.
2 Liver paste garnished with a small slice of raw carrot.

Egg

1 Three overlapping slices of hard boiled egg. Garnish the yolk with a slice of gherkin.
2 Finely chopped hard boiled egg, mixed with a little cream. Garnish with a slice of tomato.
3 Pass hard boiled eggs through a sieve and mix with mayonnaise, seasoned with mustard. Garnish with a small sprig of watercress.

Ham

1 Meat paste covered with a slice of ham. Garnish with a small rosette of mashed potatoes and a cooked pea.
2 Make a small roll of the ham slice. Garnish with a small wedge of pineapple.

Tongue

Slice of tongue. Garnish with a rosette of mashed potatoes and piece of pickled walnut.

Salami

A slice of salami wrapped around a piece of gherkin.

Smoked salmon

1 A slice of smoked salmon rolled into a cone and filled with mashed potato. Garnish with a piece of tomato.
2 A slice of smoked salmon laid flat and garnished with a small piece of lemon.

Shrimp

Select six small shrimps and arrange head to tail in the form of a rose. Pipe a rosette of butter in the centre.

Sardine

Small sardine, lightly dusted with paprika.

Tomato

Slice of tomato on which is sprinkled finely grated cheese. Garnish with a caper.

Cheese

Slice of cheese garnished with a piece of apple.

Chicken

Finely chopped chicken mixed with mayonnaise. Garnish with paprika and then pieces of green and red pepper.

Method of applying aspic

Place the canapés on a wire with a drip tray underneath. Use a dropping funnel (see page 257) to deposit sufficient aspic on each canapé to completely cover them. The surplus should run into the tray underneath.

Use the aspic warm so that it completely covers the canapé before it sets.

The varieties of canapés are endless and offer unlimited scope to the imaginative patissier. However, care is required to ensure that the items chosen complement each other in taste and colour.

Note: Aspic is a savoury stock which should set to a jelly when cold. If too soft, gelatine may be added.

Pasta

Pasta is the general term for macaroni, spaghetti, vermicelli, noodles, etc., which include any specific shape. It originates in Italy.

Noodles – nouilles

4 oz (120 g) strong flour
2 oz (60 g) eggs
½ oz (15 g) olive oil
A pinch of salt

1 Sieve the flour and salt.
2 Add the oil and egg.
3 Thoroughly mix into a well-developed, smooth dough.
4 Cover and let the dough rest for 2 hours or more.
5 Roll out very thinly into pieces approximately 3 in (7.5 cm) wide and leave to dry.
6 Cut these pieces into thin strips approx. ¼ in (6 mm) wide and leave to dry.

Notes:
1 For dusting purposes use either a strong flour or semolina.
2 Noodles are cooked in the same way as spaghetti and served in the same way as for any spaghetti recipe.
3 It may be served mixed with fresh hot cream.
4 The paste may be mixed with tomato or spinach purée for further varieties.
5 Noodles may also be used as a garnish, for example with braised beef.

Ravioli

8 oz (240 g) strong flour
1¼ oz (40 g) olive oil
3¾ oz (115 g) water
A pinch of salt

1 Sieve the flour and salt.
2 Add the oil and water.
3 Thoroughly mix into a well-developed, smooth dough.
4 Allow the dough to rest for at least 30 minutes.
5 Roll out the dough very thinly to approximately 12 in × 18 in (30 cm × 45 cm).
6 Cut into two and egg wash one half.
7 Fill a savoy bag with a large plain tube, with the ravioli filling (see over).
8 Pipe out small pieces of the filling about the size of a cherry approximately 1½ in (3.5 cm) apart on the egg-washed piece of paste.
9 Cover with the other half of paste and press down between each pile of filling to seal, taking care not to trap any air.
10 Using a serrated pastry wheel, cut the pastry between the lines of filling or cut into 1¼-in (3-cm) circles with a cutter.
11 Separate and place on a floured tray.
12 Place in gently boiling water to poach for 8–10 minutes.

13 Drain well and arrange in layers in a buttered gratin dish.
14 Pour over about ½ pt (3 dl) of jus-lie, demi-glace, or tomato sauce.
15 Sprinkle with about 2 oz (60 g) grated cheese.
16 Brown under the salamander.
17 Place dish on a flat and serve immediately.

Note: There are several different fillings for ravioli. These would normally be made for the patissier by the chef but a suitable filling is included here:

Ravioli filling

8 oz (240 g) beef or veal (braised or boiled)
2 oz (60 g) chopped onion or shallot
½ oz (15 g) fat
1 lb (480 g) spinach
1 clove of garlic
A pinch of salt
Pepper
1 egg yolk

1 Mince the meat.
2 Cook and mince the spinach.
3 Cook the onions or shallots in the fat without colouring.
4 Mix the ingredients with the egg yolk to bind the mixture and season.

Basic pasta dough for machine varieties

1 lb 4 oz (600 g) strong flour
10 oz (300 g) whole egg
3½ oz (105 g) egg yolks
1 oz (30 g) cooking oil
Salt and pepper to taste

1 Place all the ingredients in a food processor or machine and blend into a smooth dough.
2 Cover and allow to rest for 1 hour in a refrigerator.
3 Roll out and make into the various varieties with the machine.

Small pasta machines are now available for the patissier to make a variety of different products from a basic dough.

The paste is fed between rollers which can reduce it to any thickness required. Cutters can also be adjusted to cut the paste in any width of strip. The use of this machine is demonstrated in Figure 52, page 168, and the products are identified as follows.

1 Tortalini.
2 Small ravioli.
3 Small ravioli.
4 Large ravioli.
5 Spaghetti.
6 Noodles.

Gnocchi

These are small dumplings and may be made from:

1 *Chou paste* – Gnocchi à la parisienne.
2 *Semolina* – Gnocchi à la romaine.
3 *Potato and flour* – Gnocchi à la piedmontaise.

Gnocchi à la Parisienne

Yield 8 covers

10 oz (300 g) water into chou paste (see page 109)
4 oz (120 g) grated cheese
1 pt (6 dl) Béchamel sauce (see page 159)

1 Make the chou paste.
2 Add 2 oz (60 g) of the grated cheese.
3 Place in a savoy bag fitted with a plain tube.
4 Pipe out and cut with an oiled palette knife into suitable lengths ½–1 in (1.25–2.5 cm) into a shallow pan containing boiling salted water.
5 Slowly poach for 10 minutes.
6 Drain well and arrange in a buttered fireproof dish.
7 Cover with the Béchamel sauce.
8 Sprinkle over the remaining cheese.
9 Brown under the salamander.
10 Serve immediately on a flat silver dish.

Gnocchi à la Romaine

Yield 8 covers

2 pt (12 dl) milk
12 oz (360 g) semolina
3 oz (90 g) butter
3 oz (90 g) grated cheese
3 oz (90 g) grated cheese
3 egg yolks
Seasoning
Grated nutmeg

1 Boil the milk.
2 Sprinkle in the semolina, stirring continuously.
3 Allow to simmer for 5–10 minutes.
4 Season and add the nutmeg.
5 Add the egg yolk, cheese, and butter and mix in.
6 Pour onto a greased tray to a depth of approximately ½ in (1.25 cm).
7 When cold, cut out pieces with a 2-in (5-cm) round cutter or into crescent shapes.
8 Place the scraps of the cutting in an earthenware dish.
9 Arrange the rounds or crescents neatly on top.
10 Sprinkle on melted butter and the grated cheese.
11 Place under the salamander to brown.
12 Serve on a flat silver dish.

Gnocchi à la piedmontaise

Yield 8 covers

1 lb 8 oz (720 g) mashed potatoes

8 oz (240 g) flour
2 oz (60 g) butter
6 egg yolks
Seasoning
Grated nutmeg
1 pt (6 dl) tomato sauce

1 Boil or steam the potatoes.
2 Pass through a sieve and keep as dry as possible.
3 Whilst still hot, mix in the flour, butter, seasoning, and egg.
4 Mould into small balls about the size of a walnut.
5 Dust well with flour and flatten slightly with a fork.
6 Place into boiling water and poach for 5 minutes.
7 Drain carefully and place on a clean cloth to dry.
8 Arrange in a buttered fire-proof dish and cover with the tomato sauce.
9 Sprinkle with grated cheese and place under the salamander to brown.
10 Serve immediately on a flat silver dish.

Figure 52   *Pasta. Showing use of the pasta machine to produce the following products:*

1 Tortalini	4 Large ravioli
2 Small ravioli	5 Spaghetti
3 Small ravioli	6 Noodles

13 *Fermented goods*

Yeast fermentation

Before dealing with the various goods which are aerated by the fermentation of yeast, the principles of fermentation are outlined here so that the patissier will have a better understanding of what happens when yeast ferments.

Yeast is a living micro-organism existing as a cell, having a diameter of $\frac{1}{2500}$ to $\frac{1}{4000}$ in ($\frac{1}{100}$ to $\frac{1}{160}$ mm) invisible to the naked eye but easily discernible under the microscope.

When this organism is introduced to warmth, food, and moisture, it ferments, that is, it produces carbon dioxide gas and ethyl alcohol, at the same time reproducing itself. When we introduce yeast into our goods, we provide the food material and moisture and to a certain extent control the temperature, so that the yeast ferments under the best conditions to generate carbon dioxide which we need for the goods to become aerated. (The brewer or distiller requires the other by-product of fermentation, ethyl alcohol.)

However, the process of yeast fermentation is complicated and there are many factors which affect it. The best way to understand these factors is to elaborate upon each.

Food material

Yeast requires dextrose sugar (glucose) before it can ferment, but because it contains enzymes which are capable of changing both cane sugar (sucrose) and malt sugar (maltose) into dextrose, almost any sweet material (except milk sugar) will act as a source of food material. Wheat flour already contains 2.5% of these sugars so that any mixture of flour and water will readily ferment without the addition of any extra sugar.

What is important, however, is the concentration of sugar which the yeast is expected to ferment. The optimum is approximately 12½% and concentrations above this have a retarding effect. This must be remembered when doughs are made which are very rich in sugar. The yeast content must be increased considerably to compensate for this effect.

Temperature

Yeast is dormant at 32°F (0°C) but as the temperature increases so too does the activity of the yeast until, at 120°F (49°C), it becomes killed. The best working temperatures are between 70°–85°F (21°–29°C). Without understanding this, it is easy to be tempted to ferment yeast at too high a temperature. Even 85°F (29°C) feels comparatively cool to the touch. Too high a temperature causes dough skinning and the encouragement of other undesirable characteristics and it should be tolerated only for the final proof stage. It is a mistake to believe that warm water must always be used. In summer the use of water straight from the tap is recommended to achieve the right dough temperature.

Method of determining water temperature for a dough

1 Determine the temperature of the flour to be used.
2 Subtract the value from *twice* the required dough temperature.
3 The result will be the required water temperature. It can be expressed thus:

Water temperature =
(required dough temperature × 2) − flour temperature.

Salt

This commodity is invariably used in all yeast goods for the enhancement of flavour, although it has other side effects, namely:

1 Strengthens the gluten of the flour and so stabilizes the dough.
2 Produces a whiter crumb and colour and bloom to the crust.
3 Reduces staling.
4 Retards fermentation.

It is this last effect which we have to consider carefully. Bringing yeast into direct contact with salt will soon kill it or at least dangerously retard its activity. The concentration of salt usually used in a dough is tolerable by the yeast provided that at the mixing stage it is kept in a sufficiently dilute solution.

Spices

These too retard fermentation. In heavily spiced goods (for example hot-cross buns), more yeast needs to be used to compensate for this retarding effect.

Fats

These also have a retarding effect.

Time

So far we have only considered one effect of using yeast, that is to aerate. If this were the only aspect in which we were interested, there would be no purpose in allowing a dough to lie in bulk for a given time before proceeding to scale, mould, and prove.
When yeast starts to ferment, a very complicated series of enzyme changes take place, not only causing the production of carbon dioxide and alcohol but also causing the protein gluten network of the dough to become softened and more elastic. This

function enables the gluten to stretch more and retain more gas. A perfect dough is one in which this function has been allowed to reach the optimum, that is the time allowed for the dough to lie in bulk has been correct for the temperature chosen and quantity of yeast used. Below the optimum, the dough is said to be *under-ripe*; over this optimum, the dough is said to be *over-ripe*.

It follows from this that, for a perfect dough to be made, there must be perfect correlation between dough temperature and dough time for any given yeast quantity. If the temperature is reduced, the yeast quantity must be increased and vice versa.

Definitions

Bulk fermentation time (BFT)   This is the period of time from when the dough is made until when it is taken for weighing into the correctly sized pieces ready for moulding, proving, and baking.
Scaling   Dividing the dough into pieces by weight.
Moulding   Shaping the dough pieces into the appropriate shape for the purpose required.
Proving   Allowing the dough pieces to lie and grow in size before being baked. This is usually done in a cabinet in which warmth and steam are applied so that the goods are prevented from developing a skin and so grow uniform in shape. The correct degree of proof can only be learned by experience and varies with each type of goods; but, approximately, the dough pieces should at least double their size prior to being placed in the oven.
Baking   All fermented goods require a hot oven at between 400°F (204°C) and 450°F (232°C). Goods rich in sugar and fat require the lower temperature while goods such as dinner rolls, lean in sugar and fat, require the higher temperature. For the best possible baking conditions some steam should be present in the oven. When an oven is full, there is sufficient steam being generated by the goods themselves; but if the oven is only a quarter to half full it is an advantage to place in some water. This is to create a humid atmosphere and prevent the skin of the goods from setting until they have had the chance to grow slightly. Furthermore, the presence of steam will help to create moist eating goods and the production of a bloom on the crust.

Faults

The two main faults which occur in fermented goods may be attributed to under-ripeness or over-ripeness.

Under-ripeness

This is detected by all or any of the following characteristics:

1 High crust colour.
2 Small volume and bound buns, rolls, etc.
3 Poor shapes split at the sides or top.
4 Tough close textured crumb.

Note: Faults 2 and 3 may also be due to insufficient proof.

Under-ripeness is caused by insufficient fermentation and may be due to:

1 Insufficient yeast.
2 Too cool a dough temperature.
3 Too much sugar/salt/spice/fat/etc.
4 Yeast coming into contact with salt at the mixing stage.
5 Insufficient dough time.

Over-ripeness

This is indicated by:

1 Anaemic crust colour.
2 Flat shapes with no stability.
3 Loose, woolly crumb.

Note: Fault 2 may also be due to excessive proof.

Over-ripeness is caused by too much fermentation and may be due to:

1 Excessive amount of yeast.
2 Too high a dough temperature.
3 Omission of salt or the sugar in a bun dough.
4 Too prolonged a dough time.

Method of mixing fermented doughs by hand

1 Sieve flour.
2 Rub into the flour the required fat quantity.
3 Make a bay with the flour/fat mixture.
4 Calculate the water temperature (that is, required dough temperature $\times 2$ − flour temperature).
5 Measure the required amount of water at the required temperature.
6 Mix a small quantity with the yeast and the remainder with the other soluble ingredients, that is, salt and sugar.
7 Pour the solutions into the bay and lightly mix until every particle of flour is wetted.
8 Now knead the dough, stretching and pulling until it is a clear, elastic mass free of stickiness and lumps.
9 Place it aside under a cover to prevent skinning for its required bulk fermentation time.

Note: Some textbooks still state that the sugar and yeast should be creamed together. This is *bad* practice and results in a loss of yeast activity owing to the retarding effect of a high concentration of sugar.

Water quantity

This varies with the required consistency and with the strength of flour used. All fermented goods require a strong flour, but even the water absorption capacity of a strong flour can vary. Therefore, the quantity of water given in each recipe may have to be adjusted to suit individual circumstances.

Bread rolls

Yield approximately 16 rolls

1 lb 4 oz (600 g) strong flour
½ oz (15 g) milk powder
⅓ oz (10 g) salt
½ oz (15 g) sugar
½ oz (15 g) fat
⅞ oz (25 g) yeast
11½ oz (345 g) water

Dough BFT 1 hour at 76°F (24°C).

1 Mix dough as previously described.
2 Allow to rest under a cover for 1 hour.
3 Divide dough into 2-oz (60-g) pieces.
4 Mould round.
5 Place on baking trays.
6 Prove in a little steam to prevent skinning.
7 Bake in an oven at approximately 450°F (232°C) for 12–15 minutes.

Figure 53 *Fermented buns.*

Top:	Chelsea
Bottom:	Bath

Top:	Currant
Bottom:	Swiss

Top:	Cream
Bottom:	Swiss

Basic bun dough

Yield approximately 16 buns

1 lb 4 oz (600 g) strong flour
½ oz (15 g) milk powder
2½ oz (75 g) sugar
¼ oz (7.5 g) salt (see page 48)

8 oz (240 g) butter
5 oz (150 g) sultanas
1 oz (30 g) mixed peel

C
8 oz (240 g) nib sugar

D
2 oz (60 g) nib sugar

1 Mix together the ingredients of A and allow to ferment for ½ hour.
2 After this time add the ingredients of B and make into a smooth dough.
3 Leave dough to ferment for 1 hour and then mix in the nib sugar C.
4 Allow to recover for 15 minutes, during which time prepare a clean baking tin by greasing with butter.
5 Divide into pieces and lay out on the buttered tray. The appearance should be as rocky as possible.
6 Wash with egg.
7 Allow to prove *in the cold* until approximately double their original size.
8 Sprinkle some nib sugar on each piece D.
9 Bake in an oven at 430°F (221°C) for approximately 15 minutes.
10 Wash the pieces lightly with bun wash on removal from the oven.

Danish pastry

Yield 16–18 depending on varieties made

9 oz (270 g) medium strength flour
1¼ oz (37.5 g) yeast (see page 48)
5 oz (150 g) chilled milk
2 oz (60 g) egg
6 oz (180 g) tough butter or mixture of margarine
2 level teaspoonsful cardomon spice

Mixture of margarine

2 oz (60 g) pastry margarine
4 oz (120 g) cake margarine

Blend well together.

Fillings

1 Mincemeat. See page 225.
2 Almond cream. Equal quantities of ground almonds, sugar, and butter.
3 Cinnamon cream. Equal quantities of butter and castor sugar flavoured with cinnamon spice.
4 Custard. See page 185.
5 Dried fruit. Currants, sultanas, glacé cherries.

Toppings

1 Water icing. See page 289.
2 Apricot glaze. See page 289.
3 Sugar and almond nibs. Mix equal quantities.
4 Almond nibs.

1 Sieve the flour and make a bay.
2 Mix the yeast with the egg and milk and pour into the bay.
3 Mix the dough *lightly. Do not toughen.*
4 Roll out the dough to approximately 8 in × 15 in (20 cm × 37.5 cm) and cover ⅔ with the margarine or butter.
5 Fold the remaining ⅓ into the centre and fold the whole into three (as English method of making puff pastry).
6 Proceed to give it three half-turns and lastly one fold over. If the dough is not tough, this should be accomplished with about 10 minutes rest between turns.
7 Allow the dough to rest about 20 minutes and, using the fillings, make various varieties as described.
8 Once the varieties have been made, give them the maximum proof in a slightly humid prover *but not hot.*
9 Bake in a hot oven approximately 460°F (238°C).
10 When baked and while still hot, brush over with rum-flavoured apricot glaze and water icing.

Note: The secret of making good Danish pastry is to keep all the ingredients cool. To achieve this it is a good idea to store the flour etc. in the refrigerator prior to use.

Unlike puff pastry, the paste should not be too tough. It should be worked off as soon as possible, very well proved, and baked in a very hot oven. Only by observing these rules will a tender and flaky article be made.

Figure 54 *Danish pastries. Description in text*

Varieties

A great number of varieties of Danish pastries may be made according to the imagination and ingenuity of the patissier, but a useful selection is shown in Figure 54.

Baking

Ensure that only the same type of variety is baked together. Some, such as those dressed in nibbed almonds, require an oven about 20°F (11°C) cooler than that generally recommended, otherwise the almonds will take on too much colour.

Danish pastry

Explanation of varieties shown in Figure 54.

Top row (from left to right)

1 Roll the dough to approximately ³⁄₁₆ (4 mm) in thickness. Cut into squares of approximately 3 in (7.5 cm) sides. Place a small amount of the filling in each square. Egg wash the edges and fold over to form a triangle. Press edges to seal. Egg wash and dip into nib almonds before placing on to tray.
2 Roll the dough to approximately ¼ in (6 mm) in thickness and into a strip approximately 3 in (7.5 cm) wide. Place some filling down the centre of the strip. Egg wash one edge, fold the other into the centre and fold over the washed egg to overlap. Turn the strip so that the seal is underneath. Cut into pieces approximately 3 in (7.5 cm) long. Egg wash and dip into nib almonds.
3 Proceed as the previous variety. Cut slits along one edge and lay out on the tray in a curve as shown.
4 Roll out the dough approximately ³⁄₁₆ in (4 mm) thick into a strip approximately 7 in (18 cm) wide. Cut this strip into triangles having a base of approximately 3½ in (9 cm). Alternatively use the croissant cutter (see Figure 1(11) page 2). Cut a slit 1½ in (4 cm) long near the apex (point) end of the triangle and place some filling at the base end. Starting at this end roll up the triangle. Form a crescent by giving it a twist. Egg wash and place on tray.

Middle row (from left to right)

1 Roll out the dough to approximately ¼ in (6 mm) thick. Spread half with a thin layer of the almond cream and fold over to form a sandwich. Roll out this piece to a width of approximately 15 in (37.5 cm) at an approximate thickness of ¼ in (6 mm). Cut into strips approximately ³⁄₈ in (1 cm). Starting at each end and moving the hands in alternate directions give a twist to the strip. Form the twisted strip into a figure S. Dress the top with a sprinkling of almonds and nib sugar.
2 Proceed as in the previous variety but forming the strip into the shape illustrated.

3 Proceed as in the previous two varieties but form the twisted strip into a circle.

4 Roll out the dough to approximately ¼ in (6 mm) and cut into squares approximately 4 in (10 cm). Place a portion of custard filling in the centre of each square and fold the corners into the centre to form a cushion. Egg wash and place on the tray. When baked and glazed a bulb of custard may be piped into the centre. Alternatively a bulb of custard may be piped into the centre prior to baking.

Bottom row (from left to right)

1 Roll out the dough to approximately ³⁄₁₆ (4 mm) thick in a strip approximately 10 in (25 cm) wide. Spread on some cinnamon cream and cover with currants. Roll up like a Swiss roll. Cut pieces approximately ¾ in (2 cm) wide and lay on the tray.

2 Make two cuts into the above slice without severing it and arrange on the tray as a fan.

3 Proceed as in variety (1) but only cut slice into two and arrange on the tray.

4 Proceed as in variety (1) but instead of cutting the roll into slices, cut in half lengthwise. Cut these into slices approximately ¾ in (2 cm) wide and lay them on the tray with the cut surface showing.

Brioche
(Figure 55)

Yield 16–18

A
9 oz (270 g) strong flour
¼ oz (7.5 g) salt (see page 48)
1 oz (30 g) sugar
5 oz (150 g) eggs
1 oz (30 g) milk
1 oz (30 g) yeast

B
2½ oz (75 g) butter

1 Disperse the yeast with the milk and make the ingredients of A into a well-beaten dough.

2 Add the butter and beat well to form a silky, smooth toughened dough.

3 Allow to ferment for 1 hour.

4 Lightly grease some fluted patty pans.

5 After the hour, divide the brioche dough into approximately 1-oz (30-g) pieces.

6 Mould first round and then to a dumbell shape with the small end about half the size of the other.

7 Place the longer bulbous end of the piece in the pan (Figure 55).

8 Keeping the small bulb suspended make a hole in the centre of the large bulb with the finger.

9 Allow the small bulb to rest in this impression so that the shape now resembles a cottage loaf.

10 Carefully wash over with egg.
11 Allow to prove to double their size in a humid place (not too warm).
12 Bake at approximately 460°F (238°C) for 10 minutes.
13 Remove from the pan while still hot and transfer to cooling wires.

Figure 55   *Croissants brioche*

Front row: Finished croissants
Middle row: Unfilled and filled brioche
Back row: Placing brioche dough into the tins.

Croissants
(Figures 55 and 56)

Yield 20

A
10 oz (300 g) flour
½ oz (15 g) yeast
¼ oz (7.5 g) salt (see page 48)
1 oz (30 g) sugar
7–8 oz (240 g) milk

B
4½ oz (135 g) tough butter or pastry margarine

1 Make the ingredients of A into a well-toughened dough.
2 After allowing 30 minutes rest, roll out the dough to a rectangle approximately ¼ in (6 mm) thick.
3 Cover two-thirds of the dough with the butter and fold as in the English method of making puff pastry (see page 69).
4 Proceed to give three half-turns allowing a rest period between each turn.

5 Roll out the paste to approximately ¹⁄₁₀ in (2 mm) in thickness and cut into two strips 8–9 in (20–23 cm) wide.

6 Cut these into triangles as follows having a base of approximately 4–4½ in (10–11 cm) (Figure 56). Alternately use the crescent cutter as shown in (11) of Figure 1 (page 2).

7 Starting at the base, lightly shape the triangle into a crescent and lay on a clean baking sheet. Use up the paste shown in the shaded areas by adding a little to the centre of each croissant as it is being rolled.

8 Egg wash thoroughly.

9 Prove in a humid atmosphere to about double their original volume (not too warm).

10 Bake at 460°F (238°C) for approximately 10 minutes.

Note: This is a typical French pastry which is served with coffee for breakfast in many Continental countries.

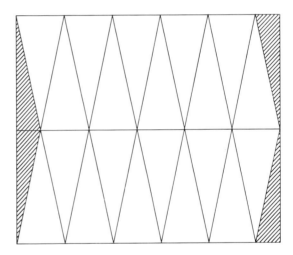

Figure 56   *Croissants. Cutting the dough for croissants*

Savarins
(Figure 57)

Yield two – each suitable for 8 covers in 7 in or 18 cm mould

Dough

4 oz (120 g) strong flour
3 oz (90 g) eggs
³⁄₈ oz (10 g) yeast
½ oz (15 g) water
2 level teaspoonsful sugar
2 oz (60 g) melted butter

Syrup

4 oz (120 g) sugar
8 oz (240 g) water (1 oz water may be replaced by 1 oz liqueur. Other flavours and/or fruit juices may be used, e.g. lemon, orange, and cinnamon)

1 Make a dough at about 80°F (27°C) of all the ingredients except the butter. Beat well into a smooth and elastic dough.
2 Allow the dough to lie for 30 minutes in a warm place (keep covered).
3 Beat in the 2 oz (60 g) of melted butter, small quantities at a time.
4 Grease or butter a savarin mould and into this pipe the savarin dough.
5 Prove fully – to the top of the savarin mould.
6 Bake at 450°F (232°C) for 20–25 minutes.
7 Remove from the mould while still warm.
8 When cold saturate with the syrup. If the savarin has been properly made it should absorb all this syrup. One recommended method is to pour the syrup into the savarin mould and replace the savarin. Leave until all the syrup has been absorbed, remove, and turn upside down onto a draining wire.
9 Glaze with boiling apricot glaze.
10 Fill centre with fruit.
11 Decorate with fresh, sweetened cream (crème Chantilly).
12 Serve on a flat dish.

Rum baba – Baba au rhum
(Figure 57)

Recipe same as for savarins except that rum is used as the liqueur, and add:

2 oz (60 g) currants

1 Proceed as for savarins.
2 When dough is ready, half fill eight greased dariole moulds and prove.
3 Continue as for savarins.
4 Serve without fruit but with crème Chantilly.

Marigans
(Figure 57, shown in foreground)

The recipe is the same as for savarins.

1 Fill barquette moulds to a third and prove to the top.
2 Bake at 450°F (232°C) for approximately 15 minutes.
3 Soak in the savarin syrup and drain.
4 Cut slits in the marigans, brush over with apricot purée and fill the slits with fresh cream.
5 Fruit can be used as a decoration.

Savarins, babas and marigans can be left overnight and be soaked with syrup the next day ready for finishing.

Croûtes

Yield 8 covers

The base of croûtes is savarin which has been allowed to stale slightly. Since even slices of savarin are required, it is best to bake the savarin in a special round, circular tin or a charlotte mould.

Fruit croûtes – Croûtes aux fruits

1 savarin cut into 8 slices
1 lb 6 oz (660 g) stewed assorted fruit
3½ oz (105 g) muscatel raisons (stoned)
8 oz (240 g) thick apricot sauce (this may be flavoured with rum or Kirsch)
Icing sugar

1 Cut the savarin into eight slices approximately ½ in (1.25 cm) thick and place on a clean baking tray.
2 Dust the slices liberally with icing sugar and glaze in a very hot oven.
3 Arrange the slices on a round, flat dish with every slice overlapping the other so as to form a crown.
4 Add the fruit to the apricot sauce and fill the centre of the dish.
5 Serve either hot or cold.

Pineapple croûtes – Croûtes à l'ananas

Yield 8 covers

8 slices of savarin
8 slices of pineapple (large)
8 red cherries
3 oz (90 g) butter
½ pt (3 dl) apricot sauce (flavoured with kirsch)

1 Fry the slices of savarin lightly in butter.
2 Place a slice of cored pineapple on each and a red cherry in the centre of each.
3 Arrange them as a crown on a flat round dish.
4 Cover with hot apricot sauce.
5 Serve hot or cold.

Apricot croûtes – Croûtes aux abricots

As for pineapple croûtes but using two apricot halves instead of one slice of pineapple. A red cherry is placed in the hollow of each apricot.

Croûtes Parisienne

As for Croûtes aux fruits but using fruit salad instead. May be served hot or cold but, if served cold, it is usual to decorate it with fresh whipped cream.

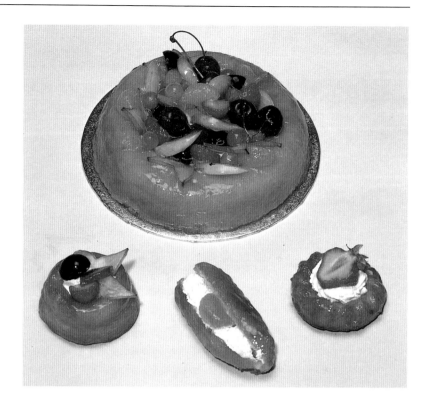

Figure 57   *Savarin, babas and marigans*

Top centre: Savarin
Bottom centre: Marigan
Others: Babas

14 _Sweet sauces_

Custard

Yield ½ pt (3 dl) = 4–8 covers

½ pt (3 dl) milk
½ oz (15 g) custard powder
1 oz (30 g) sugar
Vanilla essence

1 Mix the custard powder with a little milk in a basin.
2 Boil the remainder of the milk in a saucepan.
3 Pour onto the custard powder continuously whisking.
4 Return to the saucepan and bring to the boil stirring continuously. Flavour with vanilla.
5 Lastly add the sugar.

Almond

½ pt (3 dl) milk
½ oz (15 g) cornflour
1 oz (30 g) sugar
½ oz (15 g) ground almonds or almond essence

1 Mix the cornflour with a little milk.
2 Boil the remainder of the milk in a saucepan.
3 Pour on to the cornflour continuously whisking.
4 Return to the saucepan and bring to the boil. If almonds are used, add at this stage.
5 Boil for a few minutes.
6 Lastly add the sugar.
7 If a very smooth sauce is required pass it through a sieve.

Cold custard cream

3 egg yolks
2 oz (60 g) castor sugar
¼ pt (1.5 dl) milk
¼ pt (1.5 dl) cream
Vanilla essence

1 Whisk the egg yolks with the sugar.
2 Boil the milk and strain.
3 Whisk on to the yolks and sugar.
4 Stir over gentle heat until it is thick enough to coat the back of a spoon (_do not boil_). Add vanilla essence.
5 Cool and fold in half whipped cream.

Chocolate – chocolat

Recipe 1

Mix 2 oz (60 g) cocoa powder into a thin paste with water and add to the cold custard cream.

Recipe 2

Melt 4 oz (120 g) couverture and add to the custard while still warm and before the cream is folded in.

Recipe 3

Make a ganache with chocolate couverture and cream but add more cream until the desired consistency is reached (see page 239).

Recipe 4

Make an icing from chocolate and syrup recipe but thin it down to the desired consistency with cream (see page 239). If too sweet, adjust by replacing some or all of the couverture with unsweetened chocolate.

Recipe 5

½ pt (3 dl) milk
1½ oz (45 g) sugar
¼ oz (7.5 g) butter (see page 48)
½ oz (15 g) cornflour
1 oz (30 g) unsweetened chocolate or ½ oz (15 g) cocoa

1 Mix the cornflour with a little milk. If cocoa is used also add it here.
2 Boil the rest of the milk and strain.
3 Stir into the cornflour.
4 Return to the saucepan and bring to the boil.
5 Mix in the sugar and butter. If chocolate is used, shred and add it at this stage.

Coffee

Recipe 1

Mix 1 oz (30 g) soluble coffee powder to the cold custard cream.

Recipe 2

Replace the chocolate in Chocolate sauce recipe 5 with 1 oz (30 g) soluble coffee powder.

**Fresh egg custard –
Crème anglaise**

*½ pt (3 dl) milk
2 egg yolks
1 oz (30 g) castor sugar
Vanilla essence*

1 Whisk the sugar and yolks in a basin.
2 Boil the milk and stir it in.
3 Return to the saucepan and place on low heat.
4 Stir until it coats the back of a spoon (*do not boil*).
5 Pass mixture through a fine strainer and add the vanilla essence.

Jam

Recipe 1

*8 oz (240 g) jam
3–4 oz (90–120 g) water (according to consistency of jam)*

Boil the jam and water together and then strain. This mixture may
be thickened with a little cornflour if desired.

Recipe 2

*8 oz (240 g) fruit pulp
8 oz (240 g) sugar
2 oz (60 g) glucose
2 oz (60 g) water*

Bring to the boil and allow to simmer until correct consistency is
reached.

Apricot

Same as for jam sauce using either apricot jam or pulped apricots.
This sauce may be flavoured by the addition of kirsch, cognac, or
rum.

Lemon

Recipe 1

Add the zest and juice of 1 lemon to the cold custard cream recipe
(see page 185).

Recipe 2

*½ pt (3 dl) water
2 oz (60 g) sugar
½ oz (15 g) cornflour
1 lemon (zest and juice)*

1 Dilute the cornflour with a little water.
2 Boil the rest of the water with the sugar.
3 Add the diluted cornflour and stir continuously whilst it boils.
4 Strain and add the zest and juice of the lemon.

Mousseline

5 oz (150 g) sugar
4 oz (120 g) water
6 egg yolks
1 pt (6 dl) cream
Vanilla essence

1 Boil the sugar and water, skim, and strain.
2 Pour over the egg yolks.
3 Transfer to a bain-marie and, continually stirring, gently heat until mixture becomes like thick cream (scrape sides constantly). Add vanilla essence.
4 Remove from heat and vigorously whisk until cold.
5 Partly whip the cream and blend in.

Liqueur mousseline

Add liqueur to taste. The mousseline sauce may now take the name of the added liqueur, for example Sauce mousseline au Kirsch, etc.

Wine mousseline

Use ¼ pt (1.5 dl) wine instead of water. For very dry wines like Burgundy an extra 1 oz (30 g) of sugar should be added.

Fruit mousseline

Add 4 oz (120 g) of the designated fruit pulp, for example raspberry, strawberry, etc. A little lemon juice should also be used.

Lemon mousseline

Add ¼ pt (1.5 dl) lemon juice instead of water and the zest of one lemon. Increase the sugar to 8 oz (240 g).

Orange mousseline

Add ¼ pt (1.5 dl) orange juice instead of water and the zest of one orange.

Praline mousseline

Add 4 oz (120 g) praline paste.

Sabayon

6 oz (180 g) castor sugar
6 egg yolks
½ pt (3 dl) white wine
½ lemon (juice only)

1 Mix the ingredients together.
2 Whisk in a bain-marie over gentle heat until a thick creamy consistency is reached (*do not boil*).

Note: The sabayon may be named after the type of wine used, for example Sabayon Marsala.

Liqueur sabayon

Increase egg yolks to 8 and add 2 oz (60 g) of the desired liqueur.

Lemon sabayon

Increase egg yolks to 8 and add ¼ pt (1.5 dl) of lemon juice (instead of juice of ½ lemon) and the grated zest of one lemon.

Orange sabayon

Same as Lemon sabayon substituting oranges.

15 *Bavarois and jelly sweets*

Charlotte Russe
(Figure 58)

Yield 1 for 8 covers

Half bavarois recipe (see page 194)
24 (approx.) sponge fingers (see page 85)

1 Line a charlotte mould with sponge fingers, trimming them where necessary to make a flower-like design on the base, and a number set vertically for the sides, with the sugar-coated side of the finger against the metal.
2 Make a bavarois and fill to the level of the mould.
3 Set aside in a cool place to set.
4 Trim the edge and turn the mould out into a silver flat dish from which it is served.

Figure 58 *Charlotte russe. Pouring the bavarois mixing into a charlotte mould lined with small swiss rolls for charlotte royal. A finished charlotte russe and royal are shown in the foreground*

Charlotte Royal
(Figure 58)

Yield 1 for 8 covers

Half bavarois recipe (see page 194)
6 small Swiss rolls (see page 84)

1 Line a charlotte mould with small Swiss rolls cut into thin slices
   ⅜ in (1 cm) thick. Arrange the slices neatly so that the complete
   tin is lined.
2 Make a bavarois and fill to the level of the mould.
3 Set aside in a cool place to set.
4 Trim the edge and turn out on to a silver flat dish from which it is
   served.

Note: An alternative method, giving the charlotte a glazed finish, is
often favoured by practising patissiers.
   The mould is first lined with jelly on which the Swiss rolls are
set. These rolls may be dipped into jelly and applied to the sides of
the mould for speedy commercial finishes. To remove the charlotte
the mould would need to be momentarily placed into hot water
and then it may be turned out on to pre-set jelly on a silver dish.

Charlotte de fraises à la Royale

Same as Charlotte royal except that the bavarois has the addition of
strawberries and the charlotte is served with fresh strawberries and
whipped fresh cream.

Charlotte de fraises à la mode

Same as Charlotte Russe, except that a liqueur jelly is used to line
the bottom of the mould. Strawberries and whipped fresh cream
are also served.

Charlotte Andalouse

Same as Charlotte Russe, except that an orange bavarois is used
and served with glazed oranges and whipped fresh cream.

Charlotte Muscovite

Same as Charlotte de fraises à la mode, except that a vanilla
bavarois and a raspberry jelly are used to line the bottom of the
mould.

Other varieties

Other Charlottes may be made by using other fruits and jellies for
the top instead of sponge fingers.

Lemon jelly – Gelée citron

Yield 8 covers

1 qt (12 dl) water
4 oz (120 g) sugar
2 oz (60 g) gelatine
2 oz (60 g) egg whites
Zest and juice of 2 lemons

1 Place all the ingredients in a saucepan and bring to the boil.
2 Once it starts to boil, remove and allow to rest for ½ hour in a hot
   place, keeping it well covered.

3 Strain through a fine cloth or filter.
4 Fill into moulds.
5 When jelly has set turn out of mould by first placing it momentarily in hot water.

Note: Any fruit jelly may be prepared in the same way as lemon jelly, replacing the lemon with the fruit required. This may be an extract with the addition of colouring matter.

Liqueur jelly – Gelée liqueurs

Add to the jelly the required liqueur and colour appropriately.

Russian jelly – Gelée Moscovite

Beat cold jelly to a white froth and immediately fill the mould.

Ribboned jelly – Gelée rubanée

Lemon jelly
Orange jelly
Russian jelly

1 Prepare each of the above jellies.
2 One-third fill the mould with Russian jelly.
3 When this has set fill to two-thirds with the orange jelly and allow to set.
4 Lastly add the lemon jelly.
5 When cold and set it is ready to serve.

Bavarois

Yield sufficient to fill one 1-quart charlotte mould (8 covers) or two 1-quart Charlotte Russe, etc.

8 oz (240 g) milk
2 oz (60 g) egg yolks
½ oz (15 g) gelatine sheets (approx. 3)
1¾ oz (50 g) sugar
8 oz (240 g) cream

1 Cream the egg yolks with the sugar.
2 Boil the milk and whisk into the egg and sugar cream.
3 Replace on low heat and stir till it thickens (*do not boil*).
4 Remove from the heat and stir in the gelatine which has been previously soaked in cold water. Continue to stir until the gelatine has dissolved.
5 Strain and cool the mixture until it reaches the consistency of half whipped cream (almost setting).
6 Half whip the cream and fold it into the custard until clear.
7 Fill the mould, which may be slightly greased, and then chill.
9 Remove from mould by shaking and serve on a flat silver dish. The bavarois may be served with cream Chantilly.

Vanilla bavarois – Bavarois vanillé

To the basic recipe add either vanilla essence or extract or immerse a vanilla pod in the boiling custard. Decorate with vanilla flavoured cream.

Chocolate bavarois – Bavarois au chocolat

Add 2 oz (60 g) melted chocolate to the basic recipe, blending it into the custard. Use chocolate pieces or vermicelli in the decoration.

Coffee bavarois – Bavarois au café

Essence, extract, or instant coffee is added to the basic recipe to taste.

Orange bavarois – Bavarois à l'orange

To the basic recipe add orange flavour and colour. Decorate with orange zest, orange segments, and cream Chantilly.

Strawberry bavarois – Bavarois aux fraises and Raspberry bavarois – Bavarois aux framboises

To the basic recipe add 8 oz (240 g) washed, picked, and sieved fruit (purèe). Reduce milk content to 6 oz (180 g).

The fruit purée should be added when the custard is nearly cool and before the cream is blended in. Decorate, using whole fruit and cream Chantilly.

Individual bavarois or wine cream sweets
(Figure 59)

Bavarois recipe page 194. Wine cream recipe page 288.

Rings approximately 2 in (5 cm) diameter and 1 in (2.5 cm) in height are required for these sweets.

1 Make a sheet of Swiss roll and when cold cut out circles to make a tight fit insde the ring (to prevent seepage of mixing).
2 Place the ring with its base of sponge in a refrigerator or deep freeze to thoroughly chill.
3 Make an appropriate bavarois or wine cream, fill the rings to the brim and replace in the refrigerator.
4 When set remove from the ring by running a thin bladed knife round between the filling and the ring or by gently warming the sides with the blow torch or alternative applied heat.
5 The sweet may now be decorated with an appropriate fruit as shown in Figure 59.

Junket

Yield 8 covers

2 pt (12 dl) milk
1 oz (30 g) sugar
2 teaspoonsful rennet
Grated nutmeg
Colour and flavour

1 Warm the milk with the sugar to blood heat.
2 Add any desired flavour and colour.
3 Add the rennet and stir gently.
4 Pour into individual dishes or serving dish.
5 Leave in a warm room to set.
6 Sprinkle with grated nutmeg.
7 Serve on a doily on flat silver dish.

These may be decorated with a whirl of whipped, fresh cream if desired.

Figure 59   *Individual bavarois sweets. Description in text.*

16 *Fruit and other sweets*

Fruit sherry trifle

Yield 8 covers

Half of basic recipe for sponge or Swiss roll (see pages 82 and 83)
12 oz (360 g) tinned fruit (or one E1 tin)
1 oz (30 g) jam
1 oz (30 g) cooking sherry
1 pt (6 dl) custard (see page 185)
½ pt (3 dl) sweetened fresh cream

1 If a plain sponge has been used, sandwich with jam.
2 Cut into 1-in (2.5 cm) cubes and place half of these in the bottom of a glass bowl.
3 Soak this sponge with the fruit juice to which the sherry has been added. It is best to add the sherry to about half the juice from the tin of fruit, initially. If more soaking is necessary, the rest of the juice may be used. If fresh fruit is used, for example strawberries, use a flavoured syrup for soaking purposes.
4 Dice the fruit and lay half the quantity prescribed on the sponge layer.
5 Repeat operations 2, 3 and 4.
6 Make the custard and pour onto the layers of sponge and fruit.
7 When the custard is cold, whip the sweetened cream and cover the custard.
8 Put the remaining cream into a savoy bag with a star tube and decorate the top.
9 Finish the decoration with cherries, angelica, or chocolate pieces.

Fresh fruit salad

Before fresh fruit salad is prepared, make sure that the equipment used (knives, chopping board, etc.) is absolutely free from any odours left by vegetables (see page 4).

Any fresh fruit may be used in a fruit salad but usually a selection from the following list is made: oranges, bananas, dessert pears, dessert apples, melon, grapes, peaches, apricots, pineapple, cherries, strawberries, and raspberries.

Approximately ¼ lb (120 g) of unprepared fruit should be allowed per portion.

Basic quantities for 8 covers

2 bananas
2 oranges
2 dessert pears

2 dessert apples
4 oz (120 g) fruit liqueur or sherry (optional) or
4 oz (120 g) water or fruit juice
4 oz (120 g) cherries
4 oz (120 g) grapes
Juice of 1 lemon (omit if liqueur is used)
4 oz (120 g) sugar

1 Boil the water with the sugar and add the lemon juice. Place aside to cool preferably in the refrigerator.
2 Prepare the fruit by removing peel, stones, pips, core, etc., and cut up into either slices (Salade des fruits) or dices (Macédoine des fruits). Start preparing the hard fruits such as apples first so that they have a chance to soften in the syrup. Prepare bananas last so that the risk of browning is kept to the minimum.
3 Carefully mix the fruit with the syrup.
4 Chill in the refrigerator.
5 Place mixture in a bowl on a flat silver dish with a doily to serve.

Alternative method

1 As operation (2) above.
2 Place the fruit in layers in the bowl and sprinkle each layer with sugar and liqueur.
3 As operations 4 and 5 above.

Note: If liqueur or sherry is used, it is best to use the alternative method. In this case the lemon juice should be omitted as its use would mask the flavour of the liqueur or sherry used.

Fruit condé

A condé consists of poached or tinned fruit placed on a bed of a rice pudding mixture and glazed. Many different types of fruits could be used but the most popular are pears, bananas, pineapple, peaches, and apricots. The following recipe is for pears.

Pear condé – Poire condé

Yield 8 covers

2 pt (12 dl) milk into rice condé (see page 213)
4 dessert pears
8 oz (240 g) apricot glaze
Cherries (for decoration)
Angelica (for decoration)

1 Make a rice condé mixture.
2 Allow the rice to cool and place neatly in a bowl or silver flat dish or in individual coupes. The rice may be moulded and shaped if desired.
3 If fresh pears are used, peel, core, halve, and poach, and then leave to cool before using.

4 Drain the pears of juice and carefully arrange them on top of the rice.
5 Coat with apricot glaze.
6 Decorate with cherries and angelica.

**Poached fruits –
Compote de fruits**

Preparation of fruit

Apples and pears

Peel, remove core, and cut into quarters or halves.

Stoned fruits, gooseberries, black currants, and red currants

Wash the fruit and remove stalks and blemishes. Add extra sugar if necessary.

Rhubarb

Cut off the stalk and leaf and wash. Cut into 1½-in (4-cm) lengths. Add extra sugar if necessary.

Dried fruits

These should be washed and allowed to soak in cold water overnight. Cook the fruit gently in its own liquor adding sufficient sugar to taste. Some lemon juice may be added for additional flavour.

Soft fruits (strawberries, loganberries, raspberries)

1 Pick and wash the fruit.
2 Transfer to a glass bowl.
3 Pour over a hot syrup.
4 Cool and serve as previously described.

Note: Compotes may be served with various sauces, for example custard, mousseline, or ice-cream. They may also be flavoured with liqueurs, etc.

Compote de fruits

Yield 8 covers

2 lb (960 g) fruit
1 pt (6 dl) stock syrup (see following page)
Added sugar to taste
Lemon juice

1 Place the fruit in a shallow dish with the syrup. The size of the dish should be such that the syrup just covers the fruit.

2 Add a few drops of lemon juice.
3 Cover with a sheet of greaseproof paper.
4 Place in a cool oven to simmer slowly until fruit is soft.
5 Transfer fruit and juice into a glass bowl and serve on a doily on flat silver dish.

Note: The amount of sugar used in the stock syrup will depend upon the sweetness of the fruit used but for dessert fruit this will rarely need to exceed 50 per cent.

Fruit fool

Yield 8 covers

A   Apple, plum, rhubarb, gooseberry, banana, etc.

Purée
2 lb (960 g) fruit
8 oz (240 g) sugar
¼ pt (1.5 dl) water

1 pt (6 dl) milk
2 oz (60 g) sugar
2 oz (60 g) cornflour

1 Cook the fruit, water, and sugar to a pulp and pass it through a sieve to form a purée.
2 Add a little milk to the cornflour and sugar.
3 Boil the remainder of the milk.
4 Pour boiling milk on to diluted cornflour and stir well.
5 Return mixture to the saucepan and, on a low heat, stir until it boils.
6 Mix this with the fruit purée.
7 Pour mixture into eight coupés and allow to set.
8 Using sweetened fresh cream, decorate with a rosette and serve.

B   Strawberries, loganberries, raspberries and bananas

2 lb (960 g) fruit
8 oz (240 g) sugar
1 pt (6 dl) whipped fresh cream

1 Wash the fruit and pass it through a sieve to make a purée.
2 Add the sugar and the whipped cream.
3 Transfer to eight coupés and serve.

Baked apple – Pomme bonne femme

Yield 8 covers

8 medium-sized apples
4 oz (120 g) sugar
2 oz (60 g) butter
8 cloves
¼ pt (1.5 dl) water

1 Wash and core the apples and make an incision about ¹⁄₁₆ in (1.5 mm) round the apple about one-third of the way down.
2 Place apples in a roasting tin.

3 Fill the core hole with sugar, add a clove and a knob of butter.
4 Add the water.
5 Bake in an oven at approximately 350°F (177°C) until soft. Time of baking will depend upon the size of apple but it should take about 30–40 minutes. The apples may first be placed into the oven upside down without the sugar. After 20 minutes cooking they may be turned over, the sugar added, and baking completed.
6 Serve on a hot, flat silver dish with a little of the syrup and an appropriate sauce served separately. The sauce may be custard, honey, or cream.

Stuffed baked apple

As for baked apple except that the centre is filled with washed sultanas.

Apple meringues

These are baked apples which have been covered with Italian meringue, flashed off in a hot oven, and served on either a bed of rice, a sheet of genoese, or puff pastry.

1 Bake the apples as described above.
2 Meanwhile prepare a suitable base.
3 Once cooked, transfer the apples to the prepared base on a flat silver dish.
4 Cover the apples with Italian meringue with the aid of a savoy tube fitted with a star tube.
5 Return to a very hot oven to colour.
6 Serve with an appropriate sauce.

Apple charlotte – Charlotte aux pommes

Yield 8 covers

2 lb (960 g) stale bread
2 lb (960 g) apples (preferably dessert)
6 oz (180 g) sugar
8 oz (240 g) butter or margarine
Grated rind of lemon or a clove

1 Recipe will fill either two small charlottes or eight dariole moulds.
2 Peel, core, and wash the apples. Cut into fairly thick slices and place in the pan with about 1 oz (30 g) butter, the sugar, and the lemon rind or clove.
3 Do not add any water. Simmer apples gently until barely cooked.
4 Cut the bread into slices approximately ¼ in (6 mm) thick and remove the crusts.
5 Cut out circles of bread, one to fit the top and one to fit the bottom of the moulds.
6 Melt the butter or margarine and dip one side of the rounds which have been cut for the base. Place these rounds fat-side down in the moulds.

7 Cut the remaining bread slices into fingers 1–1½ in (2.5–3.5 cm) wide. Dip each in the melted fat and place them vertically around the inside of the mould, so that they overlap without leaving any gaps.

8 Fill the centre of the mould with the cooked apple, after removing any lemon rind or cloves which have been added.

9 Cover with the round of bread cut for the top.

10 Bake in an oven at approximately 450°F (232°C) for 35–45 minutes, until the bread lining is brown and crisp.

11 Allow to cool slightly before turning out.

12 Carefully turn out onto a hot, flat silver dish and serve with a sauceboat of apricot sauce.

Notes:

1 Dessert apples will produce a more stable purée than that obtained from cooking apples. If the apples used make a thin purée when cooked, it may be stiffened by adding bread-crumbs.

2 The base may be cut into the required portions before being placed in the mould.

3 One common fault with this sweet is that it readily collapses. The main cause of this is that the bread case is not firm enough to withstand the pressure exerted upon it by the apple filling. To overcome this fault observe the following:

(a) Use small moulds, that is, two small charlotte moulds rather than one large.

(b) Bake the bread very crisp.

(c) Do not overcook the apple filling and keep it as stiff as possible by not adding water and if necessary adding some breadcrumbs. Also use dessert apples.

Flambé fruits

Only hard fruits such as pears, apricots, peaches, pineapple, bananas, etc., can be used for this process. Tinned fruit may be used. Fresh fruits such as pears need to be poached in syrup first to soften them.

Peaches or pears flambé – Pêches/poires flambées

Yield 8 covers

8 half peaches or pears
3 oz (90 g) stock syrup (50 per cent sugar)
2 oz (60 g) liqueur or spirit (Kirsch, Benedictine, rum, etc.)
Icing sugar
8 oz (240 g) apricot or strawberry purée (for sauce added to liquor)
(optional)

1 In the dining room place a copper pan on a flambé réchaud. Pour in the syrup and allow to boil.

2 Heat the fruit in this syrup for a few minutes.

3 Sprinkle on a little icing sugar.

4 Warm the liqueur, pour over, and ignite.
5 Serve immediately with the liquor.

Bananas flambé –
Bananes flambées

Yield 8 covers

8 bananas
1 orange (juice only)
2 oz (60 g) butter
3 oz (90 g) sugar
3 oz (90 g) rum
8 oz (240 g) apricot purée
1½ oz (45 g) nibbed roast almonds (for decoration)

1 Split the bananas lengthwise on a serviette.
2 Put the orange juice, butter, and purée in the pan and bring to
  the boil.
3 Proceed the same as for Peaches flambé.

This sweet may take the name of the liqueur used; thus with
Pêches flambées à la Benedictine, Benedictine has been used.

Fruit sweets with ice-cream

A very wide variety of fruit sweets may be made in combination
with ice-cream, sometimes using a tampion of sponge (thin base,
round or shaped) and covering with an appropriate sauce, for
example, Melba, mousseline, Chantilly cream, etc.

The basic method of preparation is as follows:

1 Place a slice of ice-cream on the plate.
2 Cover with the fruit (which could be flambé).
3 Mask with a suitable sauce.
4 Decorate using glacé fruit, violets, nuts with or without
  Chantilly cream.

Variations to the method described above are described on page
206.

These sweets may either be individually prepared on plates, etc.
or more usually several portions, for example eight, are assembled
in a large dish or timbale and suitably decorated.

Yields

Fruit
Allow ½ pear, peach, etc., 4 oz (120 g) raspberries, strawberries,
etc., per portion.

Ice-cream
Allow 1½ pt (9 dl) for eight portions.

Sauce
Allow ¾ pt (4.5 dl) for eight portions.

Names of sweets

A summary of the names of some of these sweets is given here. The name of the fruit follows the name of the sweet. For example, if peaches are served under the name Hélène, the sweet becomes known as Pêches Hélène.

Name	Ice-cream	Sauce	Decoration
Adeline	Chocolate	Mousseline	Whipped cream, langues du chat, and violets
Aïda	Strawberry	—	Whipped cream and crystallized violets
Alma	Vanilla	Port mousseline	Grated chocolate
Almina	Coffee	Noyeau flavoured apricot	Chantilly mixed with praline paste
Alphonse	Pistachio	Moussline	Whipped cream and strawberries
Arlésienne	Vanilla	Kirsch flavoured apricot	Whipped cream, cherries, angelica
Balmoral	Hazelnut	Chocolate	Chantilly
Beatrice	Hazelnut	Melba	Shredded walnuts
Beauregard	Pistachio	Maraschino flavoured apricot	Whipped cream and violets
Bohémienne	Chocolate	—	Chantilly cream and pistachio nuts
Calvé	Strawberry	Kirsch mousseline	Crystallized roses
Demi deuil	Vanilla	Chocolate and Chantilly	Whipped cream
Donna sol	Vanilla	Orange mousseline	Crystallized violets
Edna	Chocolate	Apricot	Whipped cream and pistachio nuts
Ethel	Vanilla	Pistachio mousseline	Red currant jelly and crystallized violets
Fémina	Orange	Grand Marnier liqueur	—
Frascati	Almond	Strawberry	Shredded walnuts. Serve cream separately
Frou-frou	Pistachio	Apricot	Whipped cream and almond finger biscuits
Grand-maison	Vanilla	Raspberry mousseline	Glacé pineapple, grated chocolate, and praline nuts
Hélène	Vanilla	Hot chocolate sauce served separately	Whipped cream
Herman	Raspberry	Kirsch flavoured Chantilly	Red currant jelly and crystallized violets

Name	Ice-cream	Sauce	Decoration
Hilda	Raspberry	Kirsch mousseline	Strawberries
Hortancier	Vanilla	Apricot	Whipped cream and strawberries
Ilka	Apricot	Chantilly	Chocolate shavings and pistachio nuts
Madeleine	Orange	Curaçao mousseline	Orange quarters
Margaret	Lemon	Raspberry mousseline	Whipped cream and strawberries
Marquise	Apricot	Chantilly	Chocolate shavings
Mauresque	Chocolate	Chocolate	Petit chou
Melba	Vanilla	Melba	Whipped cream
Mezerdoff	Vanilla	Raspberry	Whipped cream
Mireille	Raspberry	Melba	Whipped cream and cherries
Montpensier	Coffee	Raspberry	Whipped cream and crystallized roses
Niçoise	Orange	Curaçao mousseline	Strawberries and orange quarters
Niniche	Praline	Maraschino Chantilly	Whipped cream and petit chou
Ninon	Raspberry	Chantilly	Crystallized violets
Orientale	Vanilla	Melba	Whipped cream and spun sugar
Orléans	Vanilla	Red currant	Kirsch Chantilly and broken marron glacé
Parisienne	Praline	Strawberry mousseline	Whipped cream and crystallized violets
Petit duc	Lemon	Red currant	Whipped cream
Pompadour	Vanilla	Pistachio mousseline	Whipped cream and violets
Princesse Louise	Pineapple	Apricot	Whipped cream and roasted nib almonds
Princess Olga	Apricot	Kummel mousseline	Whipped cream and crystallized violets
Printanière	Vanilla	Pistachio mousseline	Whipped cream, strawberries, and crystallized violets
Régence	Apricot	Kirsch flavoured Chantilly	Whipped cream and grated chocolate
Sarah Bernhardt	Pineapple	Curaçao mousseline	Whipped cream and crystallized violets
Savoy	Coffee praline	Anisette mousseline	Crystallized violets
Stanley	Vanilla	Chantilly	Whipped cream and grated chocolate
Sultane	Pistachio	Maraschino apricot	Glacé pineapple
Tetrazzini	Pineapple	Kirsch flavoured apricot mousseline	Whipped cream flavoured praline
Toscane	Coffee praline	Chantilly	Meringue mushroom and chocolate shavings

Other varieties

Chantecler

Place fruit on a piece of sponge sprinkled with Kirsch. Cover with Kirsch-flavoured apricot sauce and then portions of vanilla ice-cream. Decorate with whipped cream and crystallized violets.

Diplomate

Place fruit on a piece of sponge. Cover with brandy mousseline. Add portions of vanilla ice-cream. Decorate with orange quarters and violets.

Rivièra

Place fruit in a dish or timbale and cover with Melba sauce. Add portions of vanilla ice-cream. Decorate with crystallized violets.

Tyrolienne

Place vanilla ice-cream on chocolate sponge. Place fruit and cover with vanilla mousseline. Decorate with whipped cream glacé.

Use of peel

The peel or outside shell of some fruits may be used with advantage in the preparation of some sweets. These fruits are: lemons, oranges, grapefruit, melon, and pineapple.

**Grapefruit Florida –
Pamplemousse Florida**

Yield 8 covers

4 large grapefruit
3 oranges
6 oz (180 g) stoned cherries
6 oz (180 g) small strawberries or diced pineapple
3 oz (90 g) cooking sherry
4 oz (120 g) sugar
Glacé cherries (for decoration)

1 Cut the grapefruit into two, horizontally.
2 Cut out the segments, remove the skin, and mix with the skinned orange segments and other fruit.
3 Macerate the mixed fruit in sugar and sherry and chill.
4 Fill the grapefruit shells.
5 Decorate with a glacé cherry.
6 Serve very cold.

This is served as an hors d'oeuvre.

Frosted lemons

Yield 8 covers

8 lemons
1½ pt (9 dl) lemon ice (see page 296)
Angelica (for decoration)

1 Cut the lemon lengthwise about one-third of the way down.
2 Carefully remove the pulp and clean out the lemon shells.
3 Use part of the lemon pulp to make lemon ice.
4 Fill the larger shells with the ice and place the other shells on top.
5 Sprinkle with water and allow to freeze so that a frost appears.
6 Decorate with a piece of angelica and serve immediately.

Frosted oranges

Same as above, substituting oranges for lemons.

Orange or Tangerine surprise

Yield 8 covers

8 large oranges
1 pt (6 dl) orange ice (see page 296)
8 oz (240 g) Italian meringue (see page 92)

1 Cut off the top of the orange about one-quarter of the way down to form a top.
2 Carefully remove all the pulp and clean the inside of the shell.
3 Use part of the orange pulp to make the orange ice.
4 Place the larger shells on crushed ice and fill with the orange ice.
5 Mask with Italian meringue and flash off in a hot oven at 480°F (250°C) to colour.
6 Dress on a napkin and serve immediately.

Other varieties may be made with different flavoured ice-creams with diced orange segments and masked with Chantilly cream.

Melon Majestic

Yield 8 covers

1 ripe cantaloup melon
1¼ lb (600 g) small strawberries
¼ pt (1.5 dl) Chantilly cream
2 oz (60 g) Kirsch liqueur
Chocolate curls or rolls (for decoration)

1 Cut the melon a quarter of the way from the top.
2 Remove the centre seeds and liquid.
3 Carefully scoop out the flesh without damaging the shell.
4 Make the flesh into water ice (page 296, but substituting melon).
5 Macerate the strawberries in a little sugar and the Kirsch liqueur and chill.
6 Place the larger shell of the melon in a dish of crushed ice.
7 Fill with the melon ice.
8 Arrange the strawberries on top.
9 Decorate with Chantilly cream and chocolate rolls. Lightly dust with icing sugar.

Pineapple à la Ninon – Ananas à la Ninon

Yield 8 covers

1 large pineapple
1 lb 2 oz (540 g) wild strawberries
4 bananas
½ pt (3 dl) whipped cream

¾ pt (4.5 dl) raspberry sauce (Melba, see page 189)
8 boats made from sweet pastry (see page 53)

1 Cut off the top of the pineapple.
2 With a knife, cut out the flesh of the pineapple without damaging the shell and keeping the flesh in a whole piece.
3 Cut the flesh into thin slices and remove the centre core with an apple corer.
4 Macerate the pineapple slices in sugar and Kirsch and likewise the strawberries and sliced banana. Chill well.
5 Place the pineapple shell on a round dish and half fill with the strawberries and sliced banana.
6 Place the pineapple slices on top, each overlapping.
7 Fill up with whipped cream using a savoy bag with a star tube.
8 Replace the top containing the green leaves.
9 Fill the pastry boats with whipped cream, small pieces of pineapple, and strawberries, and arrange them around the filled pineapple shell.
10 Serve raspberry sauce separately.

Rice empress style – Riz à l'Impératrice

Yield 2 × 8 covers

2 pt (12 dl) milk into rice condé mixing (see page 213)
Vanilla bavarois mixing (see page 194)
4 oz (120 g) diced glacé fruits (cherries, angelica, pineapple, etc.)
½ pt (3 dl) red jelly (see page 193)
2 oz (60 g) Kirsch liqueur (optional)

1 Make the rice condé mixing.
2 Prepare the red jelly and pour into the bottom of dariole or charlotte moulds to about ¼ in (0.5 cm) in thickness.
3 Make the bavarois mixing.
4 Mix the condé and bavarois together before they have set.
5 Mix in the crystallized fruits. If used the fruit should first be macerated in the liqueur.
6 Fill the prepared moulds after the jelly has set.
7 Allow to set in a refrigerator.
8 Serve on a flat silver dish.

Variations

Tangerine rice – Riz à la Mandarine

Instead of the crystallized fruits, add the zest of six tangerines. After the mould has been turned out decorate with tangerine segments macerated in Curaçao liqueur.

Singapore rice – Riz Singapour

Instead of crystallized fruits, mix in 8 oz (240 g) diced pineapple macerated in Maraschino. Serve with cold apricot sauce, flavoured with the Maraschino in which the pineapple was macerated.

Rice Trauttmansdorf – Riz Trauttmansdorf

Instead of crystallized fruits, mix in 4 oz (120 g) diced fresh fruit in season and the maraschino liqueur in which the fruit should be macerated. Serve with ½ pt (3 dl) purée of fresh raspberries or strawberries.

Pancakes – Crêpes

Basic batter

Yield 8 covers

8 oz (240 g) flour
3 oz (90 g) eggs
1 oz (30 g) butter
A pinch of salt
1 pt (6 dl) milk
4 oz (120 g) lard

1 Whisk the egg, salt, and milk together.
2 Add the sieved flour a little at a time, whisking each portion into the liquid to make a smooth batter.
3 Mix in the melted butter.
4 Place a small quantity of lard in a clean small frying pan and heat to smoking point.
5 Pour in sufficient batter to just cover the base of the pan very thinly.
6 Cook until it is a light golden brown.
7 Turn the pancake over and cook this side to the same colour.
8 The pancake is now ready for serving in any of the following varieties.

Lemon pancakes – Crêpes au citron

Basic pancake batter
3–4 oz (90–120 g) castor sugar
2 lemons

1 Prepare pancakes.
2 Turn the pancakes on to a plate.
3 Sprinkle with sugar.
4 Fold into four.
5 Serve hot with quarters of lemon, free of pips, two per person.

If several are to be served, dress the folded pancakes neatly overlapping on a flat silver dish. Instead of fresh lemons, lemon juice could be substituted.

Jam pancakes – Crêpes à la confiture

Basic pancake batter
2 oz (60 g) castor sugar
4 oz (120 g) jam

1 Prepare pancakes.
2 Spread a spoonful of jam on each.
3 Roll up the pancakes.
4 Sprinkle with sugar and serve.

**Apple pancakes –
Crêpes Normande**

Basic pancake batter
4 apples
4 oz (120 g) castor sugar

Method 1

1 Prepare pancakes.
2 Spread on a purée made from the apples.
3 Roll up the pancakes.
4 Sprinkle with sugar and serve.

Method 2

1 Dice some cooked apple and sprinkle it into the greased pan.
2 Pour on the pancake mixture on top and cook both sides in the usual way.
3 Turn out onto a plate and sprinkle with sugar.
4 Roll up and serve.

**Orange pancakes –
Crêpes à l'orange**

As for lemon pancakes but using oranges instead.

Crêpes Suzette

These pancakes are finished at the table in the dining room by the head waiter. The patissier prepares the pancakes *very* thinly and places the number required on top of each other on a silver dish. The head waiter prepares the dish in front of the customer on a spirit stove.

16 small pancakes (2 each person)
2 oz (60 g) butter
2 oz (60 g) sugar
Zest and juice of 1 orange
1 oz (30 g) Grand Marnier
1 oz (30 g) Cognac

1 Obtain the zest and juice of the orange.
2 Add the sugar and liqueur and stir to dissolve.
3 Place the butter in the hot pan and when melted add the liquor.
4 Place the pancakes in the pan, one at a time, covering them with the sauce.
5 Fold the pancakes into four.
6 Pour over the brandy and light by holding the pan sideways over the flame.
7 Serve immediately with the sauce.

Note: It is only practicable to cook four pancakes at the same time so that, for eight persons having two pancakes each, the procedure would have to be repeated four times, using ¼ of the quantities quoted.

Crêpes soufflés

1 egg
1 oz (30 g) castor sugar
¼ oz (7.5 g) butter (see page 48)
½ oz (15 g) apricot jam
2 oz (60 g) whipped cream
2 oz (60 g) tinned or fresh fruit
½ oz (15 g) icing sugar

1 Separate the yolks from the whites.
2 Cream the sugar and yolks.
3 Whisk the whites to a stiff foam.
4 Carefully fold the whites into the yolk and sugar cream.
5 Heat the butter in an omelette pan.
6 Pour in the mixture.
7 Allow it to cook for about ¼ minute to set the base.
8 Transfer pan to a hot oven (approximately 450°F (232°C)) for about 3–5 minutes until golden brown.
9 Turn pancake out on to a clean cloth sprinkled with icing sugar.
10 When cold, spread half of the pancake with apricot jam.
11 Place on some fruit and whipped cream.
12 Fold the other half of the pancake over the fruit and cream.
13 Dust with icing sugar.
14 Serve cold.

Fritters – Beignets

Basic batter

Yield 8 covers

8 oz (240 g) flour
2 oz (60 g) olive or salad oil
½ pt (3 dl) water or milk
2 oz (60 g) egg white (stiffly beaten)
A pinch of salt

1 Sieve the flour and gradually add to the water or milk, whisking well to make a smooth batter.
2 Gradually beat in the oil and add the salt.
3 Allow to rest before using.
4 Just prior to use, add and carefully fold in the egg whites.

Apple fritters – Beignets de pommes

Basic fritter batter
1½ lb (720 g) cooking apples
½ pt (3 dl) apricot sauce (see page 187)
2 oz (60 g) flour
4 oz (120 g) icing sugar

1 Peel and core the apples.
2 Cut into ¼-in (6-mm) rings.
3 Dip into flour and shake off any surplus.
4 Dip them into the frying batter.
5 Lift out with the fingers or a long skewer and gently drop them into fairly hot fat.

6 Cook until both sides are a golden brown colour, approximately 6–8 minutes.
7 Drain well, dust liberally with icing sugar, and put under a salamander to glaze.
8 Serve on a doily on a hot flat dish.
9 Serve a sauce boat of hot apricot sauce, separately.

In place of apple, other fruits are also suitable for fritters and may be served in the same way.

Banana fritters –
Beignets de bananes

Basic fritter batter
8 bananas

Split in half lengthwise and cut in half across, each banana making four pieces.

Pineapple fritters –
Beignets d'ananas

Basic fritter batter
8 pineapple rings

If the rings are large they may be cut in two.

Apricot fritters –
Beignets d'abricot

Basic fritter batter
16 apricot halves

17 Puddings

Milk pudding

Rice pudding

Yield 8 covers

2 pt (12 dl) milk
3 oz (90 g) rice
1 oz (30 g) butter
4 oz (120 g) sugar
Vanilla
Grated nutmeg

Method 1

1 Wash the rice and place in a greased pie dish.
2 Add the sugar, milk, and flavouring and stir well.
3 Bake in an oven at a moderate heat 350°F (177°C) until the milk starts simmering. Stir.
4 Sprinkle on the nutmeg and add a few knobs of butter.
5 Reduce the heat to approximately 300°F (149°C) and cook for a total time of approximately 1½ to 2 hours.

Method 2

1 Boil the milk in a saucepan.
2 Wash the rice and sprinkle it into the milk.
3 Stir until the milk starts to boil, then simmer slowly, stirring frequently until the rice is cooked.
4 Stir in the sugar and flavouring, then transfer to a pie dish.
5 Place on a few knobs of butter and sprinkle on the grated nutmeg.
6 Either place in a hot oven until brown on top, or brown lightly under a salamander.
7 Serve on a doily on a silver dish.

Rice mould or condé

Yield 8 covers

2 pt (12 dl) milk
6 oz (180 g) rice (whole grain)
4 oz (120 g) sugar
4 egg yolks
1 oz (30 g) butter
Vanilla essence

1 Boil the milk, add the rice, and simmer gently until the rice is cooked.
2 Mix in the sugar, butter, flavouring, and egg yolks.
3 Pour into a damp mould or eight small dariole moulds.
4 Leave to become cold and set.
5 Turn out and serve with a jam sauce or with poached fruit.

Cornflour mould

Yield 8 covers

2 pt (12 dl) milk
3 oz (90 g) cornflour
4 oz (120 g) sugar
1 oz (30 g) butter
Vanilla essence

1 Blend the cornflour with a little of the milk in a basin.
2 Place the remainder of the milk in a saucepan and bring to the boil.
3 Add the boiling milk to the diluted cornflour stirring all the time.
4 Return it to the heat and allow to simmer for a few minutes, whisking all the time.
5 Mix in the butter and sugar.
6 Pour into a damp mould or eight dariole moulds.
7 Leave until it becomes cold.
8 Easing the mixture away from the sides of the mould, turn it out onto a flat silver dish.
9 Serve the mould surrounded with a cold jam sauce.

Variations

Chocolate

(a) Add 2 oz (60 g) cocoa powder (mix with the cornflour and form a thin paste with milk). Add extra 1 oz (30 g) sugar.
(b) Use 2 oz (60 g) melted chocolate.

Coffee

(a) Use 2 pt (12 dl) white coffee instead of milk.
(b) Add instant coffee to desired flavour.

Neapolitain blancmange

1 Divide the cornflour mixture into three equal parts.
2 Colour and flavour as follows:
    White   Vanilla
    Pink   Strawberry
    Green   Almond
3 Pour the pink mixing into a damp mould and leave for a few minutes to set. Keep the other mixings warm.

4 When the pink is set, pour on the white, and when this is set pour on the green.
5 Leave to cool in a refrigerator.
6 Easing the mixture away from the sides of the mould with the fingers, turn out into a flat silver dish.
7 Serve with a cold jam sauce, separately.

Semolina pudding

Yield 8 covers

2 pt (12 dl) milk
3 oz (90 g) semolina
4 oz (120 g) sugar
1 oz (30 g) butter
Lemon juice or essence

1 Heat the milk in a saucepan.
2 When nearly boiling, sprinkle in the semolina, stirring well.
3 Allow to simmer for 15–20 minutes, stirring continuously until the semolina is cooked.
4 Pour into a pie dish.
5 Either bake in a moderate oven until brown, or brown under a salamander.
6 Serve on a doily on a flat silver dish.

Semolina mould

To the pudding recipe *add* 4 egg yolks; *increase* semolina to 4 oz (120 g).

1 Proceed as for semolina pudding.
2 When mixture is made, pour into damp mould and proceed as for a cornflour mould.

Sago, tapioca, ground rice, puddings

These are made in the same way as semolina pudding using vanilla instead of lemon flavouring.

Baked egg custard

Yield 8 covers

2 pt (12 dl) milk
4 oz (120 g) sugar
9 oz (270 g) eggs
Vanilla
Grated nutmeg

1 Whisk the eggs, sugar, and vanilla flavour in a bowl.
2 Slightly warm the milk and whisk it into the eggs and sugar.
3 Pour the mixture through a sieve into a clean greased pie dish.
4 Sprinkle on a little grated nutmeg.
5 Wipe the edges of the pie dish and stand in a baking tin, half filled with water (bain-marie).
6 Cook slowly in an oven at 350°F (177°C) for approximately 45 minutes to 1 hour or until set.
7 Clean the edge of the dish and serve on a doily on flat silver dish.

Note: Never allow the water in the tin in which egg custard sweets are cooked to boil. This might curdle the custard.

Cream caramel custards – Crème caramel

Yield 8 covers

Custard

1½ pt (9 dl) milk
3 oz (90 g) sugar
9 oz (270 g) eggs
Vanilla

Caramel

6 oz (180 g) sugar
3½ oz (105 g) water

1 Make the caramel by mixing 3 oz (90 g) of the water with the sugar in a pan (preferably copper) and observing sugar boiling precautions (see page 264), heating it until it turns to an amber colour.
2 Add the remaining water (*beware of steam*) and re-boil until the sugar and water are thoroughly mixed.
3 Pour the caramel into eight dariole moulds and allow it to set.
4 Prepare the custard in the same way as baked custard.
5 Pass through a strainer into eight greased dariole moulds.
6 Place moulds in a baking tin half full of water.
7 Cook in a moderately hot oven at 380°F (193°C) until custard is set (approximately 30–40 minutes).
8 When thoroughly cold, gently loosen the edges of the cream caramels, shake to loosen, and turn out onto a flat silver dish.
9 Any caramel remaining in the moulds should be poured over the creams.

Bread and butter pudding

Yield 8 covers

2 pt (12 dl) milk into baked egg custard (see page 215)
6 thin slices buttered bread
2 oz (60 g) sultanas
1 oz (30 g) castor sugar

1 Remove the crusts from the buttered bread slices and cut into four triangles.
2 Arrange in the bottom of the pie dish with the slices neatly overlapping.
3 Sprinkle over the sultanas and cover with the rest of the bread slices.
4 Make an egg custard.
5 Pour half of the custard over the bread and allow to stand for half an hour so that the bread is prevented from floating to the surface.
6 Add the rest of the custard, dredge with castor sugar, and sprinkle on the nutmeg.
7 Bake and serve as baked egg custard.

**Cabinet pudding –
Pouding Cabinet**

Yield 8 covers

Cream caramel custard (see page 216)
6 oz (180 g) sponge cake or fingers (see page 82)
1½ oz (45 g) glacé cherries
¾ oz (25 g) sultanas
¾ oz (25 g) currants

1 Grease and sugar dariole or charlotte moulds. The base of these may be decorated with cherries and angelica if desired.
2 Dice the sponge into ¼-in (6-mm) cubes and mix with the chopped cherries, sultanas, and currants.
3 Fill the moulds half way with the mixed fruit and sponge.
4 Prepare the egg custard and pour the mixture to almost fill the moulds. Allow to stand for ½ hour.
5 Proceed as for Cream caramels. The time of cooking will depend upon the size of mould but should be 30–45 minutes. To test whether it is set, insert a knife. If it is cooked it should come out clean, without any trace of custard adhering.
6 When cooked, leave to stand for a few minutes and then turn out on to a flat silver dish.
7 Serve with an egg custard sauce or hot apricot sauce, separately.

Notes:
1 This pudding may also be steamed.
2 The diced fruit may be soaked in rum.
3 This pudding may also be served with a rum-flavoured sabayon sauce.

**Diplomat pudding –
Pouding Diplomate**

Proceed as for Cabinet pudding but serve cold. Fresh fruit may be used instead of dried fruit. Serve with jam or sabayon sauce.

Queen of puddings

Yield 8 covers

1½ pt (9 dl) milk
3 oz (90 g) butter
3 oz (90 g) castor sugar
6 oz (180 g) cake or breadcrumbs
1½ oz (45 g) jam
5 oz (150 g) eggs
3 oz (90 g) castor sugar (for meringue)
Grated rind of 1 lemon

1 Bring the milk and butter to the boil.
2 Mix the yolks of the eggs and sugar, pour on the hot milk and butter mixture and mix in.
3 Place the crumbs in a buttered pie dish.
4 Pass the custard through a strainer over the crumbs. Allow to soak for ½ hour.
5 Bake in an oven at 380°F (193°C) in a bain-marie for approximately 30 minutes until it is set.

6 Allow to cool.
7 Make an Italian meringue (see page 92) with the egg whites and sugar.
8 Spread warm jam over the top of the baked mixture.
9 Using a savoy bag and star tube, pipe on the meringue.
10 Place into a hot oven at 450°F (232°C) for the meringue to become tinged a brown colour (flashing).
11 Serve on a doily on a flat silver dish.

Apple frangipane pudding

Yield 8 covers

2 lb (960 g) cooking apples
1½ oz (90 g) water
1 lb (480 g) frangipane (use the recipe on page 62)
Sugar to taste

1 Slice the peeled and cored apples into a pan of salted water to prevent discolouration.
2 Wash in fresh water, drain, add the water in the recipe and stew. Add sugar to suit individual taste.
3 Allow to cool and spread into an 8 in (20 cm) oven proof dish.
4 Make the frangipane mixing and spread over the top of the apple.
5 Bake in an oven at 360°F (180°C) for 45–60 minutes or until golden brown in colour.
6 Serve either hot or cold with fresh cream.

Sticky toffee pudding

Yield 8 covers

A
6 oz (180 g) dried dates (stoneless)
7 oz (2 dl) boiling water
1 level teaspoonful bicarbonate of soda

B
3 oz (90 g) unsalted butter
5 oz (150 g) castor sugar
3 oz (90 g) flour (soft)
3 oz (90 g) scone flour (see page 52)
4 oz (120 g) egg

Toffee sauce

C
7 oz (210 g) soft brown sugar
4 oz (120 g) unsalted butter
5 oz (150 g) double cream
½ teaspoon vanilla essence

A

Chop or mince the dates, mix with boiling water, allow to cool to room temperature and add the bicarbonate of soda. Alternatively, mash the dates with the water in a food processor.

B

1 Cream the butter and sugar and beat in the egg.
2 Carefully fold in the flour followed by A and blend together to form a fairly sloppy mixture.
3 Put this into a deep silicone paper lined or greased 8 inch (20 cm) square baking tin and bake in a pre-heated oven at 360°F (180°C) for approximately 50 minutes or until firm to the touch.

C

4 Make up the sauce by blending all the materials together over gentle heat to dissolve the sugar, then simmer until toffee coloured.
5 Pre-heat the grill or salamander.
6 When cooked, pour some of the sauce over the pudding and place under a hot grill, allowing it to bubble and occasionally turning as needed.
7 Serve immediately while still bubbling together with the sauce. Fresh cream, yoghurt or an alternative sauce may also be served.

Suet puddings

Steamed fruit pudding

Yield 8 covers

8 oz (240 g) flour into suet pastry (see page 54)
2 lb (960 g) fruit
6–8 oz (180–240 g) approximately sugar (according to type of fruit used)
Water (according to type of fruit used)

1 Using approximately three-quarters of the paste, line a slightly greased basin.
2 Add prepared and washed fruit, sugar, and water (see below). If apples are used, add two cloves.
3 Brush the edge of the paste with water.
4 Cover with the remaining paste and seal firmly.
5 Cover with a pudding cloth or greased greaseproof paper.
6 Steam for approximately 1½ hours.
7 Clean the basin and wrap around it a folded napkin.
8 Serve in the basin on a flat silver dish with a separate sauceboat of custard.

Notes:
1 Fruits suitable for such sweets are plums, rhubarb, apple, apple and black currant, gooseberry, etc. Sharp fruits like rhubarb require more sugar than apple.
2 Soft fruits like rhubarb will not require any water added, but for dry fruits like plums up to 3 oz (90 g) may be used.

Steamed rolls

Yield 8 covers

Recipe and quantity of ingredients same as Baked jam roll recipe (page 64), using suet pastry instead of short pastry.

1 Make the same as baked jam roll.
2 Place the roll into a pudding cloth and secure both ends.
3 Steam for approximately 2 hours.
4 Serve as for baked jam roll.

Varieties

Jam, marmalade, mincemeat, date and apple, syrup.

Steamed currant roll

Yield 8 covers

8 oz (240 g) flour
½ oz (15 g) baking powder
2½ oz (75 g) sugar
4 oz (120 g) chopped suet
4 oz (120 g) prepared currants
¼ pt (1.5 dl) milk
A pinch of salt

1 Sieve the flour with the baking powder and salt into a bowl.
2 Add the suet and mix in.
3 Mix in the sugar and currants.
4 Add the milk and mix to a dough.
5 Proceed as for steamed jam roll.

Steamed suet puddings

Basic recipe

Yield 8 covers

6 oz (180 g) suet
2 oz (60 g) soft flour
4 oz (120 g) scone flour (see page 52)
6 oz (180 g) breadcrumbs
A pinch of salt
8–10 oz (240–300 g) milk or water (see operation 3 below)

1 Sieve the flour, baking powder, and salt.
2 Add the breadcrumbs and chopped suet and mix.
3 Add sufficient milk or water to make a soft dough which will drop easily from a spoon. The strength of flour used and the dryness of the breadcrumbs will affect the quantity of water needed to achieve this consistency.
4 Place in well-greased basins or moulds (sleeves).
5 Cover with greased greaseproof paper.
6 Steam for 2–2½ hours according to size.
7 Turn out on to a hot dish and serve with a custard or a jam sauce.

Varieties

Fruit pudding

Add to basic suet pudding recipe:

4–6 oz (120–180 g) selected and washed dried fruit
2–4 oz (60–120 g) sugar

Serve custard sauce separately.

Note: Fruit may include currants, sultanas, raisins, figs, dates, cherries, etc.

Golden or syrup pudding

Add to basic suet pudding recipe:

6 oz (180 g) golden syrup (for layering)

1 Prepare basic recipe.
2 Use only basins, not sleeves.
3 Deposit a layer of syrup in the bottom of a well-greased basin and then place a layer of the basic mixing on top.
4 Repeat this process to finish with a layer of the basic mixing on top.
5 Serve a syrup sauce separately.

Marmalade pudding

Add to basic suet pudding recipe:

2 oz (60 g) sugar
4–6 oz (120–180 g) marmalade (for layering)

1 Proceed as for Golden pudding, substituting marmalade for syrup.
2 Serve marmalade or custard sauce separately.

Jam layer pudding

Add to basic suet pudding recipe:

4–6 oz (120–180 g) jam (for layering)

1 Proceed as for Golden pudding, substituting jam for syrup.
2 Serve jam sauce separately.

Steamed sponge puddings

Basic recipe

Yield 8 covers

8 oz (240 g) soft flour
½ oz (15 g) baking powder
5 oz (150 g) castor sugar
5 oz (150 g) margarine
5 oz (150 g) eggs
2 oz (60 g) milk

1 Make mixing on the sugar batter method (see page 98).
2 Deposit mixture into a well-greased pudding basin.
3 Securely cover with greased greaseproof paper.
4 Steam for approximately 1½ hours.
5 Turn out onto a hot flat silver dish and serve with an appropriate sauce.

Varieties

Vanilla

Add vanilla essence to the basic mixture. Serve with a vanilla-flavoured sauce.

Chocolate

Substitute 1½ oz (45 g) flour in the basic mixture for cocoa powder. Serve with a chocolate sauce (see page 186).

Fruit (currants, sultanas, raisins)

Add 4 oz (120 g) of selected, washed, and well-dried fruit to the basic mixture. Serve with a custard sauce.

Cherry

Add 4 oz (120 g) of chopped or quartered glacé cherries to the basic mixture. Serve with almond or custard sauce.

Lemon

Add to the basic mixture the zest of 2 lemons and lemon essence to taste. Serve with a lemon sauce.

Orange

Proceed as for Lemon sponge pudding but using oranges instead. Serve with an orange sauce.

Ginger

Add ½ teaspoonful powdered ginger and 1½ oz (45 g) finely diced preserved ginger. Serve with a custard sauce.

Harlequin

1 Divide the basic mixture into three.
2 Flavour one portion vanilla, another chocolate, and the third strawberry or raspberry with sufficient colouring to make it pink.
3 Deposit into well-greased basins to form alternating layers of white, pink, and chocolate.
4 Serve with a custard or jam sauce.

Eve's pudding

Basic steamed sponge pudding recipe (see page 221)
Jam
Apple purée (see page 58)

1 Spread a little jam in the bottom of a greased pie dish.
2 Cover with a thick layer of apple purée.
3 Spread on sufficient sponge mixture to completely cover the apple purée and fill the dish.

4 Bake in an oven at 400°F (204°C) for approximately 10 minutes and then reduce heat to approximately 365°F (185°C) and allow a further 30 minutes to finish cooking.
5 Serve with a custard sauce.

Christmas puddings
Figure 60)

Yield 1 pudding at 4 lb (1920 g) sufficient for 16–20 covers.

Recipe 1

A
6 oz (180 g) suet
2 oz (60 g) flour

B
12 oz (360 g) breadcrumbs

C
8 oz (240 g) sultanas
4 oz (120 g) raisins (stoned)
8 oz (240 g) currants
4 oz (120 g) chopped peel
8 oz (240 g) brown sugar
1 oz (30 g) syrup

D
¼ oz (7.5 g) mixed spice (see page 48)
2 level teaspoonsful salt
8 oz (240 g) eggs
Zest of 1 lemon
Zest of 1 orange

Recipe 2

A
10 oz (300 g) suet
4 oz (120 g) flour
1½ oz (45 g) ground almonds

B
6 oz (180 g) breadcrumbs

C
8 oz (240 g) sultanas
8 oz (240 g) raisins (stoned)
10 oz (300 g) currants
2 oz (60 g) chopped peel
6 oz (180 g) brown sugar
1½ oz (45 g) syrup

D (optional)
2 oz (60 g) figs
1 oz (30 g) water

E
¼ oz (7.5 g) mixed spice (see page 48)
1 oz (30 g) ground almonds

F
¼ pt (1.5 dl) rum, brandy, or stock syrup

1 Finely chop the suet A.
2 Peel and core the apples B and finely chop. Add to A.
3 Chop the raisins and peel. Mix all the ingredients of C together and then add to the suet and apples.
4 Stir in the sugar D.
5 Add the ingredients of E.
6 Lastly stir in F and mix all the ingredients thoroughly together.
7 Keep for at least two days before transferring to jars.
8 Fill the jars, cover with greaseproof paper, and tie down.
9 Store in a cool, dry place until required.

Notes:
1 Mincemeat should never be used freshly made. It matures and improves on storage and should not be used until it is at least 14 days old.
2 Cool, dry storage is essential if mincemeat is to be kept for any time. Damp and warm conditions will encourage the development of mould and wild yeasts which will bring about undesirable fermentation.

Sweet omelettes

Basic recipe per person

2–3 eggs
1 oz (30 g) approx. filling
¼ oz (7.5 g) butter (see page 48)
¼ oz (7.5 g) sugar (see page 48)

Pre-preparation

First make sure that the omelette pan is well proved. Pans for omelettes should be thick-bottomed and reserved solely for this purpose. They should never be washed out but only wiped with kitchen paper. To clean the pan, make it very hot, rub the inside with salt, and wipe it with kitchen paper.

Ensure that, before starting to make the omelette, everything is ready, that is, the garnish, filling, and hot serving dish.

Once made, the omelette must be served immediately or it will become tough.

1 Break the eggs into a basin and beat the yolks and whites thoroughly together.
2 Place the butter in the pan and heat it until it is quite hot (*do not allow the butter to brown*).
3 Pour the eggs into the hot pan and stir with a fork, slowly at first and then faster as the eggs begin to set.

4 Keep a good heat but not too fierce so that a golden brown colour is achieved.
5 Place in the filling.
6 Remove from the heat and fold the edges of the omelette over to enclose the filling.
7 Shape the omelette into an oval cushion shape by tapping the handle of the pan to turn over the omelette.
8 Turn out immediately on to an oval fireproof dish or silver flat.
9 Serve immediately.

Note: The omelette should not take longer than 5 minutes to make.

Varieties of fillings

Jam – Omelette à la confiture

The jam should be warmed before folding into the omelette. To finish, dust liberally with icing sugar and, with a red hot poker, mark the top with a criss-cross pattern. Alternatively, glaze quickly under a salamander.

Fruit purée

Any sweet fruit purée may be used instead of jam.

Mincemeat

This may also be appropriately called a 'Christmas' omelette. Sprinkle with sugar, pour over warm rum, and ignite when served.

Rum or other spirits (Cognac, Kirsch, etc.) – Omelette au rhum, etc.

Prepare omelette without filling. Sprinkle with sugar, pour spirit into a heated spoon, ignite, and pour over the omelette just prior to service.

Soufflé omelette

There is often confusion between this and Crêpe soufflé because the same basic recipe is used. The following method is the one recognized for this sweet.
　Basic recipe per person:
1 egg
1 oz (30 g) sugar

1 Separate the yolks from the whites.
2 Cream the yolks with the sugar.
3 Whisk the whites to a stiff foam.
4 Carefully fold the whites into the yolk and sugar cream.
5 Butter and sugar a long oval mould or dish and fill with the soufflé mixture.

6 Dust with sugar and bake in an oven at 400°F (204°C) for approximately 15–18 minutes depending upon size.

7 When baked, place on a doily on a flat silver dish and serve at once.

Note: It is usual for this to be made for a number of covers, for example 4, and not individually.

Sweet soufflés – Soufflés d'entremets

The basic preparation up to and including the yolks may be made well in advance of the time the soufflé is required, provided it is kept in a cool place.

The stiffly beaten egg whites should be added at the last moment just before the soufflé is placed in the oven.

The beaten egg whites should be stirred into the mixing very carefully to ensure that the entrapped air is not broken down. If this does happen the soufflé will not rise.

Large soufflés should be baked in an oven 325–350°F (163–177°C) for 20–25 minutes.

Small soufflés should be baked in an oven at 400°F (204°C) for approximately 7–9 minutes.

Figure 61 *Baked soufflés. Cooked soufflés being removed from the oven*

Too hot an oven will form a crust on top too quickly and thus prevent the soufflé from rising properly. It may also cause collapsing of the soufflé when taken from the oven.

The soufflé dish should be three-quarters filled, and when baked the soufflé should rise to 1–1½ in (2.5–4 cm) above the top of the mould. A slight collapse after baking is normal.

Soufflés should always be served immediately.

Basic mixture

Yield 2 soufflés of 4 portions each

1 oz (30 g) flour
1 oz (30 g) cornflour
2 oz (60 g) butter
2 oz (60 g) castor sugar
½ pt (3 dl) milk
5 egg whites
5 egg yolks
Flavouring

Method 1

1 Grease the soufflé or cocotte dishes with clarified butter and dress with sugar.
2 Boil the milk in a saucepan.
3 Beat the butter to a cream, add the sugar, and beat well.
4 Add the flour and gently mix it into the butter/sugar mixture.
5 Pour on the boiling milk slowly, stirring vigorously to produce a perfectly smooth mixture (*panada*).
6 Return to the pan and, continuing to stir, cook the panada for a few minutes.
7 Remove from the heat and allow it to cool slightly.
8 Add the egg yolks individually, beating each well into the mixture.

At this stage the mixture may be left until required for finishing.

9 Whisk whites to a stiff snow, blend some into the mixture first to soften it, and then very carefully fold in the remainder. Do not over-mix.
10 Fill the moulds to three-quarters full.
11 Place in an oven at 400°F (204°C) to bake for 20–25 minutes.
12 One minute before they are cooked, sprinkle on icing sugar and return to the oven to glaze.
13 Serve at once in the soufflé dish, either on a doily or folded table napkin on a flat silver dish.
14 Serve with an appropriate sauce.

Method 2

1 Prepare the soufflé or cocotte dishes.
2 Make a white roux by melting the butter in a thick-bottomed pan and adding the flour.

3 Heat the milk and add it gradually to the roux stirring continuously to form a perfectly smooth mixture.
4 Cook the mixture gently, stirring continually until it thickens.
5 Add the sugar.
6 Proceed as for operations 7 to 14 in Method 1.

Varieties

Chocolate – Soufflé au chocolat

Using the basic recipe, add 2 oz (60 g) of grated chocolate to the hot milk, allowing it to melt before proceeding. Serve a custard or chocolate sauce separately.

Coffee – Soufflé au café

Using the basic recipe, add 2 oz (60 g) liquid coffee or ½ oz (15 g) instant coffee to the milk or use white coffee instead of milk. Serve with a custard sauce.

Lemon – Soufflé au citron

Add the zest of 2 lemons to the mixture prior to adding the yolks. Add the juice to the accompanying sauce.

Orange – Soufflé a l'orange or Soufflé Maltaise

Add the zest of 2 oranges to the mixture prior to adding the yolks. Part of the milk may be replaced by orange juice. Add the juice to the accompanying sauce.

Hazelnut – Soufflé noisettine

Using the basic recipe, add 4 oz (120 g) ground hazelnuts to the milk. Serve with a hazelnut sauce.

Almond – Soufflé amandines

Using the basic recipe, add 4 oz (120 g) ground almonds to the milk. Serve with an almond sauce.

Soufflé Regence

1 Line a charlotte mould with caramel (see page 216).
2 Fill with the basic soufflé mixing.
3 Serve with a custard sauce to which crushed caramel has been added.

Soufflé Montmorency

Soak 3 oz (90 g) candied cherries in a little Kirsch and add to the mixture after the egg yolks are added. Serve with a sabayon sauce.

Soufflé ananas

Same as above but using diced pineapple.

Soufflé Rothschild

Soak 3 oz (90 g) of mixed candied fruit in Kirsch or brandy and add to the mixture after the egg yolks are added. Also add vanilla flavour. Serve with a sabayon sauce.

Note: Many other varieties of soufflés may be made from this basic recipe with different flavourings.

Soufflé puddings

Basic recipe

Yield 2 soufflés of 4 portions each

2 oz (60 g) flour
2 oz (60 g) cornflour
4 oz (120 g) butter
4 oz (120 g) sugar
5 oz (150 g) egg yolks
5 oz (150 g) egg whites
½ pt (3 dl) milk
Flavouring

1 Grease the mould with butter and dress with sugar.
2 Separate the whites from the yolks.
3 Cream the butter and flours.
4 Boil the milk in a saucepan with the sugar and other flavourings.
5 Add and whisk in the creamed butter/flour and cook until the mixture thickens.
6 Allow to cool slightly and whisk in the yolks one or two at a time.
7 Whip the whites to a stiff snow, stir a little into the mixing to soften, and carefully fold in the remainder.
8 Fill the mould three-quarters full.
9 Place the filled moulds in a bain-marie on the stove and simmer until the mixture reaches the top of the mould.
10 Transfer to an oven at 400°F (204°C) and bake for 20–25 minutes.
11 Turn out on to a hot flat silver dish.
12 Serve with a vanilla sauce.

Note: These soufflés have more of a pudding consistency and are able to stand a while in a bain-marie prior to service without collapsing.

Varieties   *Chocolate, coffee, lemon, orange, hazelnut, almond*

Proceed in the same way as for the other types of soufflé described on page 230.

Pouding soufflé à l'Indienne

Using the basic pudding mixture add 2 oz (60 g) crystallized preserved ginger to the mixture after the egg yolks are added. Serve with a custard sauce flavoured ginger.

Pouding soufflé Montmorency

Same as Soufflé Montmorency (see page 230).

Pouding soufflé Maltaise

Same as Orange soufflé pudding.

Pouding soufflé Vésuvius

Cook the soufflé pudding mixture in a prepared savarin mould. When baked fill the centre with raisins in an apricot sauce. Flambé with brandy.

Pouding soufflé à la royale

Butter a charlotte mould and line bottom and sides with thin slices of apricot Swiss roll (see page 83). Fill with the pudding mixture and bake in the usual way. Serve with custard flavoured with Kirsch or apricot sauce flavoured with Madeira or Muscatel wine.

Pouding soufflé au Grand Marnier

Using the basic pudding mixture, add the zest of one orange to the milk. Add some diced macaroon biscuits soaked in Grand Marnier.

Pouding soufflé aux marrons

Add chestnut purée and piece of marron glacé. Serve with an apricot sauce.

Pouding soufflé à la Reine

Cook the pudding mixture in a savarin mould. When baked, fill the centre with candied fruit soaked in Kirsch. Serve with an apricot sauce.

Pouding soufflé sans Souci

Add currants and diced cooked apples.

**Cold lemon soufflé –
Soufflé Milanaise**

Yield 8 covers

½ pt (3 dl) cream
2 lemons
½ oz (15 g) gelatine
8 oz (240 g) sugar
5 oz (150 g) pasteurized egg (see page 18)
1 oz (30 g) roasted almond or green almond decor

1 Prepare a soufflé mould by tying a band of greaseproof or silicone paper around the side so that it is extended about 1½ in (3.5 cm) beyond the top.
2 Add the gelatine to the juice of the lemons and warm to dissolve.
3 Whisk the egg and sugar to a thick cream.
4 Add the dissolved gelatine solution.
5 Whip the cream and fold carefully into the mixture.
6 Pour into the prepared soufflé mould and allow to set.
7 Finish by removing the paper band and decorating the edge with toasted almonds or green decor. It may be further decorated with whipped cream.

Other cold soufflés

Other varieties may be made, using the same flavouring agents as used for the hot soufflé.

18 *Chocolate work*

Cooking chocolate

Although the uses described in this chapter refer to chocolate couverture, many of the techniques can be applied to cooking chocolate. The results will not be as good however, the chocolate lacking the flavour, gloss, and snap of couverture. Its advantage is the ease with which it can be used since no tempering is necessary. All one has to do is warm it to approximately 100–110°F (38–43°C) and use.

Tempering of chocolate couverture

Before chocolate can be successfully used it must be free from contamination by moisture and must be tempered. This process can be explained as follows:

Cocoa butter can be regarded as being a mixture of two fats – A with a low-melting point and latent heat, and B with a high melting point and latent heat. The A type has crystals of fat which are soft and feel greasy, whilst the B type crystals of fat impart the gloss and snap required in well-tempered chocolate.

To eliminate the A type crystals, the couverture should be completely melted, then cooled to the setting point of the A crystals, when B crystals are produced as well. The mass is now heated to the temperature at which only the A crystals will melt, leaving some B crystals. On setting, the whole mass will crystallize out in the B crystal form. (This process is known as 'seeding'.)

There are several techniques used to temper chocolate:

1 A double-jacketed pan known as a 'bain-marie' or 'porringer' is used. It consists of a small pan in which the chocolate is contained and a larger pan which is filled with warm water. The small pan is placed inside the larger one and heat is transferred by the water. To melt the chocolate this water must not exceed 120°F (49°C).

When all the chocolate has melted, transfer the small pan into another large one containing very cold water (some *ice* may be used). Stir continually until some of the chocolate sets on the bottom. Transfer again to the pan of hot water where it remains until the solid chocolate just begins to melt. Remove and stir until all the solid chocolate has melted and been dispersed. The temperature at this stage should be cool, approximately 84°F (29°C) for milk and 86°F (30°C) for plain.

2 Melt chocolate in bain-marie. Remove from heat and stir in flakes of solid chocolate, shredded from a block of well-tempered chocolate. The proportion depends on the amount of liquid chocolate and its temperature which should be sufficient to only *just* melt the shreds of solid chocolate being stirred in.

3 Once a quantity of liquid tempered chocolate has been obtained, it can be used to *seed* fresh batches of untempered chocolate. The usual procedure is to have a large bowl of liquid chocolate available and, as the tempered chocolate is used, it is replaced by the liquid untempered variety. This is how chocolate is tempered for large scale use in a factory.

Storage of chocolate

Chocolate should be wrapped, kept free from moisture and stored in a cool place (cold room but *not* a refrigerator), away from strong smelling commodities such as onion.

For the rapid setting of chocolate goods it is a mistake to put them into either the deep freeze or a refrigerator since these temperatures will cause condensation of moisture on the surface and uneven contractions in moulded goods, resulting in the fracturing of the moulded shape.

Working with chocolate

Moulding
(Figure 62)

When tempered chocolate sets, it contracts and this action makes it easy for all types of figures to be moulded. Moulds may be either metal, usually tinned, or plastic, the latter having the advantage of being flexible and so aiding release of the figure from the mould. The temperature of setting is important. Although it needs to be cool, it is a mistake to place the mould in a refrigerator. This will cause uneven contraction and result in a cracked figure.

Detailed method of moulding eggs and figures

1 Make sure that the moulds are clean, dry, and polished by rubbing cotton wool on the surface.
2 Temper the chocolate couverture as previously described.
3 Fill the figure or mould to the brim with the liquid chocolate.
4 Turn upside down and empty mould of chocolate (Figure 63).
5 Wipe the brim free of surplus chocolate and place brim downwards on greaseproof or silicone paper.
6 Place in a cool room and allow chocolate to set in the mould.
7 Repeat the operation if the coating of chocolate is too thin. Except for very small moulds, most require two thicknesses of chocolate for strength.

8 Leave the moulds in a cool room until the chocolate has contracted sufficiently for the chocolate shape to be removed from the mould. This may take as long as two hours. The release of the chocolate from the mould is easier from plastic moulds than from tin.

9 To finish off Easter eggs, the two halves have to be joined with chocolate. This is best done by heating a clean tray and placing the rim of one half of the chocolate egg on the heated tray for a few seconds so that the chocolate melts. When this happens the two halves can be secured by placing the two edges together.

10 The Easter eggs can be decorated by piping stiffened chocolate in a shell pattern around the join. Also marzipan flowers and inscriptions may be piped on.

Figure 62   *Chocolate. Moulded goods in plain, milk and white chocolate*

Figure 63   *Filling chocolate moulds*

Dipping

Chocolate may be used for sweets by dipping various centres, for example fondants. It must be well-tempered and at such a temperature that the first one has started to set whilst the sixth is being dipped.

Several varieties of pastries, marzipan shapes, and animals, are enhanced by having a part dipped in chocolate. Wholly enrobed cakes and biscuits will keep fresh and moist for very much longer periods.

Piping
(Figure 64)

When a liquid is added to chocolate, it thickens and in this state it can be piped. Piping chocolate loses its characteristic gloss and some of its snap and is not, therefore, recommended for piped off-pieces. Substances which may be added to thicken chocolate are as follows:

1 *Water or milk*   Not recommended.
2 *Glycerine*   Recommended – helps to maintain gloss.
3 *Piping jelly*   Recommended – helps to maintain gloss.
4 *Gelatine jelly*   Recommended – helps to maintain gloss.
5 *Spirits and liqueurs*   Recommended – adds to flavour.

Thinning

To make chocolate thinner we must add cocoa butter. This is useful if a very thin covering is required.

Flavouring

Chocolate or block cocoa may be used to flavour icings and creams and the crumb of cakes. Block cocoa (lacking in sugar) is especially useful to flavour very sweet mediums such as fondant. Although the chocolate is used mostly in the liquid state, solid flakes may be scattered or mixed in mediums like fresh cream.

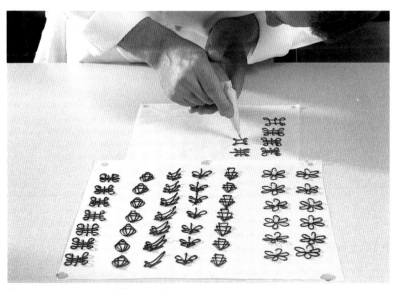

Figure 64   *Piping filigree shapes in chocolate. The flower shapes have a yellow sugar ball placed in the centre and are used to decorate the ganache torte on page 117*

Carving

The very nature of chocolate makes it an ideal medium in which figures may be carved. All that is needed is a flair for this type of sculpture work and a sharp knife. In the first instance, a sufficiently large block of chocolate has to be provided and it may be necessary for the chocolate to be first melted, tempered, and then poured into a suitably sized frame or mould.

Decoration

1 Shapes may be piped out on to greaseproof paper from drawn designs. When set, these shapes may be used to decorate gâteaux, torten, fancies, ice bombs, and special sweets.
2 Chocolate may be spread out on greaseproof paper and, when nearly set, a cutter or knife can cut out shapes which, when set, can be removed from the sheet and used for decoration.
3 Spread chocolate out on marzipan or sugar paste and, as it is setting, spread with a serrated scraper to obtain a corrugated effect. Cut out shapes with a cutter or knife when chocolate has set and use shapes for decoration.
4 Spread chocolate on marzipan or sugar paste and, before it sets, sprinkle on a variety of dressings, for example nibbed almonds, coloured decor, coconut (white and browned), violet petals, rose petals, etc. Cut out shapes as in 3.
5 Texture marzipan or sugar paste with rollers. Place melted chocolate in a greaseproof bag with a fine aperture. Pipe lines of chocolate at speed (*spinning*) over the textured paste, in different directions. Cut out shapes as in 3.
6 *Curls* (Figure 65). Pour some chocolate on to a marble slab and spread backwards and forwards until it just sets. With a sharp knife, cut the chocolate off the slab using a shearing action. The chocolate will form long curls, the thickness depending upon the length of the shearing action. *Flakes* may be done in the same way, but the chocolate has to be more firmly set.

Plastic chocolate

If confectioners' glucose and couverture are blended homogeneously together, they will form a plastic paste which may be modelled into roses etc. The proportions should be approximately two of chocolate to one of glucose, both warmed to about 90°F (32°C) before being blended together.

Faults

1 *Fat bloom.* This manifests itself with white streaks on the chocolate and is the result of using chocolate too warm.
2 *Sugar bloom.* This is a white bloom which appears on the surface of the chocolate and results from the use of chocolate at too low a temperature.

Recipes

Chocolate icing (or sauce)

Also suitable for imitation ganache

8 oz (240 g) chocolate couverture
3 oz (90 g) stock syrup (see page 257)

1 Melt chocolate in bain-marie.
2 Warm solution of stock syrup to approximately 120°F (49°C).
3 Add the syrup to the melted couverture, a little at a time, stirring each addition well in. At first the mixture will thicken and become similar to toffee but as the syrup is increased the mixture will become thinner and approach the consistency of fondant.
4 The consistency may be slightly adjusted by the use of more syrup if necessary. It is used like fondant for covering purposes. When set, it forms a skin but the icing remains soft.

Ganache

½ pt (3 dl) fresh cream
1 lb (480 g) chocolate couverture (milk or plain)

1 Melt the chocolate in a bain-marie.
2 Place cream in a clean saucepan and bring to the boil.
3 Remove from the heat and stir in the melted chocolate. Whisk until completely mixed and smooth.

Notes:
1 This mixing can be flavoured by the addition of spirits and liqueurs and its consistency varied by altering the ratio of cream/chocolate. For a thinner mixture, increase the cream and for a thicker one increase the chocolate.
2 Ganache can be used in four ways:
  (a) Used hot, it may be poured over a sponge (or similar base) like fondant when it will set into a thin, soft eating coating.
  (b) If refrigerated, it sets to a firm paste, which may be moulded into chocolate centres and sweets.
  (c) It may be whisked when slightly warm to produce a light cream which may be piped into a variety of patterns like buttercream.
  (d) As a filling, either on its own or mixed with other fillings.

Imitation ganache

Several concoctions can be made from chocolate and liquids to give a filling having similar properties to ganache (except flavour). The chocolate icing recipe, once cold, makes a passable imitation.

The best imitation is to use either artificial cream or evaporated milk instead of fresh cream.

Figure 65   *Curling chocolate using a metal scraper*

19 *Almond and other pastes*

Almond paste (Marzipan)

Recipe 1

A
4 oz (120 g) ground almonds
4 oz (120 g) icing sugar

B
4 oz (120 g) castor sugar
1½ oz (45 g) whole egg

1 Sieve the ingredients of A thoroughly together and make a bay.
2 Place the ingredients of B in a saucepan and heat but do not boil.
3 Transfer contents of saucepan to the bay.
4 Mix into a smooth paste.

Recipe 2

A
1 lb (480 g) sugar
2 oz (60 g) confectioners' glucose
¼ pt (1.5 dl) water

B
10 oz (300 g) ground almonds

C
1½ oz (45 g) egg yolks

1 Place ingredients of A in a clean copper saucepan and boil to 240°F (115°C). Observe sugar boiling precautions (see page 264).
2 Allow the boiling syrup to cool slightly, then add the ground almonds B.
3 Lastly stir in the egg yolks C and work to a smooth paste.

Notes:
1 Extra colour may be applied as desired.
2 Consistency may be adjusted by altering the egg quantity.

Sugar paste

Recipe 1

4 oz (120 g) marshmallow
4 oz (120 g) icing sugar
½ oz (15 g) cornflour
1 level teaspoonful gum tragacanth

1 Mix all the ingredients together and knead into a smooth paste.
2 Keep wrapped in polythene bag or covered with a damp cloth to prevent drying and skinning.

Recipe 2

A
½ oz (15 g) water
2 oz (60 g) water
1½ oz (45 g) glucose

B
¼ oz (7.5 g) gelatine (see page 48)
1½ oz (45 g) royal icing
11 oz (330 g) icing sugar

1 Bring the ingredients of A to the boil.
2 Stir in the gelatine until it dissolves.
3 Stir in the royal icing.
4 Add the icing sugar and knead the mixture to a firm paste.
5 Wrap in polythene bag or cover with a damp cloth.

Note: If paste is too stiff for any particular purpose, it will become more pliable if it is warmed.

Uses of sugar paste

1 Covering for all types of gâteaux and fancies. It may be coloured and flavoured. It can also be used to cover cake surfaces which have to be coated in icings or chocolate. A thin coating of sugar paste will give a flat, smooth surface which forms a good base to obtain a perfect coating of icing. This is especially useful when icing is required for the top and sides of a gâteau.
2 Rolling out the paste thinly and cutting out shapes, either with a knife or special cutters. These shapes may be flowers, leaves, animals, or shapes like diamonds or hearts. They are very useful for decorating all types of fancies, gâteaux, and sweets.
3 Sugar paste may be used in the same way as gum paste for making various models, caskets, and table pieces. It may also be modelled into flowers, animals, figures, etc., in the same way as marzipan.

**Modelling nut paste –
Almond, coconut, and
hazelnut**

6½ oz (195 g) granulated sugar
1 oz (30 g) confectioner's glucose
2 oz (60 g) water
1 oz (30 g) egg yolks or whites
4 oz (120 g) ground almonds, coconut, or hazelnuts

1 Boil sugar, glucose, and water to 245°F (118°C).
2 Stir in ground almonds or coconut.
3 Quickly stir in the egg as follows:
   Yolks – For yellow paste.
   Whites – For white paste (for coloured paste).

4 Turn out onto a slab and work down into a pliable paste.
5 Keep paste in airtight container or plastic bag to prevent paste from skinning.

Note: The coconut paste is very short and difficult to handle except for cut-out shapes. For economy purposes, the paste may be made by substituting the hazelnuts or almonds for coconut. The hazelnut paste is naturally brown in colour and is unsuitable for colouring for which white paste (using egg whites) is required. This paste is deliberately made stiff for modelling but may be softened by using water.

Varieties for modelling (Figure 66)

Use either the almond paste recipe 2 or the modelling nut paste.

Method for modelling fruits

1 Colour the paste as follows:
   Green – apples and pears
   Yellow – bananas, lemons, and peaches
   Orange – oranges.
2 Mould the paste into the required shape using modelling tools where necessary. The rough surface of the orange and lemon is obtained by rolling the shape on a cheese grater.
3 Allow the shapes to lie overnight to set firm.

Finishing

Apples
With a fine brush, paint on streaks of red and yellow colour. When set, rub on a little melted cocoa butter or cooking fat to imitate the wax-like surface of the apple. For the stems, use either brown marzipan, stalk of maidenhair fern, or a thin strip of angelica coloured brown.

Pears
Using a toothbrush and wire, scatter chocolate colour all over until required depth of colour is achieved. Use the same materials already described for the stem.

Bananas
Paint on chocolate brown marks using a fine brush. Use a little green at each end of the banana shape. When dry, rub on a little melted cocoa butter or cooking fat.

Lemons
With a brush, colour each end of the lemon shape with green colour. Glaze with confectioner's varnish or a solution of gum arabic.

Peaches

Brush on each side orange and red colour. When dry, powder with a little cornflour to imitate the bloom.

Oranges

Fill a small impression in the top of the orange with chocolate coloured marzipan to imitate the flower end. Glaze with confectioner's varnish or a solution of gum arabic.

Note: The aerograph spray may be used to colour the fruits (see Figure 26).

Figure 66 *Sugar paste and marzipan flowers and fruits. Description in text on page 247*

Pastillage (gum paste)

This is a paste made principally with icing sugar and water with a setting agent. It is used for modelling all types of shapes for decorative purposes such as caskets, etc. It sets very hard on exposure to air and therefore is not meant to be consumed. Once made it should be kept airtight by storing it in a plastic bag before working it into the required shape. There are several recipes some of which are given here.

Recipe 1

A

1 lb 4 oz (600 g) icing sugar
2½ oz (75 g) cornflour
¼ oz (7.5 g) powdered gum tragacanth (see page 48)

B

2½ oz (75 g) cold water

1 Mix the ingredients of A thoroughly together and make a bay.
2 Add the water B and knead to a clear smooth paste.

Recipe 2

1 oz (30 g) cold water
1½ level teaspoonsful powdered gelatine
1 lb (480 g) icing sugar
½ level teaspoonful powdered gum tragacanth

1 Soak gelatine in the water for approximately 1 hour.
2 Warm the bowl containing the sifted icing sugar and gum tragacanth. This is to prevent the gelatine setting before the paste is completely mixed.
3 Completely dissolve the gelatine in the water by applying gentle heat.
4 Pour the gelatine solution into the warmed icing sugar stirring with a warm spatula and knead to a clear smooth paste.

Recipe 3

1 oz (30 g) water
1 oz (30 g) white fat
½ oz (15 g) leaf gelatine
2½ lb (1200 g) icing sugar

1 Soak the gelatine in water for approximately 1 hour.
2 Melt the fat in the water of the recipe by applying heat.
3 Add the gelatine to the above 2.
4 Mix these ingredients with the sugar and knead to a stiff paste.

Recipe 4

1 teaspoonful of powdered gum arabic
5 oz (150 g) royal icing (see page 290)
Icing sugar

1 Mix the gum arabic with the royal icing.
2 Work in extra sifted icing sugar until a stiff pliable paste is made.

Notes:
These pastes should be left for at least 24 hours and well kneaded again before use in order to well distribute the setting agent.

The dusting medium may either be icing sugar or cornflour, keeping its use to the minimum.

Caskets

Gum paste, sugar paste, or almond paste may be used to make caskets. The latter, however, will need the addition of gum tragacanth at the rate of ¼ oz (7.5 g) per lb (480 g) (see page 48).

Caskets may be of any size or shape, the most popular being square, rectangular, round, or heart-shaped. They are usually filled with petits fours or sweets and are placed upon the banqueting table. Caskets may be made in coloured pastes and suitably decorated with royal icing, etc.

Making a square casket
(Figure 67)

First a full scale drawing has to be made of the top and base and of the sides as shown in Figure 68.

The slabs of paste may be accurately cut to shape and size by the following method:

1 Extend the sides of the square and rectangular shapes which represent the top, base, and sides on the drawing.
2 Transfer this drawing to a flat board and cover with a piece of waxed or greaseproof paper so that the drawing shows through.
3 Roll out the paste to sufficient thickness (about ⅛ in (3 mm)) and lay this on the paper covering the drawing.
4 Now, although the actual plan of the top, etc. is obscured, the extended lines are not and it is an easy matter to cut the paste to the accurate size and shape as shown in Figure 68.
5 Now the paper containing the accurately cut slab of paste may be transferred to another flat board to dry. The slab of paste will not become distorted in shape if kept on the paper on which it was cut.
6 After an hour or so, when the sugar piece has crusted over, lay on a sheet of clean tissue or greaseproof paper, and then lay on another board. Pressing the two boards together, turn upside down and then remove the first board which is now on top. Peel away the paper from the underside of the sugar slabs and allow this side to crust over also.
7 From time to time, keep reversing the drying out position as previously described to make sure that even drying out occurs. If this is not done, then distorted shapes will result.

Once the sugar slabs are set, they may be joined together with royal icing and then suitably decorated as shown in Figure 67.

Heart-shaped caskets
(Figure 67)

For this we need a mould round which the sides may be placed to set. A heart-shaped casket has to be made in four pieces: the base, two sides, and the top. If finding a heart-shaped mould proves difficult, a slab of 2 in thick polystyrene may be easily cut into a heart shape by a carpenter with a band saw. Besides this we need a template made from stiff cardboard and cut into a heart-shape larger than the mould.

This is used for cutting out the base and the top.

The casket shown is decorated with hand made moulded sugar paste sweet pea and carnation flowers.

Round caskets
(Figure 67)

Here the techniques are very similar to the heart-shaped casket. If size is not critical, it is easy to get a round tin of appropriate size to use as the mould. The sides in this case would be made from a strip of paste, wrapped round. When this has set it is easy to slip out the mould and cement the side onto a circular base which has been cut from a template.

The roses and leaves used to decorate the round casket in Figure 67 were made from sugar paste.

Modelling roses
(Figure 66)

Many types of flowers may be modelled from sugar or almond paste but the most popular is undoubtedly the rose. These may be used to decorate torten and gâteaux and also sugar or marzipan caskets.

The paste used for this purpose has to be smooth and pliable but stiff enough to stand up. Some gum tragacanth, at the rate of ¼ oz (7.5 g) per lb (480 g) (see page 48), improves the pliability of the almond paste and its ability to stand.

Figure 66 shows the stage by stage assembly of a rose and is explained as follows:

1 Take a ball of paste and from it fashion a shape like a rose but with a pinnacle. Leave sufficient paste attached to form a base.
2 From a ball of paste, make a petal by pressing the edges to paper thickness, keeping the centre thicker for rigidity. The very fine edge may be made by pressing the paste with the middle finger between two sheets of polythene. Damp the centre of the inside of the petal and wrap it around the pinnacle, leaving one edge furled back.
3 Repeat and put on the other petal with one edge tucked into the first petal.
4 Make a larger petal and apply it to the outside. Furl the outside edge before applying.
5 Repeat 4.

A rose may be made in two colours by inlaying paste of another colour into the petal before final shaping.

Hints

1 The number of petals on a rose is neither constant nor important to get a good effect. Usually five petals are sufficient, two for the centre bud and three surrounding it.
2 The petals are put on haphazardly, there being no regular pattern: nor are they necessarily tucked into each other.
3 For vividly coloured roses, for example carmine, powdered colours may be used to colour the marzipan and also applied by brush on the finished dried rose afterwards. To do this, the rose should first be dampened by holding it in steam.

Assembly

The roses are first removed from the base with a knife. Leaves, stems, etc., may be made from green paste, but maidenhair and dried asparagus fern may also be employed with good effect.

Marzipan and sugar paste flowers
(Figure 66)

Method 1

1 Prepare a shallow tray with a layer of castor sugar.
2 Pin out coloured marzipan or sugar paste very thinly using castor sugar as the dusting medium.

3 Cut out with a small crinkled cutter (see note) and place the shapes on to the flat bed of sugar.

4 Using the round end of a spoon handle or dowel rod, press into the centre of each cut-out. This action will make it into a cup simulating a half opened flower.

  If a crystalline appearance is not required, roll out the paste using icing sugar as the dusting medium and place the cutouts onto a sheet of plastic foam before pressing in the centres.

5 Once set the centre of these can be filled with yellow piping jelly or jam and used with angelica to decorate gateaux, fancies and caskets.

Note: Special flower shaped cutters in a range of sizes are now available with a quick release facility for the cutout shapes.

These cut-outs are shown on the circular tray in the figure on page 244 and also in front.

Method 2

Here, plastic cutters are used which not only cuts out the flower shape, but also embosses it with the features of the petals. Leaves can also be cut with their veins embossed. Such flowers and leaves were used to decorate the square casket in Figure 67.

Figure 67 *Decorated caskets*

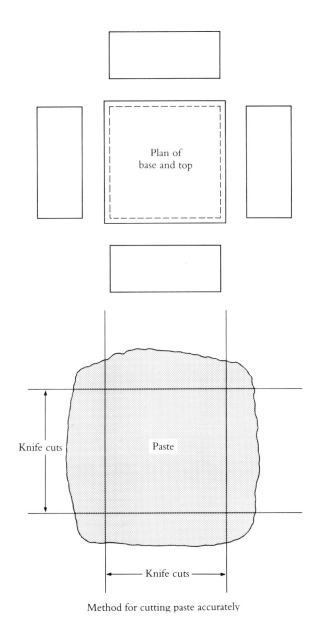

Plan of
base and top

Knife cuts

Paste

Knife cuts

Figure 68 *Square casket. Method of cutting paste*

Method for cutting paste accurately

20 *Sugar work*

Sugar syrups

For many types of patisserie goods, for example ice-cream, confiture fruits, etc., a sugar syrup of a definite density is required. This is ascertained by the use of an instrument called a 'saccharometer'. This is a hydrometer which may be calibrated in either Brix or Baumé degrees. The instrument is a hollow glass tube sealed at each end. At one end it is weighted with lead shot so that when it is placed in a solution it floats upright. The scale marked in either Brix or Baumé indicates the depth at which the tube floats. This is influenced by the density of the sugar which in turn is controlled by the ratio of sugar to water used for the solution. By the use of this instrument we can thus measure the amount of sugar in solution.

Use of saccharometer

1 Make sure that the solution to be tested is at 20°C (68°F). As the density changes with temperature, the Brix or Baumé tables have been standardized at this temperature.
2 Pour the solution to be tested into a tall cylinder (a 500 cc glass cylinder is ideal).
3 Insert the hydrometer and take the reading with the eye looking horizontally.
4 To adjust the density of the sugar solution, add a syrup with a high concentration of sugar but at the same temperature of 20°C (68°F).

The following table is adapted from the Canners' Bulletin No. 2. issued from the Campden Research Station. Although only the Baumé scale will be used in this book, reference to this table will quickly give the reader the alternative Brix scale if required. To obtain the weights of sugar used per gallon of water, multiply the weights given by ten. For practical purposes, ounces should be brought to the nearest eighth (0.125) and grams to the nearest whole number for the small quantities given in this chart.

Degrees Brix (per cent sugar by weight @ 20°C (68°F)	Degrees Baumé 20°C (68°F)	Weight of sugar to be added to each pound of water (approximately)	
		(ounces)	(grammes) (oz × 28.3)
10	5.6	1.8	50.9
11	6.1	2.0	56.6
12	6.7	2.2	62.3
13	7.2	2.4	67.9
14	7.8	2.6	73.6
15	8.3	2.8	78.2
16	8.9	3.0	84.9
17	9.5	3.3	93.4
18	10.0	3.5	99.0
19	10.6	3.7	104.7
20	11.1	4.0	113.2
21	11.7	4.3	121.7
22	12.2	4.5	127.4
23	12.7	4.8	135.8
24	13.3	5.1	144.3
25	13.8	5.3	150.0
26	14.4	5.6	158.5
27	14.9	5.9	167.0
28	15.5	6.2	175.5
29	16.0	6.6	186.8
30	16.6	6.9	195.3
31	17.1	7.2	203.8
32	17.7	7.5	212.3
33	18.2	7.9	223.7
34	18.7	8.3	234.9
35	19.3	8.6	241.4
36	19.8	9.0	254.7
37	20.4	9.4	266.0
38	20.9	9.8	277.3
39	21.4	10.3	291.5
40	22.0	10.7	302.8
41	22.5	11.2	317.0
42	23.0	11.6	328.3
43	23.6	12.1	352.4
44	24.1	12.6	356.6
45	24.6	13.1	370.7
46	25.2	13.7	387.7
47	25.7	14.2	401.9
48	26.2	14.8	418.8
49	26.8	15.5	438.7
50	27.3	16.0	452.8
51	27.8	16.7	462.6
52	28.3	17.4	482.4
53	28.9	18.1	512.2
54	29.4	18.8	532.0

Fondant

Recipe 1

14 oz (420 g) sugar
2 oz (60 g) confectioners' glucose
¼ pt (1½ dl) water

Recipe 2

1 lb (480 g) sugar
¼ pt (1½ dl) water
1 level teaspoonful cream of tartar

1 Bring the sugar and water to a clear syrup with a gentle heat.
2 Raise the temperature so that it boils vigorously. Add the glucose or acid. Observe the sugar boiling precautions (see page 264).
3 Boil to the feather degree of 240°F (115°C).
4 Pour out onto an oiled slab between toffee bars (heavy sticks of metal) or into a tray with sides.
5 Splash surface with water to prevent skinning and leave until temperature drops to approximately 100°F (38°C).
6 Now agitate with a spatula. The mass will first become creamy and, agitation continues, it also becomes thicker and white in colour.
7 When the mass is too stiff to work with a spatula, continue by hand, working it down to a smooth pliable white mass.
8 Store in an airtight tin with a little water covering the surface to prevent skinning.

Note: Hand made fondant is never as white or as smooth as the product which is manufactured for sale to the Confectionery Industry; it is therefore preferable to purchase and use the proprietary product whenever possible.

Uses of fondant

Fondant icing

1 Place some lumps of fondant in a bain-marie and apply gentle heat.
2 Add stock syrup to bring the fondant to the correct consistency for icings.

Notes:
1 The icing should not be used above 100°F (38°C) and only sufficient stock syrup should be added to adjust to the consistency required at this temperature. The fondant icing should set with a pleasing gloss, but in order to achieve this it is imperative that at no stage should the fondant be overheated. This will cause the minute crystals to grow in size and so reduce their light reflecting properties which cause the white appearance and gloss of this type of icing. The surface of the medium which is to be iced is also worthy of consideration. If the fondant

icing is poured onto an absorbent surface like a sponge, the moisture quickly migrates from the fondant to the sponge, resulting in a drying out of the icing with a loss of gloss. To prevent this, cake surfaces should be coated either with a layer of marzipan or boiled apricot purée.

2 Several things may be added to fondant to improve its gloss and flavour.

(a) *To improve gloss*   *Quantity*
   *Gelatine   1 oz (30 g) gelatine solution
                                    per lb

   *Piping jelly   Up to 2 oz (60 g) per lb
   Marshmallow   2 oz (60 g) per lb

(b) *To improve flavour*   *Quantity*
   Unsweetened couverture   Up to 3 oz (90 g) per lb
   (block chocolate)
   Instant coffee   Up to ½ oz (15 g) per lb
   Liquid coffee concentrate   Up to 1 oz (30 g) per lb
   Fruit, chocolate, or coffee ⎫
   Combined colour and   ⎪ To required taste
     flavour (combienne)   ⎬ according to strength of
   Essences   ⎪ concentrate
   Essential oils   ⎪
   Fruit juice concentrates or purée ⎭
   Juice of tinned fruit or citrus   Use as syrup for reducing
     fruit   fondant to required
                                     consistency

3 A product is available which is fondant in powder form and is reconstituted by adding a certain quantity of water. By replacing this water with fruit juice, a deliciously flavoured icing may be made.

* These additives will affect the consistency and must be taken into account when the syrup is added.

Fudge icings

By adding butter or fat to fondant, a soft fudge-like icing may be made. A recipe for a typical fudge icing is as follows.

A
4½ oz (135 g) butter
8 oz (240 g) fondant
½ oz (15 g) evaporated milk

B
1 oz (30 g) evaporated milk

1 Warm and blend together ingredients A above.
2 Add B and blend to a smooth icing.

Note: When warm (100°F (38°C)), it may be used as fondant. When cold it may be beaten and used as a buttercream.

Fondant sweets
(Figure 70)

Yield approximately 30 sweets.
These may be used for petits fours.

1 lb (480 g) fondant
2½ oz (75 g) condensed milk
½ oz (15 g) yeast water
Flavour and colour

Yeast water

1 oz (30 g) yeast
3 oz (90 g) water

Method 1 (for fondant drops)

1 Heat the fondant mixture to 150°F (65°C).
2 Transfer the fondant to a greaseproof paper cornet or savoy bag and pipe out bulbs onto silicone paper or a tray, well-floured with cornflour.
3 When set, remove the drops and store in a dry place for use as petits fours.

Method 2 (for shapes and chocolate centres)

1 For this a tray approximately 1½ in (4 cm) deep is required to be filled with corn starch.
2 In this starch impressions are made by pressing in a series of mould shapes. As an alternative one can use a special rubber mould which already has the impressions and is flexible to enable the fondants to be removed easily.
3 Fill a dropping funnel (Figure 70) with fondant and fill the impressions left in the starch or rubber mould.
4 When set, carefully remove the fondant shapes brushing off any starch which adheres.
5 Keep these shapes in a dry place until required.

There are usually two uses for these shapes as follows.

Crystallized fondants

Crystallizing syrup

1 lb 6 oz (660 g) sugar
½ pt (3 dl) water

Boil to 224°F (106°C).
Dissolve the sugar before boiling point is reached. Boil rapidly and strictly observe sugar boiling precautions. Cool at room temperature and check with saccharometer: it should be 33° Baumé. Store without any disturbance in a cool place.

1 Remove all traces of starch from the fondants. Place them on a draining wire and rest the wire in a shallow tray.
2 Gently pour the crystallizing syrup over the fondants, until they are completely covered.

3 Leave undisturbed for at least 6 hours, during which time a uniform layer of crystals will have formed around each fondant.
4 When the fondants are sufficiently covered with crystals, remove them from the wire and allow to drain for at least 4 hours.
5 Remove to a dry place and allow a further 12–16 hours for them to dry thoroughly.

Chocolate centres

1 Temper the chocolate (see page 234).
2 With a fork dip each centre into the chocolate, wipe off the surplus adhering to the bottom, and place on waxed, grease-proof or silicone paper to set.
3 Decorate using chocolate or crystrallized fruits, etc.

Stock syrup (for reducing fondant, etc.)

1 pt (6 dl) water
1 lb 8 oz (720 g) sugar

Bring the water and sugar to the boil, remove any scum, and store in a clean jar for future use.

Figure 70   *Fondant sweets and centres. Depositing warm fondant into rubber moulds for making sweets and centres*

Nougat (croquant)

Recipe 1

12 oz (360 g) sugar
4 oz (120 g) confectioners' glucose
12 oz (360 g) nibbed almonds

1 Stir the sugar and glucose over gentle heat until all sugar has dissolved and melted.
2 Raise the temperature and cook until pale amber in colour.
3 Warm and then stir in the almonds and remove mixture from the heat.
4 Turn out on to a greased or oiled slab and keep turning it over with a palette knife until cool enough to mould.

Recipe 2

1 lb (480 g) sugar
Juice of ½ lemon
12 oz (360 g) nibbed almonds

1 Stir the sugar and lemon juice over gentle heat until all the sugar has dissolved and melted.
2 Proceed as for Recipe 1.

Note: For the best decorative effect, the sugar should be amber in colour before the almonds are added so that there is a contrast between the dark colour of the sugar and the white of the almonds. However, the almonds may be added slightly earlier and cooked with the sugar to the desired colour when the almonds will also become browned. Alternatively, browned nibbed almonds may be added.

Uses of nougat

Moulding

For moulding purposes the nougat must not be allowed to go cold, otherwise it will set and become brittle. As soon as it is cool enough to handle, it should be shaped or rolled or cut out into the required pieces. Oil should be used to prevent the nougat from sticking to the slab, rolling pin, or knife. If it becomes hard and brittle before the final shaping or cutting has been done, it may be softened by placing it in a hot oven. To cement the pieces together for making a basket, etc., hot boiled sugar should be used or alternatively chocolate or royal icing.

Nougat baskets or centrepieces may be decorated either with pulled sugar (flowers, leaves, ribbon, etc.) or with royal icing. They make an attractive centrepiece for a table and provide a base on which to display petits fours, etc.

Decorative shapes

Gâteaux and torten may be decorated using shapes cut out from a sheet of nougat.

Masking

When set, nougat is easily crushed with a rolling pin. This should then be placed first in a coarse sieve to remove the very large particles (which need re-crushing) and then through a medium sieve to retain an even-sized number of nougat nibs. These are used as a dressing for masking the sides of gâteaux or torten.

Ingredients

The fine particles and dust may be mixed into fresh cream, buttercream, or ice-cream for flavouring purposes.

Paste

By putting this crushed nougat through a mill, a fine paste may be made which may also be used for flavouring purposes (praline).

Nougat Montelimart

14 oz (420 g) sugar
4 oz (120 g) water
4 oz (120 g) honey
4 oz (120 g) confectioners' glucose
1½ oz (45 g) egg whites
2 oz (60 g) chopped cherries
2 oz (60 g) pistachio nuts or green nib almonds
1 oz (30 g) nibbed almonds or hazelnuts
1 oz (30 g) flaked almonds or hazelnuts

1 Boil the sugar and water rapidly to 225°F (107°C).
2 Add the honey and glucose and continue to boil as rapidly as possible to 275°F (135°C).
3 Whip the egg whites to a stiff snow and then beat in the hot syrup. Continue beating until the mixture becomes firm in consistency. This operation is best done on a machine.
4 Warm the cherries and nuts and blend into the mixture.
5 Pour this mixture into a wafer paper-lined tray or frame, spread level, and cover the surface also with wafer paper.
6 Press down the surface with a weighted flat board and leave until perfectly cold, preferably overnight.
7 Cut into suitable sized pieces with a damp hot knife.

Petits fours

Small pieces of nougat Montelimart make ideal petits fours. They should be cut into small rectangles, turned over so that the cut surface shows, and then the base and sides dipped into chocolate.

Rock sugar

This is used for decorative effect on Christmas cakes, etc.

1 lb (480 g) sugar
6 oz (180 g) water
¾ oz (25 g) royal icing (well beaten)

1 Boil the sugar and water to 280°F (138°C) observing the sugar boiling precautions (see page 264).
2 Take the saucepan off the heat and remove surface heat by plunging the base into cold water.

3 Add the well beaten royal icing and mix quickly and thoroughly.
4 Pour quickly into a well greased bowl. When the royal icing is introduced into the boiling sugar syrup, there is considerable frothing and when it is transferred to the bowl, the mixture will rise rapidly, puffing out steam and looking much like an active stream of lava from a volcano. When it is set firm and is cool, it may be broken into pieces.

Note: For coloured rock sugar, use coloured royal icing.

Sugar boiling

The art of sugar boiling is usually acquired by patissiers through experience but is often little understood, and when faults are experienced the knowledge to ensure their correction is sometimes lacking. Therefore, before dealing with recipes and methods, some technical detail is given.

Equipment required for sugar boiling

Copper saucepans
Sugar-boiling thermometer
Scissors
Snippers
Spirit lamp
Fast table fan
Infra-red lamp
Fine sieve
Canvas
Blowing tubes, different sizes, with puffing bellows
Copper tube of $\frac{1}{8}$ in (3 mm) bore
Rolling pins, large and small
Modelling tools
Bunch of wire for spun sugar
Dipping forks for petits fours
Palette knife for turning sugar
Chisel scraper for turning sugar
Marble slab
Sugar nippers to hold sugar for warming
Knife for warming and cutting sugar
Thick plastic sheet

Some uses of boiled sugar

Fondant
Fudge, toffees
Boiled and other sweets
Dipping and glazing petits fours
Pulled sugar work
Spun sugar
Blown sugar work
Sugar models
Cast sugar

Marshmallow
Italian meringue
Nougat
Rock sugar

Theory of sugar boiling

The sugar used for this purpose is commonly known as cane sugar. It can exist in many crystalline forms (see page 23) but because it can easily become contaminated with dust from the atmosphere, preserving or lump sugar is preferred as this is sugar in its purest state. Whether cane sugar exists as a powder or a cube it is the same chemical substance called *sucrose*.

If a solution of sugar receives prolonged boiling, the sucrose undergoes a chemical change. First another molecule of water is added, and then the chemical structure is broken down into two simpler sugar molecules.

These are *dextrose* and *levulose*. Combined they form *invert* sugar, and it is largely the properties of this mixture which affects the characteristics of boiled sugar. We call this change *'inversion'*.

The change from sucrose to invert sugar by boiling is increased by the presence of an acid which acts as a catalyst. This is the reason that lemon juice or tartaric or citric acid is often used. The rate of boiling also has an effect upon the amount of inversion which takes place. The slower the boil the more invert sugar will be produced.

Crystallization

Another vital factor to be given the utmost consideration in sugar boiling is that of crystallization. To produce a saturated solution of sugar, we require approximately twice as much sugar as water but, because sugar can *melt* as well as dissolve, it is possible to get into solution by boiling three parts of sugar to one part of water. Such a solution is termed *super-saturated* and has certain properties.

If agitated, a super-saturated solution will crystallize out and give a mass of coarse grained crystals. We call this process *'graining'*. We can control the size of the crystals formed in this process in two ways: by adding sugar of a certain granular size, or by carefully controlling the rate of inversion. Since invert sugar does not readily crystallize, it follows that the more sucrose that can be 'inverted', the less sugar will remain to be crystallized. In fact, crystallization can be completely inhibited by inversion, particularly in the presence of acid. Examples of how we use these theories in practice may be given thus:

1 In fondant making, we agitate a super-saturated solution of sugar which has been boiled to 240°F (115°C) in order to produce a white thick mass which is in reality millions of minute light reflecting crystals of sugar.
2 When making fudge and cast sugar, a proportion of fondant is stirred into the mixture in order to bring about the production of fine crystals.
3 In pulled sugar, great care is required *not* to over-agitate and so induce premature crystallization.

Another substance used by sugar confectioners to modify or inhibit crystallization of the sugar syrup, is *confectioners' glucose.* This is a manufactured product, being a thick white viscous syrup containing a high percentage of dextrose along with other sugars and the gum dextrin. Many confectioners use this substance in preference to acid which can tend to carry the inversion too far. The recipes available vary in the quantities of glucose used. The glucose itself varies in its constituents and therefore the amount can vary according to its quality. For sugar boiling a glucose with a low DE (dextrose equivqalent) figure of 34 or 42 should be used.

The boiling process

Besides the chemical changes which take place, there is also a very apparent physical change which occurs. As boiling of the sugar syrup proceeds, some of the water evaporates and the resulting syrup becomes more viscous, resulting in the syrup setting firm when cold. As the syrup becomes thicker, so its boiling temperature progressively increases and so we can determine its temperature by its physical state. Indeed many experienced sugar confectioners and patissiers test their sugar by its physical state (as outlined below) instead of using a thermometer.

Hand tests for sugar boiling

Temperature °F	°C	Name of degree	How to test
220	104.5	Boiling	Effervescence
225	107	Thread degree	Touch the surface of the boiling sugar with a dry finger. Join the thumb and this finger together and separate them. An elastic thread of sugar will be formed
230	110	Pearl degree	Repeat the foregoing. The sugar will form a pearl-like bead at the ends of the thread as it breaks
235	113	Blow	When a loop of wire is inserted into the syrup and removed, a thin film will be produced which can be gently blown
240	115	Feather	At this stage the film of sugar syrup can be blown into feather-like pieces

Up to this stage, the syrup is still fairly thin although it is becoming noticeably thicker. To test the next few stages, it is necessary to take out some of the syrup and shock-cool it by plunging it into cold water to test its characteristics. This is done with the fingers by first immersing them in cold water, then plunging them into the syrup for just as long as it takes to collect a little of the syrup, then quickly putting them back into cold water again. The syrup will set and can be worked with the fingers.

Temperature °F °C	Name of degree	How to test
245 118	Soft ball	The syrup at this stage sets into a very plastic ball when mani--pulated with the fingers
250 121	Hard ball	A very much firmer ball is now formed. At this stage the syrup is becoming really thick and the temperature rises rapidly
270– 132– 280 138	Soft crack	The ball of sugar which is formed at this temperature forms a thin skin which will crack slightly
280– 138– 310 154	Hard crack	The ball of sugar now sets with a very thick skin which requires considerably pressure before it is shattered. (Many patissiers crunch this ball of sugar with their teeth to ascertain the correct degree)

Beyond this stage, the syrup begins to turn to a pale and then a dark amber colour emitting acrid fumes, until eventually a very dark, almost black, mass is formed.

310– 154– 350 177	Caramel	Very dark amber colour

Notes:
1 If glucose or acid is used, this should be added at 220°F (104°C).
2 The above sugar boiling degrees are only approximate and there are of course differences which can be detected between the extremes of 250–270°F and 310–350°F. Only a sugar boiling thermometer can give an accurate indication of the true temperature and its use is to be strongly recommended. In the final stages, the temperature at which the sugar syrup finally boils or colours is also modified by the percentage of inversion which has taken place and the percentage of confectioners' glucose or invert sugar (for example, honey) used in the initial syrup. This is because invert sugar and dextrose colour at a much lower temperature than sucrose.

Storage of boiled sugar

Boiled sugar is very hygroscopic, that is, it takes up moisture from the air. If left for a length of time, particularly in a damp atmosphere, it will first become sticky and then lose its shape. Under extreme conditions the boiled sugar will actually make a syrup with the water it absorbs and run away. This is particularly prevalent in dipped fruits and spun sugar. (The hygroscopic

4 Repeat the process for as many times as is necessary for sufficient spun sugar to be made.
5 Collect the spun sugar and use immediately to prevent spoilage due to dampness in the atmosphere.

Pulled sugar

1 Boil the sugar to the degree required, strictly observing the sugar boiling precautions.
2 If the whole of the sugar is to be the same colour (see note below) add it in the pan (*beware of steam!*), shaking carefully and then pouring out. Otherwise pour out on to a clean, slightly oiled slab and add colour as required to various portions.
3 When cool enough, fold the outsides to the centre. Continue to do this ensuring that no hard pieces are allowed to form. A uniform heat throughout is the aim.
4 When cool enough to handle start pulling by holding the sugar with one hand and pulling with the other, folding over and over so as to incorporate air and develop a silky sheen. (As long as the sugar mass is kept moving, it refrains from setting, an important factor to remember.)
5 Once the sugar is in a satisfactory conditions, it may be placed either at the mouth (opening) of an oven or at a suitable distance under an infra-red lamp.
6 This is the bulk of pulled sugar with which to work. It must be kept turned every so often to maintain uniform heat and to keep it in a solid mass. Small pieces rapidly heat up and will cause the sugar to crystallize.

Note – adding colour: Because most liquid colours contain acid which might affect the boiled sugar, it is advisable to use powdered colour mixed with a little water and added when the temperature is 257°F (125°C), so that the water boils away before the sugar reaches the final temperature.

Finished shapes like vases, fruits and flowers may also have coloured sprayed on with the air brush (see page 91).

Making flowers and leaves

Boil the sugar syrup to 290°F (143°C).

Petals (Figure 72)

Pull petals by squeezing, with thumb and first finger, the edge of a ball of sugar, making a curling twist to give a rounded edge. Pinch off with the nail of the thumb and forefinger. The edge must be as thin as possible. Ensure that the petals are cool enough to set into their pulled shape.

Roses

Make enough petal shapes to complete the rose. Build up the centre with two petals. Place three other petals around, sticking them to the centre stem by heating the base of each petal with a spirit flame. A good commercial rose may be made with five petals.

Carnations

The petals are pulled in a similar way to the rose. Cut the thin edge with inner part of a pair of scissors and quickly twist it into an S shape. Make a calyx with green sugar and on to this stick the petals in a circle. Alternate white and red petals make a good combination. For white carnations, red spots in the centre make an interesting flower.

Stems (Figure 73)

For these, thin strong wire is required. It should be pulled through the warm pulled sugar and, as it is covered, quickly shaped. Galvanized wire should first be 'burned off'. 'Tendril' shapes may be made by coiling the sugar pieces around a rod.

Leaves (Figure 72)

The sugar should be pulled into a leaf shape, i.e. round, pointed, etc. Mark in the veins of the leaf with the back of the knife and pinch round the edges if necessary. Autumn leaves can be made by partly mixing red and green sugars.

A mould can be made from metal which may be used to impress leaf shapes and veins.

Other flowers

Many other flowers may be made by copying originals, e.g. pansies, violets, anemones, daisies, etc. Careful use of colour can make them look very natural.

Orchids are made by forming a calyx, two large and three long narrow petals. They may be formed to shape by use of a rolling pin. The pistil is formed from a roll of sugar. A realistic appearance can be obtained with the right shading of colour.

Metal moulds are now available for the production of special shapes such as flowers and leaves, etc. To use, they are first immersed in iced water to cool, quickly dried with a cloth, momentarily dipped into the boiled sugar and taken out. The sugar shape sets on the mould and can be removed almost immediately.

Cabinet for boiled sugar work

Figure 78 shows a purpose built cabinet for boiled sugar work. It houses an infra-red heating lamp above a thick plastic sheet attached to a frame at the base. The height of the lamp can be adjusted so that the sugar is kept in the right temperature conditions for pulling and blowing.

Ribbons and bows
(Figure 74)

Boil the sugar syrup to at least 300°F (149°F). Use the sugar boiling recipe for storage.

1 Make strips of sugar sufficiently thick of two or more colours, for example red and white.

2 Press together and draw out carefully on a bench. Make sure that the sugar is uniform in thickness and wide enough to pull out.

3 Rub the piece down well to keep flat and uniform as the piece gets thinner and thinner.

4 After pulling a little, cut into two and press the two white edges forming a red edged ribbon. For multi stripes repeat again.

5 The ribbon must be pulled steadily at a fair speed, otherwise it will set and crack before it is thin or long enough.

6 Cut into strips of pieces which can be handled, and when warm place in position.

7 For bows, cut sufficient small pieces, warm, and make into loops, one for the centre and four for the bows.

8 Warm with the spirit lamp and put the ends of the loops inside the centre loop.

Note: The pulled sugar can be cut by the use of an old knife heated over the spirit lamp so that it melts the sugar as it is cut.

Figure 72 *Pulled sugar. Making flower petals and leaves. A spirit lamp and a leaf mould are also shown in the foreground*

Baskets
(Figures 75 and 79)

These are usually displayed on a banqueting table filled with petits fours or pulled sugar flowers.

Simple baskets

Roll out the pulled sugar and form it over an oiled tin shape. The edges may be pinched afterwards.

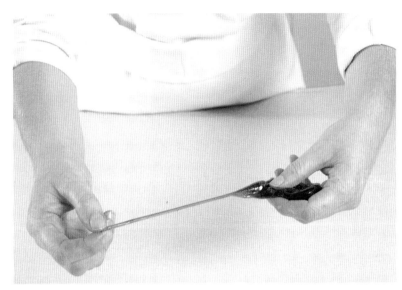

Figure 73 *Pulled sugar. Making stems*

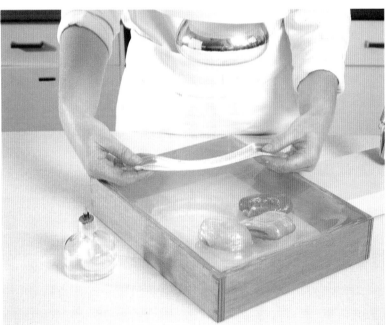

Figure 74 *Pulled sugar. Making ribbon and bows*

Woven baskets (Figure 75)

For these a base board is required fitted with an uneven number of pegs which are fairly loose and can easily be withdrawn. The board may be round or oval and both the board and the pegs should be oiled.

1 Work the sugar into a ball and then a pear shape.
2 Pull out a rope shape, keeping it uniform in thickness while coiling it in and out of the pegs. The thickness is kept uniform and at the same time the sugar is prevented from setting by twisting the sugar ball and rope end in the hand and pulling out

at the same time. Once the rope end starts to set, break off and warm slightly or restart with another ball.

3 When the basket has been woven to a sufficient height, pull some sugar into long rods to the thickness of the pegs.

4 Carefully remove the pegs and replace with the sugar rods, trimming the ends with a heated knife or a pair of small cutting pliers.

5 Prepare a base, either by rolling out pulled sugar or casting sugar into the right shape (see later).

6 Invert the basket and seal on to the base with liquid sugar.

7 Coil a rope of sugar round the top and seal off the end.

8 A handle can be made from strong flexible wire with pulled sugar coiled round in a spiral fashion (Figure 76).

Blown sugar

For this we use specialized equipment consisting of a rubber tube connected to a plastic nozzle at one end and a small hand pump at the other. This has a non-return valve to prevent air from escaping from the blown shape.

1 Boil the sugar syrup to at least 290°F (143°C).

2 Pull the sugar as previously described but keep flattening the sugar to press out any large air bubbles.

3 Cut off a bulb with scissors. Ensure that the surface is even and free from creases.

4 Press a small hole into the cut surface with the finger, heat it a little over the spirit lamp and, using two hands, attach the heated sugar firmly to the plastic tube of the pump.

5 Operate the pump and press some air into the sugar. If the sugar is not evenly warm, the warmer parts will expand more readily and it is necessary to cool those areas with the hands.

6 Use one hand to operate the pump whilst the other shapes the sugar.

7 Once the form has been achieved blow cold air on the shape with a fan or hair dryer to set the form quickly.

Note: It is important to keep the hands dry for both pulling and blowing. If they get damp or sticky it is recommended that rubber gloves be used.

Poured sugar work

Boiled sugar may be used to decorate by piping. A tube with a $1/16$-in (1.5-mm) hole in the end of the handle may be used to pour lines over sugar pieces to form a design. Bright colours may be used to give sparkle to such work.

It may also be poured criss-cross fashion over the back of an oiled ladle. The sugar sets almost immediately and can be removed to form a basket or cage which may be used to accompany individual sweets.

Cast sugar work
(Figure 81)

The casting of sugar is a relatively simple procedure although it is not necessarily easy to produce good results. It is the method used to make complete models.

We first need a mould made out of clay or plaster of Paris, constructed in sections, so that the sugar figure may be removed easily from the mould once cast.

The sugar is boiled to about 300°F (149°C) and then fondant is stirred into it so that the sugar will grain and solidify.

After pouring the sugar into the mould, allow time for draining and for it to solidify and then remove the mould section by section to release the sugar replica.

Using non-grained sugar

This is mainly used for flat moulds. These moulds are made from bent and formed 'band' metal, approximately ½ in (12 mm) wide, the strips being bent to a preconceived design with snipe-nosed pliers.

The shape is placed on oiled or silicone paper or film on a slab and the boiled sugar poured in to set (Figure 81). Use sugar boiling recipe for storage (page 265), boiled to 300°F (149°C).

If the sugar is clear it is possible to simulate 'stained glass windows'. For window displays it is usual to have an opaque sugar similar to the grained sugar. This is accomplished by mixing precipitated chalk into the sugar boil.

Different colours may be inserted by separating in sections; when one colour is cold, the other is poured in after removing the sectioning-off piece. Make sure any oil is wiped off to enable the sugar to join.

Other methods

1 Roll out plasticine, place on a design, and cut out. Oil the edges and pour in the sugar.
2 Use rubber sheeting of the required thickness (usually (¼ in (6 mm)). Make a template and cut out the required shape with a sharp cutter. Such moulds may be kept indefinitely and used repeatedly if stored correctly. Special moulds can also be purchased and their uses are illustrated in Figure 81.

Figure 75   *Pulled sugar. Making a basket*

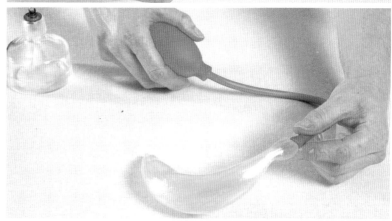

Figure 76   *Pulled sugar. Making a handle for the basket*

Figure 77   *Blowing sugar. Making a banana*

Figure 78   *Cabinet for boiled sugar work. Description in text*

Figure 79   *Pulled and blown sugar.*
Basket of blown sugar fruits

Figure 80   *A blown sugar*
vase decorated with
pulled sugar flowers

Figure 81   *Casting sugar. Pouring boiled sugar*
into rubber moulds

21 Preserves, creams and icings

Fruit preservation – jams, jellies, bottled fruit, sugar preserved fruits

In this technological age food preservation has been exploited to such an extent that all types of food are now available out of season and the patissier can usually buy most fruit, either dried, frozen, bottled, or tinned.

However, occasionally he may have to preserve a quantity of fruit for further use and in this case an understanding of this process is necessary.

Fruit may be preserved in the following ways:

1 Drying
2 Use of sugar
3 Sterilizing
4 Deep freezing
5 Use of preservatives.

Drying

This means the removal of water to the point at which micro-organisms and the natural process of decay cannot function or are slowed down. Not all fruits are suitable for this method of preservation although, with the comparatively recent advances in *accelerated freeze drying*, very good results have been obtained with fruits such as strawberries which were previously thought to be impossible to dry into an acceptable product. The drying process therefore, may be:

Normal hot air drying or natural sun drying

This is reserved for products such as dried apricots, peaches, apples, figs, etc. Such dried goods usually require a prolonged soaking (up to 24 hours) before being cooked.

Goods like dates, raisins, sultanas, etc., are usually used in their dried state, although in some cases it is an advantage for them to be soaked prior to use. The drying of many of the products in sun drenched lands is done by exposure to the sun.

Accelerated freeze drying

In this process, selected ripe fruit is first deep frozen. It is then placed into a vacuum oven between electrically heated plates. When the the deep frozen fruit is subjected to gentle heat in a vacuum oven, the moisture is rapidly removed by evaporation but in such a way that the tissue of the fruit does not collapse as it does in the normal air drying process. The dried fruit, therefore, retains its shape and size and has a porous texture.

On reconstitution, the fruit behaves exactly like a sponge, mopping up the water it lost in the drying process in a matter of minutes instead of hours. All that is necessary is for a carefully measured quantity of water to be poured on to the fruit to bring it back to almost the same state as fresh fruit. Some loss of colour and firmness may be detected but this is a small price to pay for the advantage of having any desired fruit out of season.

In the future we shall see an increased range of products being preserved in this manner.

Use of sugar

Sugar owes its powers of preservation to the fact that micro-organisms will not flourish in high sugar concentrations. Thus we can make jams and jellies which may be kept for a year or more. Confiture fruits and glacé and crystallized or candied fruits (see Chapter 20) may be kept much longer because they are impregnated with sugar to a very high concentration.

Sterilizing

This is the process adopted for bottling and canning. Since bottling is an easy and useful method for preserving fruit, fuller details are given below.

Fruit bottling

General rules

1 Always use sound fresh fruit slightly under rather than over-ripe. Large fruits should be halved or quartered.
2 Bottle in syrup rather than water so that the preserving power of sugar may be used and is allowed to penetrate the fruit. (If bottled in water and sweetened afterwards, the added sugar would merely sweeten the juice and not the flesh of the fruit, e.g. pears.)
3 Make sure that the bottles or jars and their seals are clean, dry, and in good condition.
4 The fruit should be heated gently to prevent it from breaking or rising in the jar and to ensure complete sterilization.

There are four methods of bottling:

Oven method
Sterilizer with thermometer
Sterilizer without thermometer
Pressure cooker

Oven method

1 Prepare the fruit and pack firmly, without bruising, into the clean dry bottles or jars.
2 Cover with a metal lid or saucer.
3 Place the jars, making sure that they do not touch, on slats of wood or an asbestos mat on a baking sheet in a low position in the oven. Alternatively, they may be placed in a shallow water bath.
4 Allow fruit to cook in a slow oven until the skins of the fruit begin to crack (between ¾–1¼ hours).
5 Remove the jars singly on to a folded cloth in a tray. If fruit shrinks during cooking top up from another jar.
6 Fill the jar gently with boiling syrup or water until it overflows.
7 Seal at once by any of the following methods:
   (a) Metal screw top with rubber ring and glass top.
   (b) A commercially manufactured metal cap.
   (c) A synthetic skin.
8 Leave undisturbed for 24 hours.
9 Test seal by unscrewing top and supporting the weight of the bottle by the seal.

Sterilizer with thermometer method

1 Proceed as for oven method.
2 Fill the jars to overflowing with either *cold* water or syrup.
3 Seal according to type. If using a screw top seal, first tighten then unscrew a half turn.
4 Making sure they do not touch, place the jars on a false bottom in a sterilizer, deep pan, or boiler.
5 Cover with cold water.
6 Apply heat and sterilize as follows:

Group	Fruit	Temperature after 1½ hours heating	Length of time to maintain temperature
A	Apples Apricots Blackberries Currants (red, black, and white) Gooseberries Loganberries Mulberries Peaches Raspberries Rhubarb Strawberries	165°F (74°C)	10 minutes

Group	Fruit	Temperature after 1½ hours heating	Length of time to maintain temperature
B	Apples (solid pack) Cherries Damsons Greengages Plums	180°F (83°C)	15 minutes
C	Pears Quinces Tomatoes (whole in brine)	190°F (88°C)	30 minutes

7 After cooking remove sufficient water to uncover the jars and lift them out one at time onto a cloth or slat of wood. Tighten the screw tops where necessary and leave undisturbed in a cool place. Re-tighten tops during cooling if required.

8 Test the seal after 24 hours.

Sterilizer without a thermometer method

1 Proceed as for previous method but use *hot* water or syrup for filling the jars.

2 Stand jars without touching in a water bath and completely submerge in warm water.

3 Apply heat to raise the temperature to simmering in 30 minutes and maintain for the following specified time:

Group A 2 minutes
Group B 10 minutes
Group C 20 minutes

Pressure cooking

The use of a pressure cooker will reduce the cooking time to about one-third of that of other methods. It is particularly useful for the bottling of vegetables. Details of bottling are usually given with each pressure cooker.

Pulping

Where there is a large quantity of blemished fruit a pulp may be made and preserved. This is particularly useful for the manufacture of jams and jellies.

1 Prepare the fruit by removing blemishes etc.

2 Using the minimum amount of water, stew to a pulp for at least 30 minutes.

3 Pour immediately into a very hot dry jar and seal. Complete each jar before proceeding with the next.
4 Immediately sterilize by placing it in a pan of boiling water to cover it completely. Allow to stand in the simmering water for 10 minutes.
5 Finish off as previously described.

Jams and jellies

Rather than give a large number of individual jam recipes, the process of jam making is explained as well as the factors which influence the formation of a jam recipe.

Jams and jellies are made by boiling together two basic ingredients – fruit and sugar in approximately equal quantities. The quality of the jam, however, and especially its ability to set, will depend upon the strength of a naturally occurring jellying agent called *pectin*. However, the concentration of sugar, presence of acid, and amount of moisture present also have an influence.

Pectin

This jellying agent is present naturally in all fruits but some fruits, such as strawberries and cherries, are deficient in this agent, whilst in others such as apple there is more than sufficient (see chart opposite). The pectin is extracted from the fruit during the boiling process but more will be extracted in an acid medium. In jam-making, fruits which are naturally deficient in pectin should always have an organic acid like tartaric or citric (or lemon juice) added. In commercial manufacture of jam, pectin derived from apple or citron may be added to fruits naturally deficient in this agent.

Sugar

The concentration of sugar needs to be between 63 and 66% to make a firm product and also one with sufficient preserving qualities. Below this concentration, jam is more likely to attack by wild yeasts which will ferment it (see later). However, since the sugar contributes to the setting quality of the jam, the actual quantity used will be dictated by the type of fruit used and its pectin content.

Fruit and vegetable jams

Fruit and vegetable	Acid content	Pectin content
Apple, cooking, sour	xx	xxx
Apple, dessert, acid varieties	xx	xx
Apple, crab	xx	xxx
Apple, sweet, full-ripe	0	0
Apple, sweet, full-ripe, some varieties	x	x
Apricot, ripe	x	0
Banana, unripe	0	x
Barberry	x	x
Bilberry	x	x
Blackberry, early, ripe	0–x	0–x
Blackberry, late	000	0
Blackberry, unripe, red	x	x
Bullace	xx	xx
Cherry, acid, Morello and May Duke	x	x
Cherry, cooking	0	0
Cherry, sweet, ripe	00	00
Cherry, sweet, unripe	x	x
Cranberry	xx	xx
Currant, black	xxx	xx
Current, red or white	xxx	xxx
Damson	xx	xx
Elderberry	0	0
Fig, ripe	00	00
Fig, unripe	0	x
Gooseberry, green	xx	xxx
Grape, unripe	xx	xx
Greengage	x	x
Japonica	x	x
Lemon	xxx (in juice)	xxx (in pith and some in juice)
Lime	xx (in juice)	xx (in pith and some in juice)
Loganberry	xx	xx
Marrow (vegetable)	000	000
Medlar	00	0
Melon	0	x
Mulberry	xx	x
Nectarine	0	0
Orange, bitter	xxx (in juice)	xxx (in pith)
Peach, ripe	00	00
Peach, unripe	0	0
Pear, cooking	0	00
Pear, dessert, ripe	000	000

Fruit and vegetable	Acid content	Pectin content
Pineapple	xx	00
Plum, ripe, firm	x	x
Pomegranate	x	000
Pumpkin	000	000
Quince, ripe	00	xx
Quince, unripe	00	xx
Raspberry	0	0
Raspberry, some varieties, unripe	x	x
Rhubarb	0–x	0
Rowan, mountain ash berries	xx	x
Sloe	xx	x
Strawberry	x	000
Strawberry, some varieties	x	0
Tomato	x	0

x = high   xx = very high   xxx = extremely high content
0 = low   00 = very low   000 = extremely low content

Sugar quantity

	Amount of sugar per lb (480 g) fruit
Fruits rich in pectin (apple, gooseberry, black currant, damson, red currant, etc.	1 lb 4 oz (600 g)
Fruits with medium pectin content (greengage, apricot, plum, etc.)	1 lb (480 g)
Fruits deficient in pectin (strawberry, rhubarb, marrow, blackberry, etc.)	12 oz (360 g)

Acid quantity

Fruit deficient in acid should always have some acid added (see chart, on page 279). The acid may be added as follows to each 2 lb fruit:
1 ½ lemon or 1 tablespoonful of lemon juice.
2 ½ level teaspoonful of citric or tartaric acid.
3 ⅛ pt (75 g) gooseberry or red currant juice.

Water quantity

For hard fruits, such as plum, damson, apricot, and gooseberry, up to ½ pt (3 dl) of water should be added and the fruit stewed gently before the sugar is added in order to soften the skins. Soft fruits, such as strawberry, raspberry, apple, and blackberry, require no water.

General method for making jam

1 Select sound ripe fresh fruit. The fruit is better under-ripe than over-ripe.
2 Wash and prepare. Large fruits need halving or quartering.
3 Place the fruit (and acid if used) in the boiling pan and, if it is a hard fruit, give a preliminary stewing.
4 Add the sugar and gently heat until the sugar is completely dissolved. Stir to prevent sugar burning on bottom of pan.
5 Once the sugar has dissolved, boil as rapidly as possible until the setting point of the jam is reached.
6 The setting point of the jam will vary according to the type of fruit used and may be between 2–20 minutes. Test as follows:
   (a) Remove the spoon with some jam and allow it to fall off back into the pan. When setting point is reached the last cooled drops of jam should form a flake.
   (b) Test by allowing a few drops of jam to fall on to a dry plate and leave in a cool place to set. If pushed with the fingers the surface of the jam should wrinkle.
7 Once setting point has been reached, skim carefully and remove stones.
8 Allow jam to cool slightly to thicken so that whole fruit, for example strawberries, will remain evenly suspended and not rise to the top of the jar.
9 Stir and then fill clean, dry, warm jars.
10 Cover surface of jam at once with a waxed paper disc.
11 Lastly put on the final cover, label with the type of jam and date of manufacture, and store in a cool place.

Faults in jam

1 *Sugar crystallizing.* This will happen if:
Concentration of sugar is too high.
There is insufficient acid present.
Jam has been insufficiently boiled.
Jam has been too long in storage.
2 *Mould formation on surface.* Mould growth will occur on almost any medium which is moist and left in still air. It only requires one mould spore to find its way to the jam before it is covered for a luxurious growth of mould to appear eventually. The jam must be sealed whilst still very hot to prevent contamination by the mould spores floating in the air. Jam contaminated with mould is not harmful. The mould can be removed from the surface of the jam which will leave the remainder quite wholesome and fit for use.
3 *Fermentation.* This is caused by the presence of wild yeast cells which will reproduce on the jam causing an evolution of carbon-dioxide gas. It can be traced to contamination at the covering stage, although jam already opened is much more likely to be attacked and to ferment.
   Watery jams, where the sugar concentration is low, are much more prone to attack of this kind.
   If jam is opened for any length of time before it is used, it is always a wise precaution to bring it to the boil before use.

Fermented jam is usually completely spoiled, having an objectionable sour acid taste.

4 *Too thick.* (a) Too much sugar. (b) Insufficient water.

5 *Too watery.* (a) Not enough pectin. (b) Insufficient sugar. (c) Insufficient acid. (d) Too much water added.

6 *Poor colour.* All fruits lose a certain amount of colour when they are cooked and this is reflected in the jam they produce. Most jam manufacturers use artificial colours to make their jam brighter and the private producer can do the same. However, the presence of a dirty colour in jam is usually because it has not been boiled properly or it has become contaminated by a dirty pan.

7 *Opaqueness.* Jam and jellies should be clear and almost transparent. Opaqueness is a sign that the boiling was unduly prolonged or that there is some contamination. Premature crystallization of the sugar will also cause this to happen.

Some selected jam recipes

Apricots (made from dried apricots)

8 oz (240 g) dried apricots
1½ pt (9 dl) water
Juice of ½ lemon
1 lb 8 oz (720 g) sugar

1 Wash the dried fruit thoroughly.
2 Place in a basin with the water and allow it to soak for at least 24 hours.
3 Place the fruit and the liquor in which it has been soaked in a preserving pan and add the lemon juice.
4 Bring to the boil and boil gently for ½ hour, stirring occasionally.
5 Add the sugar and continue boiling until the setting point of the jam has been reached. Stir constantly.
6 Fill the jars and immediately cover.

Note: This jam can be sieved to make an ideal purée for glazing and other purposes.

Greengage/apricot/ peach/plum/damson

1 lb (480 g) fruit
1 lb (480 g) sugar
¼ pt (1½ dl) water

Same method as for apricot jam, using water to stew and soften fruit before adding sugar.

Green gooseberry/ black currant

1 lb (480 g) fruit
1 lb 8 oz (600 g) sugar
8 oz (240 g) water

Same method as for apricot jam, using water to stew and soften fruit before adding sugar.

Strawberry

1 lb (480 g) fruit
12 oz (360 g) sugar
Juice of ½ lemon

1 Cut strawberries in half. This helps in the extraction of their limited pectin content.
2 Gently simmer with the lemon juice.
3 Add sugar and boil rapidly until setting point is reached.

Notes:
1 Instead of lemon juice, a teaspoonful of tartaric acid may be used or 2 oz (60 g) red currant juice.
2 Because of this jam's poor setting properties, it is often blended with jams which are rich in pectin, for example apple, red currant, etc.

Strawberry (using red currant to aid setting and increase bulk)

1 lb (480 g) strawberries
8 oz (240 g) red currants
1 lb (480 g) sugar

1 Wash and string the red currants, place them into a pan with a little water, and simmer gently until tender.
2 Pass through a cloth or hair sieve to obtain the juice.
3 Add to the washed strawberries and sugar and proceed to make the jam as previously described.

Raspberry/loganberry

1 lb (480 g) fruit
1 lb (480 g) sugar

Same method as for strawberry jam.

Note: It is best to use under-ripe fruit for this recipe.

Raspberry and red currant

8 oz (240 g) raspberries
8 oz (240 g) red currants
1 lb (480 g) sugar
⅓ pt (2 dl) water

1 Wash and string the red currants and place in the preserving pan with the raspberries.
2 Add the water and simmer on gentle heat until the fruit is cooked.
3 Add the sugar and proceed to make the jam as previously described.

Marmalade

1 lb (480 g) seville (bitter) oranges
3 lb (1440 g) sugar
3 pt (18 dl) water
½ lemon

1 Wash, wipe the oranges and cut in half.
2 Remove the pips, tying them in a muslin bag.

Recipe 2 (opaque)

Apricot purée
Fondant

Use equal quantities in same method as Recipe 1. Adjust consistency with stock syrup.

Red glaze

1 Use sieved red currant or raspberry jam or jelly instead of apricot.
2 Colour arrowroot glaze (see below) with red colour.

Arrowroot glaze

1 pt (6 dl) fruit juice
1 oz (30 g) arrowroot
Sugar (depending on sweetness of fruit)
Colour and flavour

1 Mix arrowroot with a little of the fruit juice.
2 Boil the remainder and gently pour it on the diluted arrowroot stirring continuously.
3 Pass through a strainer.
4 Use while still hot.

Jelly glaze

1 pt (6 dl) water
¾ oz (20 g) gelatine
2 level teaspoonsful citric acid
6 oz (180 g) sugar
Colour and flavour

1 Heat the water and stir in the gelatine.
2 Add the sugar, acid, and flavour.
3 Use when the glaze is near to setting.

Royal icing – Glacé Royale

3 oz (90 g) egg whites pasteurized or processed albumen (see page 18)
1 lb (480 g) icing sugar
Lemon juice

1 Beat the egg whites with two-thirds of the sugar and the lemon juice until white and thick (approximately 10 minutes continuous beating).
2 Add the remaining sugar and beat until stiff.
3 Keep covered with a clean damp cloth to prevent skinning.

Notes:
1 The more beating the mixture has in 1, the less it will required in 2, and the easier it will be to beat.
2 Royal icing should not be too aerated, stiff enough to hold its shape and yet feel soft when piped out. When exposed to the atmosphere it will set very hard and brittle. If this is not required, a teaspoonful of glycerine may be added to the above recipe which will cause the icing to set much softer.
3 Royal icing may be used for the decoration of all types of cakes, nougat baskets, petits fours, etc.

Mirror glaze (for decoration of French torten)

Recipe 1

1 lb 4 oz (600 g) apricot jam
6 oz (180 g) glucose
3 oz (90 g) sugar

1 Heat all the ingredients to boiling point and then allow the mixture to cool to room temperature.
2 Whip on top speed for one minute.
3 Use as a topping for chocolate, vanilla and caramel gateaux.

Recipe 2

1 lb 4 oz (600 g) glaze
½ oz (15 g) cocoa powder

1 Same method as 1 above.
2 Use as a topping for chocolate gateaux.

Recipe 3

1 lb 4 oz (600 g) apricot jam
6 oz (180 g) glucose
9 oz (270 g) appropriate fruit purée

1 Same method as 1 above.
2 Use as a topping for fruit gateaux.

22 *Ices*

Process of making ices

Scrupulous cleanliness must be observed in every stage of ice-cream making because the materials used can so easily become contaminated and give rise to the development of food poisoning organisms. For the production of ice-cream, a special compartment should be reserved, appropriately fitted-out and kept solely for this purpose. Moreover, the equipment used should also be reserved solely for ice-cream making. An abundant supply of hot and cold water for washing purposes is also essential.

Modern ice cream freezers consist of a container which has a refrigerated jacket cooled by a refrigerant as used in a normal refrigerator. Inside the container is driven a tightly fitted paddle which stirs the mixture as it is being frozen, imparting smoothness as well as aeration.

Causes of faults

Good quality ice-cream should be perfectly smooth, free from any lumps, ice crystals, or sugar crystals, and be nicely aerated.

Lumps

1 Mixture was not sieved before placing in the freezing container.
2 Paddle does not make absolute contact with the sides and base so that some of the mixture is not being stirred.
3 Hard ice-cream is mixed with soft, that is, not all the mixture is of the same temperature.

Ice crystals

1 The action of the paddle is to break up and disperse the ice crystals as they form. If the mixture is left unstirred in a frozen condition in the initial stages of making, ice crystals will form.
2 The size of the ice crystals depends upon the speed and hence the temperature at which the mixture is frozen. The quicker the operation, the finer these crystals will be and the less risk of their detection in the finished ice-cream.
3 Sometimes water gets into the finished ice-cream (especially with tub equipment). In these circumstances, it is obvious that such water will form ice and this can become dispersed throughout the mixture.

The presence of small ice crystals in ice-cream is called 'sandiness' because this describes how the ice-cream feels and tastes. Slow freezing is usually the cause.

Sugar crystals

Since an ice-cream mixture contains sugar in solution, it follows that under certain circumstances, if the mixture contained too much sugar, the sugar could crystallize out. This rarely happens when the ice-cream contains glucose or acid, as in lemon ice-cream. If the mixture is made properly and then quickly frozen, this fault should not appear.

The use of the saccharometer to adjust the density of the sugar solution is described on page 250.

Storage of ice-cream

Ice-cream should be stored at the lowest temperature possible but in any event not higher than −5°F (−20°C). However, at this temperature the ice-cream is very hard and unsuitable for service. It should be brought out of storage deep freeze the day prior to service and stored at normal refrigerator temperature of 10–20°F −12 to −6°C) according to the type of ice-cream used and the consistency required for service.

Types of ices

Cream ices	– contain cream and/or milk.
Fruit or water ices	– made from fruit purée or pulp and stock syrup.
Fruit cream ices	– made from fruit purée or pulp, sugar, and cream and/or milk.
Special ice mixtures	– bombes, gateaux, cassatas, etc.
Other preparations	– coupes, sundaes, baked Alaska.

Yields

The number of portions obtained from ice-cream depends upon the size of the server used and the amount of aeration the ice-cream has received in its manufacture.

Many patissiers rely upon commercial ice-cream which can now be obtained in a good variety of flavours and combinations and is always of an excellent uniform standard. However, such ice-cream has to be economically produced to be sold at a competitive price and thus the variety tends to be limited and the quality restricted. Ice-cream made by the patissier can be of superior quality and a very good reputation can be built with specialities of the house. The following ice-cream recipes are of continental origin and well recommended for a first class restaurant.

Ice-cream

Vanilla ice-cream

1 pt (6 dl) milk
5 oz (150 g) cream
1 oz (30 g) confectioners' glucose
5 oz (150 g) sugar
4 oz (120 g) egg yolks
Vanilla essence

1 Whisk together the egg yolks, sugar, and essence.
2 Add the glucose to the milk and bring to the boil.
3 Whisk the boiling milk into the yolks and sugar and thoroughly blend together.
4 Transfer to a clean saucepan and gently heat (*do not boil*).
5 Stir the mixture continuously until it coats the back of the spoon.
6 Pass mixture through a fine sieve.
7 Leave to cool and then add the cream.
8 Freeze immediately.

Several different flavoured ice creams can be made from this basic recipe by deleting the vanilla and substituting other flavours as follows.

Chocolate ice-cream

Using 4 oz (120 g) chocolate couverture make a thick sauce with 1½ oz (45 g) stock syrup (see page 295). Stir this into hot milk, prior to it being added to the egg yolks and sugar.

Coffee ice-cream

Add ½ oz (15 g) instant coffee to the hot milk.

Praline ice-cream

Add a little of the hot milk to 2 oz (60 g) of praline paste and mix to a smooth thin paste. Mix this into the yolks and sugar before the hot milk is whisked in.

Pistachio ice-cream

Add:
2 oz (60 g) ground almonds
2 oz (60 g) ground pistachio nuts
1 oz (30 g) fondant
Maraschino essence
Green colour

Stir the mixed ground nuts into the yolks and sugar before the boiling milk is added. Dissolve the fondant in the boiling milk. Add appropriate quantity of flavour and colour to the mixture just prior to incorporating the cream.

Caramel ice-cream

Melt the sugar and glucose and heat until amber shade is reached. Add hot milk, a little at a time until the caramel mixture is dissolved. Add this to the beaten egg yolk and continue as previously described.

Fruit ices with cream

Strawberry or raspberry ice-cream

To the vanilla ice-cream recipe add:
½ pt (3 dl) strawberry or raspberry pulp
2 oz (60 g) sugar
Red colouring

Stir into the warm milk and egg mixture prior to adding the cream.

Banana ice-cream

5 large ripe bananas
1 pt (6 dl) stock syrup (see below)
½ pt (3 dl) cream
Juice of ½ lemon

1 Mash the bananas into a fine pulp and pass through a sieve.
2 Add the stock syrup to the bananas and adjust the density to 17°B with water (see page 250).
3 Add the lemon juice and lastly stir in the cream.
4 Freeze in the usual way.

Basic fruit ice recipe

1 pt (6 dl) fruit pulp
1 pt (6 dl) cream
1 pt (6 dl) milk
Sugar (see below)
1 lemon (juice only)
Colouring

1 Heat the fruit pulp, lemon juice, and sugar to about 200°F (93°C) stirring constantly.
2 Leave to cool.
3 Mix in the cream and milk and necessary colour.
4 Freeze.

Because different fruits contain different amounts of sugar, the sugar content of this recipe has to be adjusted accordingly as follows:

Raspberry and strawberry	12 oz (360 g)
Pineapple	10 oz (300 g)
Peach	10 oz (300 g)
Black cherry	8 oz (240 g)
Black currant	12 oz (360 g)
Orange and tangerine	10 oz (300 g)
Apricot	12 oz (360 g)

Stock syrup for ice-creams

½ pt (3 dl) water
1 lb (480 g) sugar

1 Bring the sugar and water to the boil.
2 Remove any scum.
3 Store in a clean jar for future use.

Punch à la Romaine

Yield 8 covers
This is the classical name given to sorbets in which dry, white wine or champagne is used for the mixing and rum (3 oz (90 g)) is added afterwards or poured over the sorbet prior to service.

Note: If a special fruit juice has been used, the sorbet may be named according to the fruit used, for example Lemon sorbet – Sorbet au citron.

Liqueur ice – Glacé au liqueurs

1 pt (6 dl) stock syrup
2 oz (60 g) liqueur
White wine or water

1 Mix the liqueur with the stock syrup.
2 Test with the saccharometer and adjust to 18°B by adding white wine or water.
3 Freeze in the usual way.
4 When served, a little of the liqueur may be sprinkled on.

Granites

Made in the same way as ordinary water ice but the density is adjusted to 12–14°B with water or wine. They should be granular in texture after freezing.

Marquises

These are sorbets in which the meringue has been replaced by unsweetened whipped cream.

Coupes and sundaes

Coupes and sundaes are made up from ice-cream, fruit, and a suitable sauce, and decorated with fresh whipped cream, fruit, nuts, etc. The fruit may be flavoured with liqueur or spirit. Coupes are served in special tall glasses or silver cups, whereas sundaes are served in shallow dishes. Both are usually accompanied with wafer biscuits or petits fours. It is wise to use cups or dishes which are large enough to prevent the contents spilling over the sides when they are eaten. The make-up of each coupe varies little but there are two basic ways as follows.

Method 1

1 Place the fruit in the base of the cup.
2 Cover with a scoop of ice-cream.
3 Pour over a suitable sauce.
4 Decorate with cream.
5 Garnish with fruit, nuts, chocolate, etc.

This method is usually reserved for macédoine of fruit.

Method 2

1 Place a scoop of ice-cream in the base of the cup.
2 Cover with the fruit.
3 Proceed as outlined in Method 1.

This method is used where whole or halves of fruit are used.

Notes:
1 Fruits must always have their stones, pips, and skin removed before putting into coupes or sundaes.
2 Where liqueur is mentioned this can also refer to wine or spirits. Fruit such as cherries and diced fruits is usually allowed to soak in the liqueur some hours beforehand. The liqueur is only poured on to solid fruit such as pear and peach halves.
3 Where two or more ice-cream mixtures are used, it is usual to place the fruit between.
4 Since many of the recipes are of continental origin, pistachio nuts are often mentioned. These are difficult to obtain and expensive, but an acceptable alternative is green coloured nib almonds.

Varieties of coupes and sundaes

The variety of coupes and sundaes which it is possible to make is enormous when one considers the number of permutations which can be made in the use of various flavoured ices, types of fruit, liqueurs, and sauces. A number of them are summarized on the following pages.

Name	Ice	Fruite base	Liqueur	Sauce	Decoration
Malmaison	Vanilla	Peeled and stoned grapes	–	Curaçao mousseline	Whipped cream, crystallized violets, and spun sugar
Marguerite	Strawberry	Half peach	–	–	Whipped cream and wild strawberries
Marie Brizard	Coffee and anisette	Cherries	–	–	–
Marie Louise	Vanilla	Raspberries	–	Raspberry	Whipped cream
Marquise	Vanilla	Strawberries	–	Melba	Whipped cream and wild strawberries
Mercédès	Vanilla	Apricots	–	–	Chartreuse whipped cream and shredded chocolate
Metternich	Raspberry	Diced pineapple	–	–	Vanilla whipped cream
Mexicaine	Tangerine	Pineapple	–	–	–
Midinette	Vanilla	Half peach on small meringue shell	–	Kirsch-Melba	Whipped cream
Mireille	Half vanilla, half red currant	Stoned nectarines and white currants	–	–	Whipped cream
Miramar	Pineapple	Diced pineapple and tangerine	Kirsch	Chartreuse mousseline	Serve with savoy biscuits
Miss Helyett	Raspberry	Apricot	–	–	Vanilla whipped cream
Mistinguette	Almond and strawberry	Macédoine	Cointreau	–	Rosettes of whipped cream and a green cherry
Mizette	Vanilla	Half peaches	Curaçao mousseline	–	Whipped cream and strawberries
Monte Carlo	Pistachio	Macédoine	Kirsch	–	–
Monte Cristo	Lemon and pistachio	Diced peach, orange, and banana	Kirsch	–	–
Montmorency	Vanilla	Cherries	Kirsch	Melba	Raspberry whipped cream
Montreveille	Vanilla	Half peach	–	Apricot	Whipped cream
Morland	Apricot	Diced melon	–	Apricot	Whipped cream
Moscovite	Almond with chopped glacé fruits	Cherries	Kümmel	Raspberry	Whipped cream and roasted nib almonds
Mozart	Vanilla and almond	Sliced peaches	–	Raspberry	Whipped cream and roasted nib almonds
Nébuleuse	Chocolate	Cherries	–	Kirsch–raspberry	Whipped cream, praline nibs, and crystallized violets
Niçoise	Orange	Macédoine	Curaçao or Grand Marnier	–	–

Name	Ice	Fruite base	Liqueur	Sauce	Decoration
Nina	Vanilla	Strawberries	–	Curaçao mousseline	Whipped cream. Cover with spun sugar
Orientale	Pineapple	Diced pineapple	–	Apricot	Whipped cream and roasted nib almonds
Petit Duc	Vanilla and lemon	Red currants and half peach	–	–	–
Princesse	Praline and orange	Raspberries	–	–	Whipped cream and strawberries
Princesse Olga	Apricot	Strawberries	–	Kümmel mousseline	Whipped cream and crystallized violets
Rêve de Bébé	Pineapple and strawberry	Strawberries soaked in orange juice	–	–	Whipped cream and crystallized violets
Rose Chéri	Pineapple	Strawberries	–	White wine sabayon	Crystallized roses
Royale	Vanilla	Macédoine	–	–	–
Sans Gêne	Vanilla	Red currants	–	–	Whipped cream
Savoy	Coffe and praline	Raspberries	–	Anisette mousseline	Crystallized violets
Silésienne	Vanilla	Marron glacé	Kirsch	–	Whipped cream
Stella	Vanilla	Half apricot on meringue shell	–	Apricot	Pistachio nuts
Suzanne	Pineapple	Diced pineapple	Rum	Red currant	Whipped cream
Tétrazzini	Pistachio	Half peach	–	Raspberry mousseline	Whipped cream and orange segments
Thaïs	Vanilla	Macédoine and marron glacé	Kirsch	–	Whipped cream
Tripolitaine	Strawberry and lemon	Diced peach, orange, and strawberry	–	–	–
Tutti Frutti	Strawberry, pineapple, and lemon	Macédoine	Kirsch	–	–
Vénus	Vanilla	Half peach	–	Curaçao mousseline	Whipped cream, strawberries, and spun sugar
Verdoot	Vanilla	Half peach, strawberries, and raspberries	–	Quince jelly	Crystallized violets
Victoria	Half strawberry, half pistachio	Macédoine	Champagne	–	–
Zaza	Raspberry	Quartered fig	–	Apricot	Whipped cream

Sundaes

Name	Ice	Fruit base	Liqueur	Sauce	Decoration
Créole	Lemon	Diced pineapple and banana	Rum	–	Chantilly cream
Banana Royal	Vanilla	Banana split lengthwise	–	–	Whipped cream, crushed pineapple, chopped walnuts, and glacé cherry
Imperial Palace	Ginger and pistachio	Stoned and diced lychees	–	–	Maraschino whipped cream and chopped walnuts
Longchamps	Vanilla and pistachio	Three savoy biscuits soaked in Benedictine	–	Purée of strawberries	Benedictine flavoured whipped cream and chopped pistachio nuts
Morocco	Chocolate	Pistachio with whipped cream and nougat	–	–	Chantilly cream and chocolate petal shapes
Ninon	Vanilla	Morello cherries	Rum	–	Chantilly cream
Osborne	Vanilla	Sliced banana	–	Maple syrup	Whipped cream and finely chopped figs
Peach Royal	Vanilla	Sliced fresh peaches	–	Crushed pineapple	Whipped cream with nougat nibs and glacé cherry
Pineapple	Vanilla	Diced pineapple	Kirsch	–	Chantilly cream
Rainbow	Pistachio and strawberry	Split banana	–	–	Whipped cream, orange segments, and chopped pistachio nuts
Strawberry Whip	Strawberry	Crushed strawberries with whipped cream	–	Raspberry	Whipped cream
Temptation	Vanilla, strawberry, and chocolate	–	–	Chocolate	Chantilly cream, chopped pistachio nuts, and glacé cherries
Tutti Frutti	Strawberry, lemon, and pineapple	Diced candied fruits	Kirsch	–	–
Viennese	Coffee ice cream softened with sweet black coffee *or* Chocolate ice cream softened with ganache	–	–	–	Chantilly cream

Figure 83 *Ice bomb. Two ices are used for the making of this bomb*

Ice bombes (Figure 83)

Like coupes, ice bombes too can be prepared in a great number of combinations.

The preparation is as follows.

1 Thoroughly chill the bombe mould by placing it on crushed ice or in the deep freeze compartment.
2 Line the mould with the frozen ice cream to a depth of approximately ¾ in (2 cm). This is best done with a large spoon, pressing the mixture to the sides of the bombe mould.
3 Fill to the top with the bombe mixture into which glacé fruit, chocolate, praline, nuts, etc., may be mixed.
4 Cover either with a sheet of white paper, or preferably a disc of thin sponge cut to the same size as the mould.
5 Seal the mould with fat and freeze, either in ice and freezing mixture or in the deep freeze compartment.
6 When required for use, dip the mould into warm water for a few seconds, remove the base plug to release the vacuum, and allow the bombe to slide out. To cut out a wedge use a knife the blade of which has first been immersed in very hot water.
7 Decorate and serve immediately.

Note: Treat the fruit used in the same way as for coupes. Where liqueur is mentioned, it is either incorporated in the basic bombe filling or used to marinade fruit if used.

Basic bombe fillings (parfait)

Yield 4–5 bombes

Recipe 1

½ pt (3 dl) stock syrup (see page 295)
6 egg yolks
7½ oz (225 g) cream (slightly whipped)

Recipe 2

½ pt (3 dl) stock syrup
11 egg yolks
½ pt (3 dl) cream (slightly whipped)

1 Mix the yolks and stock syrup gradually together.
2 Heat the mixture in a bain-marie, whisking continuously until it becomes thick like the consistency of mayonnaise.
3 Remove, place on ice, and continue whisking until the mixture is cool.
4 Add any desired flavour, liqueur, etc., and fold in the cream. In some recipes it is recommended that the cream should be stiffly whipped to increase lightness and bulk. This makes it very difficult to blend in the other ingredients; therefore excessive whipping is not recommended. Continue whisking until mixture is perfectly smooth.

In the following list, unless otherwise stated, the filling used is the basic one above.

Iced charlottes – Charlottes glacées

These are made in charlotte moulds in the same way as charlotte russe or royal. The mould is lined with sponge fingers or Swiss roll and then filled with various ice creams, bombe or mousse mixtures with fruit, etc., and then deep frozen until required. They are often served with a cold sauce.

Ice gâteaux

These are ice cream mixtures made in the form of a gâteau which is first frozen and then served in slices or wedge-shaped portions.
    The make up of these is as follows:
    Two or three layers of thin sponge (roll mixing) are sandwiched with ice cream mixtures to which fruit, nuts, etc., may be added. The sponge may be splashed with liqueur. Once frozen the gâteau may be decorated with whipped cream, fruits, nuts, chocolate, etc.

Rolls

These consist of ice-cream mixtures in the form of a roll around which is wrapped a thin sponge roll mixing. They are cut into slices for serving.

Bricks

Ice-cream mixtures frozen in brick-shaped moulds. Also served in slices. If a bombe mixture is used and frozen into a brick shape it is called 'Iced biscuits' (Biscuits glacés).

Note: For sponge recipes see Chapter 4, page 81.

Iced mousses

Iced mousses are used either on their own or as a centre for the iced bombes. There are two types: cream and fruit.

Cream ice mousse

Yield 8 covers

½ oz (15 g) water
7 oz (210 g) icing sugar
7 oz (210 g) pasteurized egg (see page 18)
1 pt (6 dl) whipped cream
Flavouring

1 Beat the egg water, and sugar together in a bain-marie over gentle heat until it is foamy.
2 Transfer to ice and continue whisking until cold.
3 Add the flavouring.
4 Fold in the whipped cream.

Note: The flavouring may be chocolate, coffee, praline, vanilla, liqueurs, etc.

Fruit ice mousse

Yield 8 covers

½ pt (3 dl) stock syrup
½ pt (3 dl) fruit purée
Few drops lemon juice
1 pt (6 dl) whipped cream

1 Mix the stock syrup with the fruit purée and lemon juice.
2 Gently fold in the whipped cream.

Note: This type of mousse can only be made with fruits such as bananas, peaches, apricots, raspberries, strawberries, etc., which give a thick purée. Watery fruits like melons, oranges, etc., are unsuitable.

Iced soufflés – soufflés glacés

Ice soufflés are made in special soufflé moulds or straight sided silver timbales. Around the edge at least 2 in (5 cm) higher is wrapped a strip of greaseproof paper and secured with a piece of thread. The mould is filled to within ½ in (12 mm) of the top of this greaseproof paper band and frozen. When the soufflé is served it looks as if it has risen 1½ in (4 cm) above the mould as a baked soufflé is expected to do.

Usually the mixtures used for soufflés are either the iced mousse or bombe but other mixtures can be used as shown overleaf. Besides fruit, broken sponge fingers soaked in liqueur, crushed nougat, etc., may be incorporated.

Iced fruit soufflé glacé aux fruits

Yield 8 covers

1 lb (480 g) Italian meringue (see page 92)
½ pt (3 dl) fruit purée or pulp
¾ pt (4.5 dl) whipped cream

Add the fruit purée to the meringue and fold in the whipped cream.

Iced chocolate soufflé

Yield 8 covers

¼ pt (1.5 dl) stock syrup
1 oz (30 g) unsweetened chocolate
5 oz (150 g) Italian meringue
1 pt (6 dl) whipped cream

1 Melt the chocolate.
2 Blend the stock syrup.
3 Mix in the Italian meringue.
4 Gently fold in the whipped cream.

Other varieties of iced soufflés

The iced chocolate recipe may be used for other varieties as follows.

Coffee

In the above recipe substitute ½ oz (15 g) soluble coffee powder for the unsweetened chocolate.

Liqueur

Replace the unsweetened chocolate with 1–2 oz (30–60 g) of the required liqueur according to its strength.

Praline

Replace the unsweetened chocolate with 3 oz (90 g) of crushed praline or praline paste.

Cassata

These are usually made in bombe moulds, being first lined with three different types of ice, with the final filling a meringue/cream mixture containing a good quantity of glacé fruits, and then frozen.

Filling

8 oz (240 g) Italian meringue
5 oz (1½ dl) whipped cream
8 oz (240 g) finely diced glacé fruits
Flavouring

Varieties

Name	Ice creams	Mix with Cassata filling
Napoletana	Vanilla, chocolate, strawberry	Diced glacé fruits
Siciliana	Lemon, orange, chocolate	Diced angelica, halved pistachio nuts, and crystallized water melon
Tortoni	Praline, pineapple, chestnut	Noyau and diced marron glacé
Tosca	Pineapple, apricot, praline	Glacé cherries and pineapple

Figure 84   *Plated sweets. Description in text*

Baked ice-creams (baked Alaska)

These are ice-cream sweets which are covered with meringue and placed in a hot oven for a minute or so, for the meringue to take on an attractive colour (flashing).

1 Prepare a base of thin sponge (roll mixing). This may be sprinkled with liqueur.
2 Mould the ice-cream to the shape of the sponge base and put back into the freezer for a little while.
3 Cover with Italian meringue (page 92) using a savoy bag. Simple decoration can be applied using a star tube.
4 Immediately place in a hot oven at 450°F (232°C) until the meringue is coloured.
5 Serve immediately.

Individual Alaska with fruit

1 Prepare a base of sponge about ½ in (1.25 cm) larger than the fruit which is to be, that is, peach, pear, etc.
2 Place the fruit on the sponge base.

3 Cover with a scoop of ice-cream.
4 Place in the freezer for ½ hour or so.
5 Cover with Italian meringue and flash off in a hot oven.
6 Serve immediately.

Ice-cream and meringue

See page 93.

Ice-cream with fruit

See page 203.

Plated sweets
(Figure 84)

An attractive way to present sweets to the customer is to first cover the plate with an appropriate sauce.

Lines or drops of a sauce of a contrasting colour are then added and feathered or marbled (see page 126) with the point of a knife or a cocktail stick.

Explanation of varieties in Figure 84:

Top left	A slice of the chocolate torte (page 123). After feathering in thin cream, chocolate pieces are added as well as a sugar rose.
Top right	The petit gateau described on page 124 is placed on a plate with the strawberry sauce which is feathered with lightly whipped cream.
Bottom centre	The small orange bavarois described on page 195 is placed into a brandysnap basket (see page 152) before being placed onto the sauce. Drops of red coloured sauce are piped on and feathered into heart shapes.

Glossary

French and English patisserie names and terms

Fruits/nuts

Almond	*Amande*
Apple	*Pomme*
Apricot	*Abricot*
Banana	*Banane*
Blackberry	*Mûre de ronce*
Blackcurrant	*Cassis*
Cherry	*Cerise*
Chestnut	*Marron*
Cranberry	*Cannenberge*
Currant	*Raisin de Corinthe*
Currant, white	*Groseille blanche*
Currant, red	*Groseille rouge*
Currant, black	*Cassis*
Damson	*Prune de damas*
Date	*Datte*
Fig	*Figue*
Filbert	*Aveline*
Gooseberry	*Groseille verte*
Grapefruit	*Pamplemousse*
Grapes	*Raisins*
Greengage	*Reine-claude*
Hazelnut	*Noisette*
Lemon	*Citron*
Melon	*Melon*
Mulberry	*Mûre*
Nectarine	*Brugnon*
Nut	*Noix*
Olive	*Olive*
Orange	*Orange*
Tangerine Orange	*Mandarine*
Peach	*Pêche*
Pear	*Poire*
Pineapple	*Ananas*
Pistachio	*Pistache*
Plum	*Prune*
Pomegranate	*Grenade*
Quince	*Coing*
Raspberry	*Framboise*
Red currants	*Groseilles*
Strawberry	*Fraise*
Walnut	*Noix*

Others

Bakery	*Boulangerie*
Bomb	*Bombe*
Cakes	*Gâteaux*
Chilled	*Frappé*
Cream	*Crême*
Dried	*Sec (Sèche)*
Fingers	*Tranchettes*
Fritters	*Beignets*
Frosted	*Givré*
Iced	*Glacé*
In cases	*En caisses*
Jelly	*Gelée*
Panada	*Panade*
Patties (small)	*Bouchées*
Patties (large)	*Vol-au-vent*
Paste	*Pâte*
Pastry	*Pâtisserie*
Pie	*Pâté*
Pudding	*Pouding*
Rolled	*Roulé*
Rolls	*Paupiettes*
Salted	*Salé*
Savoury Jelly	*Aspic*
Souffle	*Soufflé*
Sliced	*Trancher*
Wafer	*Gaufre*

Culinary and technical terms used in Patisserie

(Not all the terms explained here appear in this book but they are included to assist the practising patissier.)

Absorb – To take in.

Adsorb – To hold by surface tension.

Aerate – Incorporating air or carbon dioxide gas during one or more stages of production to make goods more palatable and digestible. Air can be introduced by whisking, beating, or mixing. Carbon dioxide gas is introduced by the use of either baking powder or yeast. The expansion of air and steam during baking also contribute to the total aeration.

Albumen – One of many proteins. Generally it refers to the whites of eggs.

Almond paste – A mixture of not less than 23.5% of dry almonds. Not less than 75% of the remainder shall be solid carbohydrate sweetening matter.

Angelica – The young leaf stalks of a plant which are candied and used for decoration.

Aspic – Savoury jelly.

Bain-marie – (i) A container of water in which foods may be placed either to cook or to keep hot.
(ii) A double jacketed saucepan the lower part of which contains water and the top, material to be heated.

Bake blind – Baking unfilled flan or tartlet cases for filling later.

Baking – Cooking in an oven at correctly controlled temperatures.

Baking powder – Chemicals which when moistened and heated generate gas (usually carbon dioxide) which aerates bread and cakes.

Baking sheet – A metal plate on which cakes, etc., are baked.

Batch – Entire mixing or contents of oven.

Batter – Soft completed cake mixture.

Baume – Degrees on the scale of a saccharometer (sugar hydrometer).

Bavarois – A light sweet dish which includes gelatine and cream.

Bay – A well, made in a heap of flour or other dry materials, to receive liquid ingredients of a mixing.

Beat – The aeration of materials by beating together.

Béchamel – A basic white sauce.

Beignets – Fritters, sweet or savoury.

Benedictine – A liqueur made resembling Chartreus distilled at Fécamp in Normandy.

Blackjack – The dark, caramelized sugar syrup used for colouring rich fruit cake mixings.

Blanch – Removing the skins of nuts by plunging them first into hot water and then into cold.

Bloom – The healthy sparkle on baked goods. Fat and sugar bloom (see Chapter 18, page 238).

Bombe – Ice cream speciality of different flavours in a bomb shape.

Bouchées – Small puff pastry open cases.

Boulangerie – The bakery department.

Brake – A machine having two adjustable metal rollers for rolling and reducing the thickness of pastry or dough. They may be mechanically or hand operated.

Brioche – A fancy yeasted cake used as a breakfast roll.

Buckwheat – A cereal grown on the continents of Europe and America. The flour is usually made into pancakes.

Bun – A small cake aerated either chemically or by yeast.

Bun wash – A liquid brushed on yeasted buns immediately on removal from the oven to impart a glaze.

Cake – Baked mixture of fat, sugar, eggs, flour, etc.

Cake hoop – A metal ring in which a cake is baked.

Cake tins – Metal shapes in which cakes are baked.

Canapé – A piece of toast, pastry or biscuit on which various savoury foods are served, either hot or cold.

Candied – Preserved by immersion in super-saturated sugar solution. Subsequent drying results in a coating of sugar crystals.

Caramel – (i) Sugar heated above its melting point.
(ii) Sugar solution boiled above 312°F (155.5°C) until it turns amber brown.

Caramel fruits – Grapes, orange segments, etc., dipped in sugar solution boiled to at least 280°F (138°C).

Caramelize – Change in the sugar during baking a cake causing crust to colour (see *Caramel* above).

Caramels – Toffees composed of butter, cream, etc.

Carbonate of ammonia – Known as VOL to the baker and confectioner, it is a mixture of ammonium bicarbonate and ammonium carbamate. When heated it changes to carbon dioxide and ammonia gases which aerate certain goods, e.g. biscuits and chou pastry.

Carbon dioxide(CO_2) – A heavy gas produced by baking powder or yeast fermentation which aerates cakes, buns, etc. It is also incorporated under pressure in fruit drinks to make mineral waters and carbonated refreshments.

Cassata – An ice cream speciality.

Celsius – Temperature scale (constructed by Celsius, 1701–44) in which 0° represent the freezing point and 100° the boiling point of water at normal atmospheric pressure. The degree Celsius is very often called the degree Centigrade, as they are the same thing; however, 'degree Celsius' is the preferred term.

Centres – Moulded fondants and other sweet meats ready for dipping into chocolate couverture or boiled sugar to make sweets or petits fours.

Charlotte – Kind of pudding made in a special shape for which a charlotte mould is required.

Cheese curd – A curd produced by adding rennet to warm milk or by souring. When set, the whey is drained away to leave the curd.

Chinois – A fine meshed conical strainer.

Chocolate vermicelli – Polished granules of chocolate used as a decorative medium.

Clarify – (i) Removal of all extraneous material from a liquid or jelly in order to improve its transparency.

(ii) Removal of water from butter, etc. by gentle heating.

Coagulate – Partial or complete solidification of a protein in suspension. This may be caused by heat or acid.

Coat – Cover a cake with icing, paste, chocolate, etc.

Coffee drops – Small sweets resembling coffee beans.

Comb scraper – A plastic scraper with a serrated edge used to create patterns on icings, chocolate, etc.

Compote – Stewed fruit.

Compound fat – A fat, white in colour, made from hydrogenated oils. It is almost 100% fat.

Cones – Rice or maize, coarsely ground, used as a dusting medium for dough.

Concasser – To roughly chop or dice.

Constituent – One ingredient or component part of the whole.

Coralettes – Small nibs made of almonds, etc., and coloured.

Corbeille de fruits – A basket of fruits.

Coupe – An individual serving bowl.

Cream – (i) To beat two or more ingredients together to a creamy, light, and fluffy consistency, e.g. fat and sugar.

(ii) Fresh dairy cream – fat content of fresh milk.

(iii) Generic term used to describe buttercream, etc. In Great Britain, confectioners can only use this term to describe dairy cream.

Cream of tartar – Potassium hydrogen tartrate. One of the acid components of baking powder in which two parts are mixed with one of sodium bicarbonate.

Cream powders – Refers to many types of organic acids sold as substitutes for cream of tartar for use in baking powder.

Crême – Cream.

Crêpes – Pancakes.

Crimping – Giving a decorative edge to various pastes, e.g. shortbread, almond paste, etc., either with the thumb and finger or with special pincers.

Croquant – Melted sugar with nuts. The mixture can be moulded into shapes when hot or crushed when cold. It may also be made into a paste known as praline paste or nougat.

Crystallization – Formation of crystals deliberately in various sugar boiling operations.

Cup cakes – Small cakes baked in small paper cases.

Curd – A cooked mixture like a custard, e.g. lemon curd.

Curdle – Separation of the emulsion formed when fat, sugar, eggs, etc. are beaten together to form a cake batter. It is usually caused by adding the liquid too quickly or too cold.

Cut-outs – Units cut out of a mass of paste, etc., with either a knife or a cutter.

Cutters – Implements used to cut out pastries, etc. in various shapes. They may be plain, fluted, or made in a special shape, e.g. holly leaf or flower.

Gloss – The fine reflective surface on goods such as chocolate and fondant.

Glucose, confectioners' – A thick, viscous, colourless syrup used in boiling sugar preparations, etc.

Gluten – The insoluble protein of wheat after it has been hydrated. It is the elastic substance which assists in trapping the carbon dioxide gas in a dough, thereby enabling it to be aerated.

Glycerine – A colourless and odourless syrup with a sweet taste, used in cakes for its hygroscopic property in order to delay staling.

Gnocchi – Type of small dumpling made from potato, semolina, etc.

Graining – Re-crystallizing a super-saturated sugar solution by agitation.

Gratinate – Sprinkle with cheese etc. and colour brown in an oven or under the salamander.

Grease – Brush or cover baking tins with fat.

Gum arabic – The dried gum of the acacia plant. Used as a glazing or setting agent.

Gum paste – Special paste made from icing sugar, starch, water, and gum tragacanth, used for modelling purposes.

Gum tragacanth – A gum obtained from the spiny shrub of the Astragalus genus. Used as a setting agent.

Hard flour – Flour containing a good quantity of gluten. A strong flour.

Hors d'oeuvre – Appetizing dishes served as a first course.

Hotplate – A heated flat metal plate on which certain goods like pancakes can be baked.

Hydrometer – An instrument for determining the approximate specific gravity of a liquid at a certain temperature.

Hygroscopic – The power of attracting moisture, e.g. glycerine.

Icing – Sugar mixtures used for coating and decorative purposes, e.g. royal icing, fondant, etc.

Icing sugar – Finely powdered and sieved sugar.

Jelly – A soft, stiff, semi-transparent food chiefly derived from gelatine or other gummy substances. In patisserie there are several different types of jellies, namely aspic, pectin, piping, starch, gelatine, etc.

Jigger – A tool with a serrated wheel used for cutting pastry with a crinkled edge. It may be made of either brass or wood.

Jus-lié – Gravy which has been thickened.

Knead – Work into a mass, e.g. flour and water into a dough.

Kirsch – Liqueur made from cherries and used for flavouring various sweets.

Lamination – Formation of a number of layers as in the making of puff pastry.

Lecithin – A powerful emulsifying agent.

Line – To cover the inside of a baking tin with a mixture such as pastry etc.

Liqueurs – Spirits with an alcohol content of at least 30% vol. sweetened with sugar and flavoured with essences, essential oils, distillates or fruit juices.

Macédoine – (i) A mixture of fruit or vegetables.
(ii) Cut into ¼-in (3-mm) dice.

Macerate – To steep in a liquid to soften. Generally applied to fruit which is sprinkled with liqueur to improve flavour.

Maidenhair fern – A fern which is dried and pressed and used in the decoration of cakes.

Mandolin – Utensil used for slicing vegetables.

Manipulation – Term used to describe handling and shaping of a dough, paste, etc.

Maraschino – Liqueur made from cherries and used for flavouring various sweets.

Marinate – Place food in a liquid to tenderise or flavour it.

Marble icing – Decorative effect caused by inlaying one coloured icing into another in the form of a design. Also called 'feathering'.

Marzipan – A cooked paste made from two-thirds blanched almonds and one-third sugar.

Masking – Covering a cake surface with icing, buttercream, roasted nuts, etc.

Maw seeds – Seeds from a species of poppy, used for sprinkling on rolls etc. Available as either 'blue' or 'white'.

Menu – Bill of fare.

Mincemeat – Mixture of dried fruit with apples and suet flavoured with spice, lemon juice, and rum or brandy.

Mise en place – Basic preparations prior to the service.

Mould – (i) Shaping of a dough or paste.
(ii) A hollow form made from metal, plaster, plastic, wood, etc. in which pastes like marzipan may be cast.
(iii) Special hollow forms by which chocolate goods may be moulded.
(iv) Minute fungi which grow in damp conditions.

Mousse – A dish which is light in consistency, served either hot or cold.

Musty – A taint which develops usually in raw materials when stored under unsuitable conditions.

Nibs – Small fragments, such as almond or sugar nibs.

Nougat – (i) A confection made from sugar, honey, and egg whites, with added glacé fruits and nuts, e.g. Montelimar
(ii) Mixture of melted sugar and almonds ground to a paste and mixed with chocolate.
(iii) Mixture of melted sugar and almonds known as praline – croquant.

Orange flower water – A delicate flavoured distillate obtained from the flower of the orange tree used for flavouring almond and ices, etc.

Palette knife – A special knife having a thin flat blade with a rounded edge used for spreading purposes.

Parfait – Ice cream mixture made from syrup, egg yolks, and cream, and frozen in moulds.

Pastillage – Paste made from icing sugar and gum tragacanth or gelatine mucilage.

Pastries – Term used to describe all goods made by the pastrycook and confectioner.

Pasty – Small savoury containing meat and vegetables.

Patty – Small pie baked in a patty pan.

Pectin – The natural jelly agent found in most fruits and vegetables. It is available processed in either a liquid or a powder form. Used in cold set jelly and in jam and jelly recipes in which fruit used is naturally deficient in this agent.

Peel – (i) A flat wooden or metal blade attached to the end of a long handle. Used for setting and drawing bread and cakes, etc., from the oven.

(ii) The candied rinds of citrus fruits. Available either as halves (*caps*) or cut into small dices.

Petits fours – Very small pastries which can be placed in the mouth in one piece. There are two types:

(i) *Petits fours secs* – dry biscuit types.

(ii) *Petits fours glacés* – finished with icing.

Pie – A dish covered with pastry and containing fruit, meat, fish, etc.

Pincers – A tool consisting of two springy metal prongs, the ends of which are either shaped or serrated. They are used to pinch a design onto the edge of various pastes.

Pinching – Use of the above tool or the use of the thumb and forefinger to give a decorative edge to various pastes.

Pinning – Rolling out a paste with the rolling pin.

Piping – The operation of forcing a mixing from a bag through a small orifice which may be plain or shaped (cut) to leave a decorative impression.

Plaiting – The weaving of a rope of dough, paste, boiled sugar, etc., into an ordered design.

Plaster moulds – Moulds made from plaster of Paris.

Poach – Simmer dishes gently in boiling water or liquid without allowing the contents actually to boil.

Praline – Croquant which has been milled into a smooth paste. Used for flavouring purposes.

Precipitate – To throw out of solution. Deposit of a solid from a solution.

Profiteroles – Small puff paste balls, filled with fresh cream and served with a chocolate sauce.

Prove – The aeration of a yeasted dough with gas prior to its being baked.

Prover – A cabinet in which yeasted goods are placed to prove before baking. A warm, humid atmosphere must be provided for this purpose.

Pudding – A soft mixture, either sweet or savoury, baked or steamed in a basin or dish.

Puff pastry – Laminated structure built up from dough and butter or fat.

Pulled sugar – A solution of sugar containing glucose or weak acid, boiled to at least 300°F (149°C), poured onto a slab, and then pulled to attain a sheen. Used for fashioning ornamental shapes for table decoration and display pieces.

Punch – Frozen mixture of fruit syrup and Italian meringue.

Purée – Food passed through a sieve to make a thick pulp, e.g. apricot puree.

Quark – A salt free, fat free soft cheese made from skimmed milk.

Réchauffer – To re-heat.

Recipe – Formula containing weights of materials used for a particular type of dish. Yields, temperatures, times, etc., should also be recorded.

Recovery time – The time required by doughs to lose their toughness, brought about by manipulation.

Reduce – Concentration of a liquid by boiling.

Rennet – An infusion from the stomach of a calf which contains the enzyme rennin. Used to coagulate milk for the manufacture of curd and cheese.

Retardation – Arrest of the activity of fermented goods usually by keeping them at a low temperature of 34–38°F (1–3°C).

Rice flour – Rice milled into a fine flour. Used in some mixings and also for dusting purposes.

Ripening – Usually refers to the mellowing of the gluten in fermented goods, making it less tough and more extensible. May be brought about by the action of fermentation, manipulation, temperature, or use of additives.

Rock sugar – An aerated decorative material made from boiling sugar and royal icing.

Rolls – Small shapes made from bread. They may be soft crisp and of any shape.

Roux – Flour and fat cooked into a thick mixture.

Royal icing – Mixture of icing sugar and egg whites used for decorative purposes.

Rub in – Term used to mix flour and fat when the amounts in a recipe are either equal or the fat less than the flour. The ingredients are rubbed together by hands or by the beater of a machine to reduce the fat to small particles before the rest of the ingredients are added.

Sabayon – Sauce made from the yolks of egg and either water or wine.

Saccharometer – A special hydrometer for determining the density of sugar solutions. They are usually calibrated in degrees Baumé.

Sack – Unit of 280 lb in which flour is invoiced from the miller. It is delivered in two 140-lb bags.

Saffron – Dried stigmas of the saffron crocus. The deep orange coloured infusion is used for flavouring and colouring various specialities.

Salamander – A type of grill heated from above.

Salpicon – Mixture of small diced foods.

Sandwich plates – Shallow round metal tins in which sponge sandwiches are baked.

Saturated solution – A solution holding the greatest amount of another material without precipitation occurring. Usually it refers to a sugar solution.

Savoy bag – A cone shaped bag of cloth, nylon, or plastic in the end of which a tube can be inserted. Used to deposit or pipe all types of soft mixtures onto baking sheets or for decorative purposes.

Savoy tube – A nozzle made of metal, nylon, or plastic, either plain or shaped, through which various mixtures may be forced in either plain or decorative shapes.

Scaling – Operation of weighing dough or cake into units before baking.

Scoop – Small shovel for handling small quantities of dry materials.

Scraper – (i) A flat piece of flexible plastic material used to scrape mixings from the sides of the mixing bowl.

(ii) A flat piece of rigid metal fixed into a wooden handle and used for scraping baking tins or bench surfaces

Either type of scraper may be used to smooth the sides of cakes coated with royal icing, buttercream, etc. Patterns cut into the edge of such a scraper may be used to give decorative effects.

Season – Dulling the shining surface of new pans and baking tins by leaving them in a hot oven for a few hours. This is to improve their heat absorption properties.

Seasoning – Adding a mixture of salt and pepper with other aromatic flavouring substances to savoury dishes.

Setting – Filling an oven with bread or cakes.

Sherbets – Very light ices made from fruit juice.

Shortpastry – A friable mixture made from flour and fat with either egg, milk, or water to bind. It may be either sweet or savoury.

Shredded – Cut into fine strips.

Sieve – Utensil with a mesh made of either wire or nylon, through which dry or liquid materials and mixtures can be strained. It can be used to screen small particles from larger ones.

Skinning – The hard surface which is formed if dough is left uncovered, due to the evaporation of moisture.

Slab cake – Cakes baked in large frames weighing about 5–7 lb (2½–3 kilos).

Slack dough – A dough containing extra water to make it soft.

Snow – Term used to describe the foam caused when egg whites are whipped.

Sodium bicarbonate – The alkali constituent of baking powder which liberates carbon dioxide gas in the presence of the correct quantity of acid.

Soft flour – A flour with a weak gluten content.

Sorbet – A very light fruit ice.

Soufflé – A very light dish. It may be hot or cold, sweet or savoury.

Spatula – A flat spoon-shaped utensil used for mixing purposes.

Spin – Pipe chocolate under pressure through a very fine aperture tube and moving it to and fro over goods such as meringues, japs, etc for a decorative effect.

Splash – Sprinkling water or liquid over goods.

Sponge – (i) A light cake made by beating eggs and sugar and then blending in the flour.

(ii) A thick fermented batter.

Spun sugar – Threads of sugar formed from a boiling sugar solution. Used for decorative purposes.

Stencil – A pattern cut from suitable material through which icings or mixings may be deposited in a certain shape.

Stock syrup – Solution of sugar and water used to reduce fondant etc.

Strong flour – A flour containing a strong gluten.

Sugar paste – A paste made principally from sugar.

Sundaes – Ice cream dishes to which fruit is added.

Super-saturated solution – A highly saturated solution in an unstable condition which, when agitated, will rapidly crystallize.

Tamis – Cloth which is used to strain thick sauces.

Tart – A baked pastry case filled with fruit or some type of mixing.

Tea bread – Small yeasted goods made from an enriched dough.

Tight dough – Stiff dough containing insufficient water.

Timbale – A deep round silver dish.

Tranche – A slice or cut.

Turntable – A piece of equipment upon which a cake can be rotated in order to apply an even coating of icing or cream.

Velouté – A basic sauce made from stock.

Vol-au-vent – A large case made of puff pastry.

Wafer paper – Edible paper-like sheets on which macaroons etc. may be piped. Sometimes referred to as rice paper.

Wash – To brush goods with eggs, milk, or water prior to baking, or to apply icing or a glaze on baked goods.

Washbrush – Soft haired brush used for applying the wash etc. to goods.

Whip – Rapidly aerate by beating with a whisk.

Whisk – An implement made from wire used to whip mixings.

Yeast – Living minute fungi which ferment carbohydrate to form alcohol and carbon dioxide. Used to aerate bread and confectionary products.

Yield – Quantity of units calculated from any particular recipe.

Zest – The coloured outside rind of citrus fruits. This contains the essential oils of the fruit.

Temperature conversion table

The numbers in heavy type can be either °C or °F if the heavy type number is °C, the equivalent in °F is on the right. If the heavy type number is °F, the equivalent in °C is on the left.

°C		°F	°C		°F	°C		°F	°C		°F
−40	−40	−40	−1.1	30	86.0	18.2	65	149.0	43	110	230
−34	−30	−22	−0.6	31	87.8	18.8	66	150.8	49	120	248
−29	−20	−4	−0	32	89.6	19.3	67	152.6	54	130	266
−23	−10	+14	0.5	33	91.4	19.9	68	154.4	60	140	284
−17.7	−0	+32	1.1	34	93.2	20.4	69	156.2	65	150	302
−17.2	1	33.8	1.6	35	95.0	21.0	70	158.0	71	160	320
−16.6	2	35.6	2.2	36	96.8	21.5	71	159.8	76	170	338
−16.1	3	37.4	2.7	37	98.6	22.2	72	161.6	83	180	356
−15.5	4	39.2	3.3	38	100.4	22.7	73	163.4	88	190	374
−15	5	41.0	3.8	39	102.2	23.3	74	165.2	93	200	392
−14.4	6	42.8	4.4	40	104.0	23.8	75	167.0	99	210	410
−13.9	7	44.6	4.9	41	105.8	24.4	76	168.8	100	212	413
−13.3	8	46.4	5.5	42	107.6	25.0	77	170.6	104	220	428
−12.7	9	48.2	6.0	43	109.4	25.5	78	172.4	110	230	446
−12.2	10	50.0	6.6	44	111.2	26.2	79	174.2	115	240	464
−11.6	11	51.8	7.1	45	113.0	26.8	80	176.0	121	250	482
−11.1	12	53.6	7.7	46	114.8	27.3	81	177.8	127	260	500
−10.5	13	55.4	8.2	47	116.6	27.7	82	179.6	132	270	518
−10.0	14	57.2	8.8	48	118.4	28.2	83	181.4	138	280	536
−9.4	15	59.0	9.3	49	120.2	28.8	84	183.2	143	290	554
−8.8	16	60.8	9.9	50	122.0	29.3	85	185.0	149	300	572
−8.3	17	62.6	10.4	51	123.8	29.9	86	186.8	154	310	590
−7.7	18	64.4	11.1	52	125.6	30.4	87	188.6	160	320	608
−7.2	19	66.2	11.5	53	127.4	31.0	88	190.4	165	330	626
−6.6	20	68.0	12.1	54	129.2	31.5	89	192.2	171	340	644
−6.1	21	69.8	12.6	55	131.0	32.1	90	194.0	177	350	662
−5.5	22	71.6	13.2	56	132.8	32.6	91	195.8	182	360	680
−5.0	23	73.4	13.7	57	134.6	33.3	92	197.6	188	370	698
−4.4	24	75.2	14.3	58	136.4	33.8	93	199.4	193	380	716
−3.9	25	77.0	14.8	59	138.2	34.4	94	201.2	199	390	734
−3.3	26	78.8	15.6	60	140.0	34.9	95	203.0	204	400	752
−2.8	27	80.6	16.1	61	141.8	35.5	96	204.8	210	410	770
−2.2	28	82.4	16.6	62	143.6	36.1	97	206.6	215	420	788
−1.6	29	84.2	17.1	63	145.4	36.6	98	208.4	221	430	806
			17.7	64	147.2	37.1	99	210.2	226	440	824
						37.7	100	212.0	232	450	842
									238	460	860
									243	470	878
									249	480	896
									254	490	914
									260	500	932

Index